T0297813

Affective Computing

Affective Computing

Rosalind W. Picard

The MIT Press
Cambridge, Massachusetts
London, England

First MIT Press paperback edition, 2000

© 1997 Massachusetts Institute of Technology

All rights reserved. No part of this book may be reproduced in any form by any electronic or mechanical means (including photocopying, recording, or information storage and retrieval) without permission in writing from the publisher.

This book was set in Stone Serif and Stone Sans by Windfall Software using ZzT$_E$X.

Library of Congress Cataloging-in-Publication Data

Picard, Rosalind W.
  Affective computing / Rosalind W. Picard.
    p.   cm.
  Includes bibliographical references and index.
  ISBN 978-0-262-16170-1 (hc.: alk. paper)—978-0-262-66115-7 (pb.: alk. paper)
  1. Human–computer interaction. 2. User interfaces (Computer systems). I. Title.
QA76.9.H85P53   1997
004'.01'9—dc21   97-33285
                                                                         CIP

The MIT Press is pleased to keep this title available in print by manufacturing single copies, on demand, via digital printing technology.

To Len and Michael,
with love

Contents

Preface

I never expected to write a book addressing emotions. My education has been dominated by science and engineering, and based on axioms, laws, equations, rational thinking, and a pride that shuns the "touchy-feely." Being a woman in a field containing mostly men has provided extra incentive to cast off the stereotype of "emotional female" in favor of the logical behavior of a scholar. For most of my life my thinking on emotions could have been summarized as: "Emotions are fine for art, entertainment, and certain social interactions, but keep them out of science and computing."

Clearly, some kind of conversion has happened; this is a book about emotions and computing. Moreover, it is not about how people *feel* about computers, but about something of more questionable cause: giving emotional abilities to computers. This will no doubt sound outlandish to some people, who may wonder if I have not lost a wariness of emotions and their association with poor judgment and irrational behavior. I have not. The adjective "emotional" evokes negative connotations which are in many cases justified. Computers do not need poor judgment and irrational behavior. One of the things I will show in this book, however, is that in completely avoiding emotion, computer designers may actually lead computers toward these undesirable goals.

I ran into a fundamental and relatively unknown role of emotions while investigating what scientists assume to be the *rational* mechanisms of perception and decision making. I was trying to understand how people perceive what is in a picture—how they decide what the contents of an image are. My colleagues and I have been trying for decades to make computers "see"—to help catalog and search the contents of images and video, to help physicians find abnormalities in medical imagery, to help robots navigate or computers inspect industrial parts, and to help achieve many other goals. Most of my research has focused on the problem of modeling mechanisms of vision and learning, and has had nothing to do with emotions.

But what I ran into, in trying to understand how our brains accomplish vision, was emotion. Not as a corollary, tacked on to how humans see, but as a direct component, an integral part of perception. The story of how emotion influences perception, along with other important roles of emotion, will be saved for later in this book, but suffice it to say that this marked a turning point in my thinking. The role of emotions in "being emotional" is a small part of their story. The rest is largely untold, and has profound consequences—not just for understanding human thinking, but specifically for computing.

The latest scientific findings indicate that *emotions play an essential role in rational decision making, perception, learning, and a variety of other cognitive functions*. Emotions are not limited to art, entertainment, and social interaction; they influence the very mechanisms of rational thinking. We all know from experience that too much emotion can impair decision making, but the new scientific evidence is that *too little emotion can impair decision making*. This conclusion is not obvious from introspection. It comes from studies of unusual patients who essentially have too little emotion. These patients, in rather eerie ways, are similar to today's computers—particularly in how they malfunction. However, there has been almost no emphasis on the problem of "too little emotion," despite its pronounced implications for computer science, cognitive science, and for all who are interested in intelligence.

Today's evidence indicates that a healthy balance of emotions is integral to intelligence, and to creative and flexible problem solving. Indeed, the most objective scientists use emotions in creative and flexible problem solving, although they have rarely included emotions in models of these activities.

I have come to the conclusion that if we want computers to be genuinely intelligent, to adapt to us, and to interact naturally with us, then they will need the ability to recognize and express emotions, to have emotions, and to have what has come to be called "emotional intelligence." My goal in this book is to explain what these abilities consist of, why it is important to do this, what it can lead to, and how we can accomplish it. I have tried to do all of this in a way that is accessible to readers with a variety of backgrounds—including computer science, cognitive science, psychology, engineering, and philosophy.

Affective computing is nascent; most of the work I describe here is just beginning. Very little of it is ready for products; most falls into the domain of research. I have gathered many bits of recent and ongoing research, and combined these with my own theories to construct a framework of affective computing. Nonetheless, with almost as much heat as in an abortion debate, one might argue whether the bits of affective computing that presently exist constitute "insignificant tissue" or "a budding life." Are the ideas in this book something we can think about and discard at our convenience, or are they the germs of a future generation of computing? I think the evidence gathered here makes a strong case for the latter—that the development of affective computers is just a matter of time. Of course, the specific amount of time will depend on future strides in research and development, and in our understanding of emotions.

Most of us in technical fields cannot claim any special emotional competence, myself included. If we spent more time with machines that paid attention to our affect, that placed importance upon it and helped it to be communicated, then perhaps we might improve some of our affective communication abilities, even slightly. As I have learned since digging into the emotion theory literature, there are compelling reasons to develop emotional skills. Those of you who are emotionally savvy no doubt find it of great amusement that anyone would have to turn to the literature to see how important emotion is; but be forewarned, researchers have found the influences of emotion to be far deeper than even you may realize.

Affective computers are not a substitute for affective humans. In the course of this work I have come to appreciate all the more our own human needs for emotional development. It is my hope that this direction of research will encourage and enable us in this development—by no longer ignoring human emotions in human-computer interaction, by helping us become more aware of how we communicate, by providing testbeds for theories of emotion in learning and other functions, through animation of emotional characters and playful scenarios with which children can interact, by assisting scientists in collecting affective patterns, by helping advance research on understanding the role of emotion in preventive medicine, and more. It is my hope that affective computers, as tools to help us, will not just be more intelligent machines, but will also be companions in our endeavors to better understand how we are made, and so enhance our own humanity.

I would like to acknowledge several people who helped shape this book and my research on this topic. Books by Antonio Damasio, Richard E. Cytowic, and Manfred Clynes were the first to capture my interest in emotion, persuading me to take a more objective look at its role. Nicholas Negroponte has greatly inspired me through his own willingness to take risks and embrace unconventional ideas, and through his support of my research. I am grateful to Sandy Pentland for his steady encouragement of my ever-evolving ideas, and for much helpful advice along the way. Peter Hart nudged me to set aside many other fine distractions and pursue affective computing wholeheartedly. I am privileged to work with an outstanding faculty at MIT, and am especially grateful to my colleagues at the Media Lab; their exuberant creativity and collaborative spirit make the Media Lab the greatest place for giving birth to new ideas.

The development of affective computing has benefited from discussions with MIT students and colleagues, especially those in the "AC Reading Group" and "AC Seminar." I would particularly like to thank my graduate students at the time of writing this book: Fang Liu, Kris Popat, Steve Mann, Tom Minka, Martin Szummer, Jennifer Healey, Raul Fernandez, and Jonathan Klein, who have greatly impacted my thinking and contributed much fun to the learning process. Jonathan, Jennifer, Raul, and Steve, together with Fanya Montalvo, Pattie Maes, Jocelyn Riseberg, and Thad Starner provided helpful comments on drafts of some chapters. Alan Wexelblat read the whole book, and provided advice that has improved it in many ways. I appreciate the feedback of several colleagues on sections where I wove their research into the affective computing framework: Aluizio Araujo, Bruce Blumberg, Janet Cahn, Dolores Canamero, Clark Elliott, Irfan Essa, Nico Frijda, Tomoko Koda, Scott Neal Reilly, Andrew Ortony, Ira Roseman, Deb Roy, Aaron Sloman, Masanao Toda, Juan Velásquez, and Yasser Yacoob. I would also like to acknowledge influential discussions with Tim Anderson on emotions and creativity, Carl Hewitt on indeterminism in computers, Barry Kort on emotions in learning, Jerry Lettvin on emotions and physiology, Iain Murray on text-to-speech applications, and Aaron Sloman on emotion and meaning. Ken Haase, Beth Link, and Len Picard gave me enjoyable science fiction pointers. Laurie Ward, Caraway Seed, and Kate Mongiat have served as helpful administrative assistants to my research, especially tracking down numerous books and articles. I also wish to thank Bob Prior and Julie Grimaldi at MIT Press for their enthusiastic support of this book project.

My dear family and close friends, especially Charlene MacPherson and Cheryl Overs, have provided invaluable support to me. My new son, Michael, has lifted my spirit with his beautiful smiles. I wish to express my deepest gratitude to my husband, Len Picard, who has unselfishly demonstrated the greatest example of love, and holds my highest respect and admiration. Let me end with humble acknowledgement of God, the source of wonder and inspiration available to us all, whom machines do not yet appreciate. *Soli Deo Gloria.*

Introduction

This book proposes that we give computers the ability to recognize, express, and in some cases, "have" emotions. Is this not absurd? Computers are supposed to be paradigms of logic, rationality, and predictability. These paradigms, to many thinkers, are the very foundations of intelligence, and have been the focus of computer scientists working fervently to build an intelligent machine. After nearly a half century of research, however, computer scientists have not succeeded in constructing a machine that can reason intelligently about difficult problems or that can interact intelligently with people.

Three decades ago, Nobel laureate Herb Simon, writing on the foundations of cognition, emphasized that a general theory of thinking and problem solving must incorporate the influences of emotion (Simon, 1967). Emotion theorists have also argued for the role of emotion as a powerful motivator, influencing perception, cognition, coping, and creativity in important ways. Other results have emerged from neuroscience, cognitive science, and psychology, indicating a pivotal role for emotion in attention, planning, reasoning, learning, memory, and decision making. Some scientists have argued that the demands of a system with finite resources operating in a complex and unpredictable environment naturally give rise to the need for emotions, to address multiple concerns in a flexible, intelligent, and efficient way. Nonetheless, the consideration of emotions for computing has been largely ignored.

Although scientists bicker about a definition of emotion, they agree that emotion is not logic, and that strong emotions can impair rational decision making. Introductory psychology texts have described emotion as "a disorganized response, largely visceral, resulting from the lack of an effective adjustment."[1] Acting "emotionally" implies acting irrationally, with poor judgment. Emotional responses tend to be inappropriate, and even embarrassing. At first blush, emotions seem like the last thing we would want in an intelligent machine.

However, this negative face of emotion is less than half of the story. Before telling the rest of the story, it is prudent to acknowledge that emotions have a stigma, especially among those who prize rational thinking, such as scientists and engineers. Emotions are regarded as inherently non-scientific. Scientific principles are derived from rational thought, logical arguments, testable hypotheses, and repeatable experiments. There is room *alongside* science for "non-interfering" emotions such as those involved in curiosity, frustration, and the pleasure of discovery. Curiosity drives much of scientific inquiry— and the greatest reward of the scientist is often the pure joy of learning. Fear also contributes to science. One can argue that scientific funding via defense budgets has been prompted by fear, such as the fear of not being able to protect our children from attack by another country, or the fear of losing technical superiority. Despite these influences, emotions are usually regarded as acceptable only when they are on the sidelines. If brought more actively into scientific thinking and decision making, then we assume they are negative—wreaking havoc on reasoning. If emotions play a direct and positive role, then it has been overshadowed by this negative one. The negative bias has repelled many a scientist from careful analysis of the role of emotions.

Why do I propose to bring emotion into computing, into what has been first and foremost a deliberate tool of science? Emotion is probably good for something, but its obvious uses seem to be for entertainment and social or family settings. Isn't emotion merely a kind of luxury, that, if useful for computers, would only be of small consequence? This book claims that the answer is a solid "no." Scientific findings contradict the conclusion that human emotions are a luxury. Rather, the evidence is mounting for an essential role of emotions in basic rational and intelligent behavior. Emotions not only contribute to a richer quality of interaction, but they directly impact a person's ability to interact in an intelligent way. Emotional skills, especially the ability to recognize and express emotions, are essential for natural communication with humans.

What about emotion and computers? Shouldn't emotion be completely avoided when considering properties with which to endow computers? After all, computers control significant parts of our lives—nuclear power plants, phone systems, the stock market, airplane flights, automobile engines, and more. We need computers to be predictable and reliable, with clear rational judgment. Our lives sometimes depend on it. Who wants a computer to be able to "feel angry" at them? To feel contempt for any living thing? In the worst case, the consequences might be life-threatening, as in the film "2001" where the emotional computer HAL kills its crewmates, ostensibly out of fear. These questions skitter across the much deeper subject at hand, and I will devote a chapter to potential ethical concerns and less-than-desirable uses of this technology.

In this book I will lay a foundation and construct a framework for what I call "affective computing," computing that relates to, arises from, or deliberately influences emotions. This is different from presenting a theory of emotions; the latter usually focuses on what human emotions are, how and when they are produced, and what they accomplish. Affective computing includes implementing emotions, and therefore can aid the development and testing of new and old emotion theories. However, affective computing also includes many other things, such as giving a computer the ability to recognize and express emotions, developing its ability to respond intelligently to human emotion, and enabling it to regulate and utilize its emotions. Along the way I will weave in both existing work and my own ideas, to begin to fill in the framework.

To complicate matters, nobody knows the answers to basic questions in emotion theory such as: "what are emotions?" "what causes them?" and "why do we have them?" For a list of twelve open questions in the theory of emotion, see Lazarus (1991). These are all openly debated, and evidence lacks on all sides of the debates. To minimize speculation, my treatment of these topics will be limited to those questions essential to the development of affective computing. I will also make suggestions as to how affective computing can help us get closer to answering these important theoretical questions. On the practical side, I will describe new applications of affective computing to areas such as computer-assisted learning, perceptual information retrieval, creative arts and entertainment, and human health and preventive medicine. Most of these are implementable in the near to distant future, but some are being realized today.

I should state a couple of things that I do not intend "affective computing" to address. The first is the pursuit of computers to perform surgical procedures such as cingulotomies—the making of small wounds in the ridge of a part of the brain's limbic system known as the cingulate gyrus, a controversial operation to aid severely depressed patients. Although the use of computers in "tele-surgery" and other medical advances is a significant area of research, such uses are not the focus here. Nor do I plan to discuss how people feel about their computers, and how and why their feelings evolve as they do, even though these are important topics.[2]

On the other hand, I will address how *computers* will be able to recognize, express, and "have" some of these "feelings." The reason for the quotes on "have" and "feelings" will be clarified later, when I carefully describe these concepts. Affective computing is an area of research in need of diligent and sensitive exploration, since machines with affective abilities will need to be skillful and prudent in their use of such abilities. The potential contributions of this research are significant both theoretically and practically—for progress in understanding emotion and cognition, for improvements in how computers reason about and solve problems, for advances in how we may communicate with them, and for how they will influence our own human development.

Songs vs. Laws

Let me write the songs of a nation; I don't care who writes its laws.
—Andrew Fletcher

Emotion pulls the levers of our lives, whether it is love that leads to an act of forgiveness, or curiosity that drives scientific inquiry. As humans, our behavior is greatly influenced by the so-called "song in our heart." Parents, rehabilitation counselors, pastors, and politicians know that it is not laws that exert the greatest influence on people—there are laws prohibiting murder, but there are still murders. Instead, to change the way people behave, one cannot merely change the laws; people's hearts must change. The death penalty has not lowered the murder rate in states where it has been instituted as law; however, murder rates are significantly lower in certain cultures, e.g., in Japan vs. in the United States.

Music, sometimes called "the finest language of emotion," is an apt metaphor, whether it refers to people being influenced by the cultural "tune" or refers to someone with different behavior as "marching to a different drummer." Of course there is no audible tune, and no actual drummer; rather, the metaphor is one of subtle and powerful influence on our behavior—not described simply by laws or rules. To illustrate this influence, imagine the following scenario:

Your colleague keeps you waiting for an important engagement to which you are both strongly committed. You wait with reason, but with increasing puzzlement at her unusual tardiness. You think of promises this delay is causing you to break, except for the promise you made to wait for her. Perhaps you swear off future promises like these.

She is completely unreachable; you ponder what you will say to her about her irresponsibility. But you still wait, because you gave her your word. You wait with growing impatience, frustration, and anger. You waver between wondering "is she ok?" and feeling so irritated that you mutter under your breath, barely joking, "I'll kill her when she gets here."

Finally you give up on your promise to wait. Then she appears. How do you respond?

Whether you greet her with rage or relief, consider the effect of her expression on your response. Suppose she shows up looking carefree and unabashed. You may feel angry and lash out at her. Or suppose she shows up harried, apologetic, with woeful, grieving countenance. You might feel a sudden mixture of relief and forgiveness, and question her compassionately. In other words, the look on her face—her expression of affect—may powerfully influence how you respond. A small communication of emotion can change an entire course of behavior.

In saying that emotions, or "songs," pull the levers of our lives, I am *not* suggesting that laws are unimportant. The legal system has its raison d'etre, despite its notorious abuses and shortcomings. Similarly, systems of laws or rules used by computers have useful applications, despite the acknowledged brittleness of artificial intelligence (AI) rule-based expert systems. Laws are clearly important. However, laws and rules are not sufficient for understanding or predicting human behavior and intelligence.

In fact, evidence indicates that laws and rules do not operate without emotion in two highly cognitive tasks: decision making and perception. Some of the emotional influences for perception have even received special names—such as the fear-induced phenomenon of "tunnel vision," or the joy-induced state of "seeing through rose-colored glasses." But what other evidence is there besides such subjective experiences? Let's consider the role of emotion in perception and decision making, beginning with a somewhat bizarre scenario about perception. Perception is a task that, until recently, was presumed to be primarily cortical, occurring in the highest parts of the brain, together with other high-level rational processes.

Limbic Perception

"Oh, dear," he said, slurping a spoonful, "there are not enough points on the chicken."
—Michael Watson, from *The Man Who Tasted Shapes* (Cytowic, 1993)

Some people feel shapes on their palms as they taste food, like the "points" Michael usually feels when the chicken dish is seasoned correctly. Others see colors as they hear music. These are not drug-induced or voluntary experiences, but rather happen in a natural and involuntary way to people with *synesthesia*, a condition that occurs in an estimated ten people out of every million. A synesthete's brain behaves as if the senses are cross-wired, as if there are no walls between what is seen, felt, touched, smelled, and tasted. The result is heightened perceptual experience. But these crossed perceptions are not explained merely by neurologically "crossed wires."

One would expect that during synesthesia, there would be an increase in cortical activity because of the heightened perceptual experience. The cortex is the physically highest part of the brain, and contains the visual cortex and auditory cortex, the well-studied sites for processing the senses of vision and hearing. The neurologist Richard E. Cytowic studied a variety of aspects of synesthetic experience (Cytowic, 1989), in search of an understanding for how it occurs. He expected to find his explanations in parts of the brain where the senses come together, perhaps in the parietal lobe's tertiary association area where the three senses of vision, touch, and hearing converge. However, to his surprise, Cytowic found that scans of cerebral blood flow[3] during synesthesia episodes indicated a collapse of cortical metabolism. An overall increase of brain metabolism occurred, but it was not in the "higher" cortex, where it was expected.

Instead, Cytowic's studies pointed to a corresponding increase in activity in the limbic system. The limbic system (or more accurately, *systems* since it involves many individual components and functions) is a collection of parts of the brain that lie predominately between the brain stem and the two hemispheres of the cortex (see the "triune brain" in Fig. I.1). Although there is not complete agreement on what parts of the brain constitute the limbic system, it is typically considered to include the hypothalamus, the hippocampus in the temporal lobe, and the amygdala. The limbic system is the seat of emotion, memory, and attention.[4] It helps determine valence (i.e. whether you feel positive or negative toward something) and salience (i.e. what gets your attention). In so doing, the limbic system contributes to the flexibility, unpredictability, and creativity of human behavior. It contains vast interconnections with the neocortex, so that brain functions tend not to be purely limbic or cortical, but a mixture of both.

The degree of limbic activity during synesthesia indicates that the limbic system plays a significant role in perception. In other words, perception is occurring not just in the cortex, but also below the cortex, in the region of the brain that is the primary home of the emotions. Things are not being perceived without going through a system that attaches valence to the memory—positive or negative, like or dislike.

Research on synesthesia is only one of many examples that points to an intervening role for emotions in perception. For example, studies have shown that mood influences perception of ambiguous stimuli. If healthy subjects are asked to quickly jot words they hear, then they are more inclined to spell "presents" than "presence" if they are happy, and to spell "banned" than "band" if they are sad. Subjects resolve lexical ambiguity in homophones in a mood-congruent fashion.[5] Similar results occur when subjects look at ambiguous facial expressions. Depressed subjects judge the faces as having more rejection and sadness.[6] Moods also bias perception of the likelihood of events—an individual in a negative mood perceives negative events as more

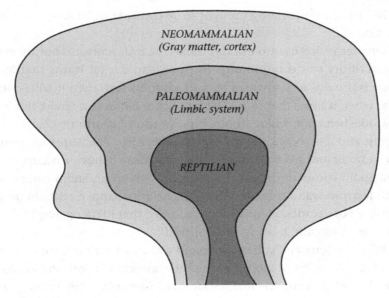

Figure I.1
Paul MacLean's "triune brain" divided the brain into three regions: neocortex, limbic system, and reptilian brain (MacLean, 1970). The neocortex is traditionally the best studied, and contains the visual cortex and auditory cortex; it is where the majority of perceptual processing has been assumed to occur. The limbic system is considered the primary seat of emotion, attention, and memory. Although clear dividing lines are shown here, the functions of the regions are not neatly divided.

likely and positive events as less likely, and the reverse holds true for people in positive moods.[7] In the words of the prominent emotion theorist Carroll Izard, emotion is "both a motivating and a guiding force in perception and attention" (Izard, 1993).[8]

The Limbic-Cortical Tangle

The distinction here between cortical and limbic functions is for emphasis only; in practice, normal limbic and cortical brain areas do not operate in isolation, but are functionally intertwined. The two areas have been artificially separated in how they have been studied, with most emphasis on the cortex. The cortex is easiest to probe as it lies closest to the scalp, and hence has been easiest to study. The limbic system lies below the cortex. Its common adjective of "subcortical" reinforces the old impression that it functions at a level lower than the cortex. However, discoveries such as that of the limbic role in the "high" function of perception imply that a high or dominating function is not necessarily cortical. Even more strongly than the synesthesia findings mentioned above, the research of Joseph LeDoux has shown that other kinds of processing thought to be cortical can be achieved *without* the cortex.

One surprising example of this is that the audio cortex is not always needed for auditory fear conditioning. In particular, if a rat learns that an audible tone is usually accompanied by a shock to its feet, then it will soon exhibit fear when it hears that tone. The rat cannot tell us it is afraid, but it exhibits fear-like behavior, where its blood pressure and heart rate change, it startles easily, and if in a cage, it "freezes" its movement. The surprising result found by LeDoux and his colleagues is that the same behavior occurs even when the audio cortex of the rat is removed. Without an audio cortex, a rat can still learn to fear a tone. But how can hearing happen without an auditory cortex? For decades scientists have assumed that higher perceptual functions such as vision and hearing were cortical.

What LeDoux and colleagues found was that for simple tones, the subcortical structures could recognize the tone, associate it with the likelihood of a shock, and generate the fear response. In particular, they found parts of the thalamus and midbrain that process auditory signals *before* they go to the cortex. Lesions in these regions eliminated the rats' ability to learn to fear the tone. Looking more closely, they found fibers going not only from these regions to the cortex, but also going to the amygdala, a structure central to the limbic system. After extensive careful experiments, they determined that the amygdala is where the learning for fear conditioning occurs initially (LeDoux, 1990). Moreover, this agreed with earlier results found in rabbits and other mammals—and the mechanisms are thought to be similar in all animals that exhibit fear conditioning, including humans (LeDoux, 1994).

Of course, not all perceptual processing occurs in the limbic system. More complex auditory stimuli have been found to require cortical processing. In other words, within its massively parallel system, the brain appears to have at least two paths for perception. The first path—"quick and dirty"—goes straight to the limbic system. When you spontaneously jump out of the way of a suddenly looming large object, then the processing probably occurred by this first path. The second path goes through the cortex and is slower, but more accurate. It allows us to recognize, a moment later, that the big object was an inflatable beach ball, and there was no need to be afraid.

There are substantially more connections from the limbic system to the cortex than vice-versa. These discoveries suggest that not only can the limbic system "hijack" the cortex, such as when it tells you to jump out of the way, but the limbic influence may actually be the greater of the two.[9] This might seem to imply that we are "run by our passions" as might be spoken of someone who does not act reasonably; however, more accurately it implies that even reasonable behavior is neurologically directed by these so-called passions.

Although for decades people have thought that the higher cortical parts of the brain control the lower parts, it is clear now that the lower can also control the higher. Nonetheless, it is commonplace to overlook the role of the lower systems, and especially the pervasive role of emotions and feelings. Cytowic, in remarking on the subtle pervasiveness of emotion's influence, points out that we often hear people say, "Sorry, I wasn't thinking," but we almost never hear "Sorry, I wasn't feeling." Whatever our perception of the role of low-level feelings, the sub-cortical limbic system is a crucial player in our mental activity. It is hard to say conclusively which system of the brain is *directing* the show, but it is clear that the limbic system is a vital part of the performance, even if it is not in the limelight.

Reevaluating Decision Making

Perception is not the only function mistakenly thought of as being purely cortical. Decision making, especially rational decision making, is thought of as a higher cognitive function in the human brain. We all know that "emotional decisions" are generally undesirable—that emotions can derail a rational decision-making process. However, emotions also play a more important role. Let us look at a surprising neurological finding that indicates a critical and paradigm-changing role for emotions.

The Thinking–Feeling Axis

"Scientific conclusions must be decided with the head; whom you choose to marry may be decided with the heart."
—folk advice

"Head" and "heart" are English-language metaphors for thinking and feeling. Most people consider that both head and heart are useful for decision making, as long as they are used suitably for separate purposes, as in the folk advice above. In fact, a tendency is to polarize thoughts and feelings, as if they were opposing phenomena.

The popular Myers-Briggs personality-type indicator provides a good example of this polarization. It characterizes personality via four axes, one of which has the labels "thinking" (T) and "feeling" (F) as opposite endpoints. Most students in technical graduate research programs are biased toward the "T" side. These types of personalities place relatively small emphasis on emotions or feelings relative to thoughts and logical reasoning. Since the developers of computers are largely members of this unusually biased population, it is no surprise to see affect marginalized in models of intelligence constructed by computer scientists.

The Myers-Briggs personality type indicator, when applied to large populations of men and women, reveals a gender bias along only this T-F axis. Two-thirds of men tend to lie closer to the "T" side and two-thirds of women tend to lie closer to the "F" side (Kroeger and Thuesen, 1992). This bias agrees with male-female stereotypes, and is increasingly supported by studies examining what men and women value in communication.[10] It is reasonable to expect that these differences might also extend to how men and women prefer to interact with computers.

Acknowledging the gender bias, affective computers might tend to be considered more feminine for incorporating emotions. However, this conclusion is short-sighted. The human brain, in both males and females, relies on emotion in normal *thinking*. In other words, even the most rational thinking requires participation from the emotion-mediating parts of the brain. Consequently, affective computers should not be considered more feminine, but more human.

The notion of a triune brain simplifies how we look at the systems involved in thinking and feeling, but its simplicity is also a bit dangerous. In particular, it is wrong to deduce from it that there is a clean line between "thinking" and "feeling." Any such line is particularly blurred when we look at decision making. In fact, we find something completely unexpected. First, recall that the brain does not separate cortical and limbic activity. Quoting from the *The Neurological Side of Neuropsychology* (Cytowic, 1996):

Authorities in neuroanatomy have confirmed that the hippocampus is a point where everything converges. All sensory inputs, external and visceral, must pass through the emotional limbic brain before being redistributed to the cortex for analysis, after which they return to the limbic system for a determination of whether the highly-transformed, multi-sensory input is salient or not.

Not only do functions traditionally thought of as cortical pass through the limbic brain, but the experience of emotion also engages parts of the cortex. In particular, the "frontal lobe" part of the cortex, which lies approximately behind the forehead, communicates significantly with the limbic brain. Damage to this area impairs the normal cortical-limbic interaction, effectively leaving a person with too little emotion.

Too Little Emotion Impairs Decision Making

We all know that too much emotion can wreak havoc on reasoning, but now there is evidence that *too little* emotion also can wreak havoc. This evidence requires a shift from the usual notion of how people separate emotions and rationality. I will give a brief explanation below, and refer the reader to the careful arguments and references assembled by Antonio Damasio in his book, *Descartes' Error* (Damasio, 1994), for the justification such a far-reaching paradigm shift demands.

Damasio's patients have frontal-lobe disorders, affecting a key part of the cortex that communicates with the limbic system. Otherwise, the patients appear to have normal intelligence, scoring average or above average on a variety of tests. At first encounter, these patients appear to be like *Star Trek*'s Mr. Spock—unexpressive of emotions and *unusually rational*. Consequently, one might expect them to be highly intelligent, like Spock.

In real life, however, Damasio's patients make disastrous decisions. Suppose they lose a lot of money with an investment. Unlike healthy people who would learn that the investment is a bad one and stop investing in it, they might continue to invest until all their money is gone. Moreover, this pattern of behavior repeats itself with relationships and other social interactions, usually resulting in the loss of jobs, friends, family, colleagues, and more. Such behavior is far from intelligent. These patients with impaired emotional abilities are, ironically, unable to act rationally.

This disorder is exemplified by "Elliot," whose IQ and cognitive abilities are all normal or above average, but who suffered damage to frontal lobe brain tissue as the result of a brain tumor. When confronted with a simple decision such as when to schedule an appointment, Elliot will disappear into an endless rational search of "Well, this time might be good," or "Maybe I will have to be on that side of town so this time would be better," and on and on. Although a certain amount of indecisiveness is normal, in Elliot it is apparently not accompanied by the usual feelings, such as embarrassment, if someone is staring at you for taking so long to make up your mind. Instead, Elliot's tendency is to search an astronomically large space of rational possibilities. Moreover, Elliot seems to be unable to learn the links between dangerous choices and bad feelings, so he repeats bad decisions instead of learning otherwise. Elliot's lack of emotions severely handicaps his ability to function rationally and intelligently.

Damasio has hypothesized that Elliot's brain is missing "somatic markers" that associate positive or negative feelings with certain decisions. These feelings would help limit a mental search by nudging the person away from considering the possibilities with bad associations (Damasio, 1994). These markers are those that healthy people identify as subjective feelings, "gut" feelings, or intuition.

Apparently, a balance is needed—not too much emotion, and not too little emotion. I suggest that computers, with the exception of some science-fiction creations, have erred on the side of having too little emotion. Artificial intelligence systems produced so far are not too unlike Elliot—they have above average knowledge of some area of expertise, usually encoded as huge set of rules, but they are relatively unintelligent at making decisions. They are unable to associate judgments of value and salience with important decisions. These judgments are products of interactions between the limbic system and the cortex. Little has been done to imitate them in computers.

Damasio's findings point to an essential role of emotion in rational thinking. This is not the first time researchers have come to this conclusion. Johnson-Laird and Shafir have written to the cognition community about the inability of logic to determine which of an infinite number of possible conclusions are sensible to draw, given a set of premises (Johnson-Laird and Shafir, 1993). Even the massive parallelism of the human brain cannot fully search the large spaces of possibilities involved in many day-to-day decisions. How do you decide which paths to search? There is not time to consider *every* possible logical constraint and associated path.

By no means should anyone conclude that logic or reason are irrelevant; they are as essential as the laws of a nation. Additionally, the neurological evidence describes an essential role for emotions, the "songs of the nation" that Fletcher implied were so influential. Therefore, these findings indicate that further study of emotion is essential if we are to understand human cognition, perception, and decision making.[11] The implications are significant also for computer science and industry: computers, if they are to be truly effective at decision making, will have to have emotions or emotion-like mechanisms working in concert with their rule-based systems. If not, we can expect them to have problems like those of Elliot and others who suffer from inadequate emotional abilities. "Pure reason" may continue as a Platonic ideal, but in successful cognitive systems, it is a logical howler.

Tests of Thinking and Intelligence

In normal human cognition, thinking and feeling are partners. If we wish to design a device that "thinks" in the sense of mimicking a human brain, then must it also "feel?"

Consider briefly the classic test of whether or not a machine can think: the Turing test.[12] This test examines whether, in a typical conversation between two participants who have no sensory contact with each other, a human tester cannot tell if the replies are being generated by a human or a machine. There have been competitions to see if a machine could pass this test and, in limited domains, some machines have passed. However, some intelligent people have *not* passed. The test cannot *prove* that a machine (or person) does or does not think; nonetheless, it is a terrific exercise in thinking about thinking.

A test of true thinking must involve emotion. Consider that one might converse with the computer passionately about a song or a poem, or describe to it the most tragic of accidents. To pass the test, computer responses should be indistinguishable from human responses. If a human is put into a highly emotional situation, then he or she will tend to respond with emotion. This observation is an old one, even recognized by Aristotle when he wrote about audiences in his *Rhetoric* :

Indeed they are always in sympathy with an emotional speaker even when there is nothing in what he says; and that is why many an orator tries to stun the audience with sound and fury.

A Turing test of an affective computer needs to include stunning it with sound and fury, so to speak. To fool the test-giver, the computer would need to be capable of recognizing emotion and synthesizing a suitable affective response.

Although the Turing test is usually performed with text communication, so that sensory expression such as voice intonation and facial expression does not play a role, this does not mean that emotions are not communicated. The power of influencing emotion through language was a primary tenet of Aristotle's *Rhetoric*. In fact, most users of text email find that recipients infer emotion from the email, regardless of whether they intended to communicate emotion through the mail. A machine, even limited to text communication, will communicate more effectively with humans if it can perceive and express emotions.

The crux of testing a computer's intelligence is in determining what questions should be asked of the computer. Hofstadter has suggested that "humor, especially emotion," would comprise the acid test of intelligence for a "thinking machine" (Hofstadter, 1981). The media have exploited this idea in movies where, for example, a human is finally convinced of a robot's intelligence when the robot understands a joke.

Debates still rage, however, about what constitutes thinking, and especially intelligence. As Howard Gardner establishes in his landmark book *Frames of Mind*, human intelligence consists of multiple forms, including social intelligence, which consists of interpersonal and intrapersonal skills (Gardner, 1983). Peter Salovey and John Mayer identify these latter skills as *emotional intelligence*, which they define as "the ability to monitor one's own and others' feelings and emotions, to discriminate among them and to use this information to guide one's thinking and actions" (Salovey and Mayer, 1990). The importance of these skills has been underscored by Dan Goleman in his book, *Emotional Intelligence* (Goleman, 1995), which argues that emotional abilities are more important than traditional IQ for predicting success in life.

Emotional intelligence involves factors such as self-motivation, empathy, self-awareness, impulse control, persistence, and social deftness. Empathy, in particular, requires an ability to recognize and express emotions and, in humans, the ability to experience another's emotions as one's own. Such abilities are tricky to test, and no widely accepted tests exist yet. Nevertheless, emotional skills have profound consequences for how humans perform and interact. I will discuss what these affective abilities would mean for computers in Chapter 2.

Affective Communication

Today it is easy to find people who spend more time interacting with a computer than with other humans. Every day people enter the online communities of the Internet where they communicate with each other *through* computers. Daily interaction between humans and computers has billions of dollars of economic impact, not to mention psychological impact, which is harder to quantify. I will not take space here to review the field of human-computer interaction, which is covered in numerous books and conferences; however, I would like to describe one set of intriguing studies, to motivate another reason for creating affective computers.

This particular set of studies was conducted by Clifford Nass, Byron Reeves, and their colleagues at Stanford University, and is described more fully in their book, *The Media Equation* (Reeves and Nass, 1996). They performed a number of classical tests of human social interaction, substituting computers into a role usually occupied by humans. Hence, a test that traditionally studies a human-human interaction was used to study a human-computer interaction.

For example, one experiment examined how what is said by human A about human B's performance changes when A gives the evaluation face-to-face with B, versus when A gives the evaluation about B to another presumably neutral person. Studies of human social interaction indicate that, in general, humans are nicer face-to-face. In a variation on the traditional test, human B is replaced with computer B. Human A now has to evaluate the computer's performance, say, after the computer gives him a short lesson. Human A gives B its evaluation "face-to-face," and then is asked by a different computer for an evaluation of how B did. The classic human-human results still hold, for example the tendency to be nicer face-to-face remains.

Numerous similar experiments were done by Reeves and Nass, revealing that the classic results of human-human studies are maintained in human-computer studies. The findings hold true even for people who "know better," such as computer science students who know that computers don't have emotions. After accounting for potential biasing factors, the researchers concluded that individuals' interactions with computers are inherently natural and social.[13] Affect is a natural and social part of human communication; therefore, people naturally use it when they interact with computers.[14]

It is not unusual for intelligent people to attribute emotion to things that clearly do not have emotion. For example, someone might wind up a toy dog to make it wag its tail, and say, "How cute—it likes us." Although people *know* that wind-up toys and computers do not have emotions, their default model for relating to others apparently assumes them, most likely because humans are strongly biased for human-human interaction.

Emotion plays an essential role in communication, even in its subtlest form where it merely indicates that communication has succeeded—that we are understood. If you reprimand someone and their facial expression does not change, then the inclination is to continue your communication until you receive a visible or verbal sign that your communication has succeeded. For example, when a look of pain or sorrow appears on their face, then you know you have been understood, and you can cease your reprimand. Body language is also read for signs that communication has succeeded. People watch each other's body language for a response signal to indicate that their message has been interpreted, often repeating their message until the response signal occurs. This tendency to repeat sending the same message may be at the root of the practice of many computer users to repeatedly type the same wrong thing at the computer, or to repeatedly click on something that does not work, as if the computer would notice their increasing frustration and acknowledge it in some way.

Affect recognition and expression are necessary for communication of understanding, one of the greatest psychological needs of people.[15] Suppose someone is terribly upset at you, and you gleefully respond "I understand!" They are not likely to feel understood at all. In contrast, a reflection of their emotion, a sign of empathy, is a sign of understanding. Nicholas Negroponte, in *Being Digital*, reminds us that even a puppy can tell when you are angry with it (Negroponte, 1995). How do we know it can tell? Because it signals this understanding to you. It does not keep wagging its tail during a rebuke, but may put its ears back, its tail down, and drop its head. These are signs that communication has succeeded, that in some simple form, the puppy understands your feelings.

Basic affect recognition and expression are expected by humans in communication. However, unlike the puppy, computers today cannot even tell if you are pleased or displeased. They will scroll screenfulls of information past you regardless of whether you are sitting forward eagerly in your seat, or have begun to emit loud snoring sounds. Computer-based communication is affect-blind, affect-deaf, and generally speaking, affect-impaired. A quantum leap in communication will occur when computers become able to at least recognize and express affect.

Example: The Effective and Affective Tutor

Before moving to the key issues and challenges in affective computing, let's consider an example of its use. One of the research interests at the MIT Media Lab is the building of better piano-teaching computer systems; in particular, systems that can grade some aspects of a student's expressive timing, dynamics, phrasing, etc. This goal contains many challenges, one of the hardest of which involves expression recognition, distilling the essential pitches of the music from its expression. Recognizing and interpreting affect in musical expression is important, and I will return to it later. But first, consider another influence of expression, in a scenario where you are receiving piano lessons from a personal computer tutor:

Imagine you are seated with your computer tutor, and suppose that it not only reads your gestural input, musical timing and phrasing, but that it can also read your emotional state. In other words, it not only interprets your musical expression, but also your facial expression and perhaps other physical changes corresponding to your emotional feelings—maybe heart rate, breathing, blood-pressure, muscular tightness, and posture. Assume it could have the ability to distinguish the three emotions we all appear to have at birth—distress, interest, and pleasure.[16] Given affect recognition, the computer tutor might gauge if it is maintaining your interest during the lesson, before you quit out of frustration and it is too late for it to try something different. "Am I holding your interest?" it would consider. In the affirmative, it might nudge you with more challenging exercises. If, however, it detects you are frustrated and making lots of errors, then it might slow things down and proffer encouraging feedback. Detecting user distress, without the user making mechanical playing errors, might signal to the computer the performance of a moving requiem, or the presence of a sticky piano key, or the need to ask the user afterward for more information.

The computer tutor should not always just try to make the user happy. Nor should it simply make the lesson easier if the user is upset. Instead, there are intelligent responses that, if given information about what the user is experiencing, can improve the pupil's learning experience. Having access to the user's affective expression is a critical aspect of formulating an intelligent response.

The principles in the piano tutor scenario hold also for non-musical learning tasks—learning a software package, a new game, a foreign language, and more. The topic can vary, but the problem is the same: how should the computer adapt the pace and presentation to the user? How can it know when to provide encouraging feedback or to offer assistance? Certainly, the user should have the option to ask for this at any time; however, it has also been demonstrated that systems that proactively offer suggestions can provide a better learning experience.[17] The tutor probably should not interrupt a user who is doing well, but it might offer help to one who has been getting increasingly frustrated. Human teachers know that a student's affective response provides important cues for discerning how to help the student.

Book Overview

This book is written in two parts: Part I provides the intellectual framework for affective computing and is written to be accessible to all readers. Part II is written for those who are interested in the design and construction of affective computers—fellow researchers, scientists, and engineers—and provides descriptions of tools and progress in this area. Even in Part II, however, I have tried to keep explanations at a level that can be understood by a broad audience.

Part I provides background, motivation, main ideas, applications, and a discussion of potential concerns that arise with affective computing. Chapter 1 overviews relevant concepts from emotion theory, since most readers will not be specialists in that area. Chapter 2 takes what is known about human emotions, and constructs requirements for computers that would have the ability to recognize, express, and "have" emotions. It also discusses emotional intelligence, which will likely have to accompany the other affective abilities if affective computing is to become successful. Chapter 3 describes potential applications of affective computing, including both some that are practical now, and some that are in the indeterminate future, but which allow us to think differently about how computers and our relationships with them might advance. Affective computers, especially those that "have" emotion, raise moral and ethical dilemmas, as well as a number of social and philosophical questions, which are broached in Chapter 4.

Part II provides more depth for those who wish to help realize the ideas and applications in Chapters 2 and 3. Low-level representations of emotions, moods, and human physiological signals are addressed in Chapter 5. Chapter 6 poses human affect recognition as a pattern recognition and learning problem, proposes some models for its solution, and highlights results in affect recognition and expression. Chapter 7 describes models for synthesizing emotions and their influences in computers, particularly in software agents. Finally, Chapter 8 describes the development of affective wearable computers, devices that not only have many exciting future applications, but that also can potentially help advance fundamental understanding of human emotions.

I   *Envisioning Affective Computing*

1   *Emotions Are Physical and Cognitive*

How do you recognize another person's emotional state? What is it about their face, their voice, their gait, or other mannerisms and behaviors that communicate how they feel? What are the links between someone's emotions and what their body expresses? How reliable, or how universal, are physiological measurements such as heart rate and skin conductivity as indicators of mood or emotion? What is the difference between mood and emotion? What causes emotions, and how do they influence decisions and behavior? How do you know if someone "likes" someone or something? How are emotions "induced?" Are emotions purely "cognitive" like thoughts, purely "physical" like the pounding of a heart, or some kind of combination? Why do we need emotions?[1] These are a handful of the questions that arise when considering how computers might recognize, express, and "have" emotions. Unfortunately, the literature on emotion and cognition has no clear answers to most of these questions; in fact, emotion theorists still do not agree even on a definition of emotion. Nearly a hundred definitions of emotion have been recorded and categorized (Kleinginna and Kleinginna, 1981).

It is tempting to entirely avoid the word "emotion" since it is so imprecise. However, avoidance is an extreme position since ill-defined words can still be very useful. To quote John McCarthy, "We can't define Mt. Everest precisely—whether or not a particular rock or piece of ice is or isn't part of it; but it is true, without qualification, that Edmund Hillary and Tenzing Norgay climbed it in 1953. In other words, we can base solid facts and knowledge on structures that are themselves imprecisely defined." Given that most people's intuitive concept of emotion is well-established and that the word remains in broad use, I will continue to use the word and base solid facts and knowledge upon it.

There is a wealth of literature overviewing theories in emotion and cognition, including Plutchik and Kellerman's (1980–1990) edited collections of research on emotion, as well as several other books by prominent emotion theorists that set forth their own theories as well as provide general backgrounds (Buck, 1984; Mandler, 1984; Frijda, 1986; Lazarus, 1991). This book will not repeat the efforts of these extensive resources. However, the reader is also not assumed to be familiar with emotion theory. Instead, this chapter distills the issues necessary to provide a background for the development of affective computing. The sections below clarify terminology to be used in this book, and provide background material for those unacquainted with emotion theory. The focus will be on the issues most relevant to giving computers affective abilities.

Physical vs. Cognitive

The myriad theories on emotion can be largely examined in terms of two components: 1) emotions are cognitive, emphasizing their mental component; and 2) emotions are physical, emphasizing their bodily component.

Research on the cognitive component focuses on understanding the situations that give rise to emotions; for example, "That was an important goal to me and you prevented my attaining it; therefore, I am angry." Numerous "cognitive appraisal theories" exist to delineate which mental appraisals give rise to which emotions; I will say more about these in Chapter 7, since a few of them have inspired computer implementations. Historically, the focus on the brain-centered aspects of emotion is attributed to Walter Cannon, who emphasized that emotion is experienced centrally by the brain, and that its experience is possible without sensations of or from the body (Cannon, 1927).

Research on the physical component emphasizes the physiological response that co-occurs with an emotion or rapidly follows it. Historically, William James was the major proponent of emotion as an experience of bodily changes, such as your heart rate increasing or your hands perspiring (James, 1890). This view was challenged by Cannon and again much later by Schachter and Singer who argued that the experience of physiological changes was not sufficient to discriminate emotions. Schachter and Singer conducted experiments that induced the same state of bodily arousal in subjects, but placed the subjects in different situations. The subjects reported different moods afterward. Schachter and Singer argued that physiological responses such as sweaty palms and a rapid heart beat inform our brain that we are aroused, and that then the brain must appraise the situation we are in before it can label the state with an emotion such as fear or love (Schachter 1964).

Today we know that both brain and body interact in the generation of emotion and its experience. Not only can thoughts lead to emotions, but emotions can occur without obvious cognitive evaluation, such as by changes in bodily chemistry. Moreover, there is growing evidence that emotions can be discriminated by distinct physical signatures (Ekman, Levenson, and Frieson, 1983; Winton, Putnam and Krauss, 1984; Frijda, 1986; Cacioppo and Tassinary, 1990; Levenson, 1992; Scherer, 1993; Vrana, 1993; Bradley, Cuthbert, and Lang, 1996). The viewpoints on the relative importance of the physical or cognitive components today depend largely on how "cognitive" and "physical" are defined. At the root of the division is a debate rooted in Descartes' separation of mind and body—where thoughts, and often the brain, are treated separately from the rest of the body. In this book I will emphasize emotions in both mind and body, and the role of *both physical and cognitive* components for affective computing.

The distinction—are emotions physical first or cognitive first—is not as important to us as the question, "How can emotions be generated in computers, recognized by computers, and expressed by computers?" What is the mapping that connects the emotion that you are cognitively or physically experiencing to the way in which it is expressed to others? In particular, there are usually visible or audible signs of emotion. If a computer is trying to recognize or understand your emotion, it should be able to get information not just from you telling it the name of your emotion, but also from looking at your face, listening to your voice, noticing your gestures, and appraising the situation you are in. The development of affective computers requires understanding of both physical and cognitive components of emotion.

The Wheelchair Scenario

Rafe's friends always describe him as a happy person. He likes to play tennis and finds great enjoyment in watching the top professionals play the game. After watching his favorite player win in the semifinals of a grand prix tennis tournament, Rafe contentedly stood in line under a hot August sun waiting to get a cool drink. As the glow of his vicarious victory faded, the heat and humidity became more and more oppressive. Suddenly, Rafe felt a piercing pain from a blow to his lower back. Rafe turned rapidly with an angry expression and clenched fist. Rafe saw that he had been hit by Rebecca, a person with hemiplegia whose wheelchair had gone out of control and caused her to crash into Rafe and to spill her drink on her dress. Rafe's understanding that the cause of his pain was an uncontrollable event that had embarrassed Rebecca immediately changed his anger to sadness and sympathy. Though still in pain, his happy nature surfaced, and he began helping Rebecca recover from the accident.[2]

In this scenario, there are a variety of factors that activate Rafe's emotions. They include bodily responses to heat, humidity, and pain, as well as cognitive responses such as the appraisal that the collision was unintentional and now presented an opportunity to help Rebecca.

Note that it is possible to fiddle with semantics and erase these distinctive causes—for example, one could argue that cognitive responses include all responses of the brain, which includes neurophysiological controls and subconscious appraisal mechanisms, and therefore all emotions are cognitive. On the other hand, one could argue that all cognitive events reduce to physiological events, and therefore all thoughts and emotions are purely physiological. What is clear however, is that emotions can be caused by thoughts and they can be caused by physical mechanisms of which we are not conscious. One can emphasize both cognitive and physical aspects of emotion. In this chapter, I'll consider the two components separately—first, the physical, and second the cognitive. This division is not precise, and the terms "physical" and "cognitive" are deliberately not carefully defined, but are used in their most common senses.

Terminology

Before proceeding, it is helpful to clarify a few pieces of terminology: "Emotional" and "affective" will be used interchangeably as adjectives describing either physical or cognitive components of emotion, although "affective" will sometimes be used in a broader sense than "emotional." I will occasionally use the adjective *sentic* from the Latin *sentire*, the root of the words "sentiment" and "sensation," interchangeably with the adjectives *emotional* and *affective*, especially when I emphasize physical mechanisms of emotion expression. "Sentic" was coined by Manfred Clynes (Clynes, 1977), a pioneer in linking emotional states to physical measurement.

An emotional *state* refers to your internal dynamics when you have an emotion. The state is multi-variate—including aspects of both your mental state and physical state. It changes with time and with a variety of other activating and conditioning factors. Emotional state cannot be directly observed by another person, but may be inferred. In the wheelchair scenario when Rafe was standing in line, the strangers next to him could not reliably guess his emotional state. However, when he turned around with clenched fists, they could infer that he was in a state of anger.

An emotional *experience* refers to all you consciously perceive of your own emotional state. In the wheelchair scenario, Rafe's emotional experiences probably included contentment, mild distress, anger, sympathy, and happiness. Some authors equate emotional experience with emotional "feelings." However, sometimes the word "feelings" is used strictly for sensory stimuli, e.g., feeling a slimy surface or pinprick. To add to the confusion, some theorists lump feelings such as hunger and pain in with emotions, while others distinguish feelings such as hunger as "drives"[3] and feelings such as pain as "sensations." This book will not treat hunger or pain as emotions, but will recognize that they can influence the activation of emotional states. For example, hunger can increase irritability, and pain can spur anger. Generally, the term "feelings" refers to not just sensations as of pain and hunger, but also to subjective experience of affective phenomenon, which will become an important topic later in this book.

The term emotional *expression* will be used to describe what is revealed to others, either voluntarily, such as by a deliberate smile, or involuntarily, such as by a nervous twitch. Emotional expression via the motor system or other bodily systems, or "sentic modulation," is usually involuntary, and provides clues that others may observe to guess your emotional state.[4]

Finally, the term *mood*, although defined in many different ways in the literature, will be used to refer to a longer-term affective state. The precise duration is not well-defined, although moods can apparently last for hours, days, and maybe longer. In contrast, psychologists say that emotions are events that last at most a few minutes. A mood may arise when an emotion is repeatedly activated, for example a bad mood may arise during a half hour of reinforced negative thoughts or actions, or may be induced by taking drugs or medication.

Physical Aspects of Emotion: Sentic Modulation

The emotional character is expressed by a specific subtle modulation of the motor action involved which corresponds precisely to the demands of the sentic state.
—Manfred Clynes, in *Sentics* (1977)

A bodily component of emotions is accepted by most theorists today, although they differ on its nature. In particular, William James's 1890 view of this response *being* the emotion is not generally accepted today.[5] Nonetheless, the motor system acts as a carrier for expressing emotional state. The influence of emotion on bodily expression is what I'll call "sentic modulation."

Sentic modulation, such as voice inflection, facial expression, and posture, is the physical means by which an emotional state is typically expressed, and is the primary means of communicating human emotion.[6] In fact, few people are good at articulating their emotional state, but expressing it through sentic modulation is natural, and usually subconscious. A number of emotion and cognition theorists have studied the physiological correlates of emotions, arguing that each emotion probably has its own unique somatic response pattern. Paul Ekman, the foremost authority on facial expressions, has argued that there are "basic" emotions, each of which has its own set of unique facial muscle movement patterns (Ekman, 1992).

If computers are to utilize the natural channels of emotional communication used by people, then when computers learn to recognize human emotion, they will have to rely primarily on sentic modulation, as opposed to having people explicitly tell them the names of their emotional feelings. To give computers affect recognition requires understanding the physical manifestations of emotion.

Facial Expression

Facial expressions are one of the most widely acknowledged forms of sentic modulation. Beethoven, after he became deaf, wrote in his conversation books that he could judge from the performer's facial expression whether or not the performer was interpreting his music in the right spirit. The face is where our eyes linger during conversation. In a videoteleconference, where the camera is free to point anywhere, the default is to have it point to the faces of the people in the room. Whether in person or over a videotelephone, we tend to communicate most affectively "face-to-face."

Facial expressions are subject to what Ekman has termed "social display rules" that limit the range of acceptable expression, such as in business or social settings. For example, it is inappropriate for a businessman to contort his face in extreme disgust or disappointment during a negotiation session. In serious meetings he knows to express only mild emotion, regardless of his feelings. However, at a sporting event the social display rules are different. There he is not only free to contort his face, but also to vociferate, to wave his arms and torso, and to jump up and down.

In his 1862 thesis, Duchenne identified independent expressive muscles in the face, such as the muscle of attention, muscle of lust, muscle of disdain or doubt, and muscle of joy (Duchenne, 1990). Based on his work, Ekman and his colleagues have developed a "Facial Action Coding System," that provides mappings between muscles and an emotion space. Presently, most attempts to automate recognition of facial expression are based on Ekman's system. Some of the latest results in this area will be described in the second part of this book.

Vocal Intonation

The second widely acknowledged form of sentic modulation is vocal modulation. Emotions in speech can be understood by young children before they can understand what is being said (van Bezooyen, 1984). Dogs can recognize vocal affect, even though they presumably cannot understand what is being said. If Fido is on the sofa and you yell angrily, "Get down off the sofa!" he may not only get down, but he will probably acknowledge the emotion

Table 1.1
Some forms of sentic modulation are easily perceived by other people, while other forms require physical contact such as a handshake, or measuring devices such as a blood pressure cuff.

Apparent to others:

Facial expression

Voice intonation

Gestures, Movement

Posture

Pupilary dilation

Less apparent to others:

Respiration

Heart rate, pulse

Temperature

Electrodermal response, perspiration

Muscle action potentials

Blood pressure

---

physically, with the position of his ears, tail, and head. The same behavior will likely result if, when he is on the sofa, you yell with the same angry tone of voice, "Get *up on* the sofa!" Voice, of course, is why the phone tends to communicate affective information more accurately than email or a written letter. Spoken communication transcends the message of the words—alerting the listener to states such as anxiety, nervousness, or love.

Most emphasis on computers and speech has focused on teaching computers to understand *what* is said. More recently, researchers have focused on teaching the computer to recognize *who* is speaking. The challenge for affective computers is to understand *how* something is said. In fact, often it is not what is said that is most important, but how it is said.

Vocal inflection is also important in applications where people and computers depend upon the use of synthetic voices. Many people who have lost the ability to speak rely on typing at a computer, and having the computer synthesize speech for them. However, they are still handicapped when it comes to being able to raise their voice in anger when anger peaks during an argument, or soften it lovingly when they feel loving. Their synthetic voices are much more useful if they include affective intonation. It would be especially beneficial if the computer could directly sense the typist's affect, and modulate the synthetic speech accordingly. Some early results getting computers to synthesize and recognize affective expression in speech will be presented in the second part of this book.

Motor Forms of Expression

Alternate forms of sentic modulation have been explored by Clynes (1977). One of his principles, that of "sentic equivalence," allows a person to select an arbitrary motor output of sufficient degrees of freedom for expressing emotion. For example, a device called a "sentograph" measures pressure along two degrees of freedom—vertical pressure and horizontal deflection—from a person pushing with a finger on the device while expressing an emotion. Measurements of these two pressure signals represent an "essentic form," a precise spatiotemporal form produced by the nervous system, which carries the emotional message.

A note on "essentic form" is appropriate, as the work of Clynes is controversial among psychologists. What is it in a piece of music that makes it sound sad to listeners? Or in a piece of animation that makes it tender, joyful, touching? Clynes has suggested that there is a spatiotemporal form, with clear beginning and end, that embodies the emotional message. It can exist in a human's movement, in a piece of music or art, or in a variety of forms. In sentic modulation, the essentic form is captured from various motor system outputs—a finger moving, a foot moving, whatever can express sufficient degrees of freedom. Through essentic forms, emotions can be communicated by many means, not just facial and vocal expression.

The motor output explored most carefully by Clynes is the transient pressure of a finger during emotional expression. In these experiments the subject deliberately expresses an emotional state by pressing against a measuring surface while experiencing that state. The person does not feel the surface move, but a sensor underneath the surface records pressure changes horizontally and vertically. The person repeatedly expresses a given emotion, pressing upon the device with each expression, as the felt emotion builds in intensity. The resulting pressure traces are hypothesized to be indicative of an underlying essentic form, the carrier of the emotional message. To emphasize the existence of an underlying form, independent of the channel of expression, Clynes measured other channels of motor output. For example, he measured also foot pressure and chin pressure, the latter for a patient who was paralyzed from the neck down. These different channels of motor expression revealed comparable characteristic essentic forms.

Although this form of emotional expression is contrived in the sense that it is not a natural form of communication that people usually use, nonetheless it has been measured for thousands of people and found to provide repeatably stable distinct traces for states such as no emotion, anger, hate, grief, love, joy, sex, and reverence (Clynes, 1977). The repeatability holds across groups of individuals, and to some extent, cultures. People who observed the forearm and hand of someone expressing emotion with the sentograph recognized which emotion was being expressed with significantly higher than chance probability. It should be emphasized that the pressure curves are made with deliberate expression, as frequently done in experiments where an actor or actress is asked to express an emotion. The person is consciously and willingly trying to feel and communicate the particular emotional state, while applying pressure to the recording device. Hence, this factor may influence the results, as deliberate expression can differ from spontaneous or naturally generated expression, although to the extent that physiological feedback is at work, these distinctions become blurred.

Other Physiological Responses

There are many physiological responses that vary with time and that might potentially be combined to assist in recognition of emotional states. These include heart rate, diastolic and systolic blood pressure, pulse, pupilary dilation, respiration, skin conductance and color, and temperature.[7] The most commonly measured of these are summarized in Table 1.1. These forms of sentic modulation will be revisited later in this book in discussions about computer recognition of affect, particularly when the computers are "wearable." Wearable computers can be in long-term physical contact with a person.

Here are some examples how emotions can map to physical expression: Given that a person is experiencing an emotion, e.g., hate, then sentic modulation may result in a tense voice, glaring expression, or finger pressure strongly away from the body. Respiration rate and heart rate may also increase. In contrast, given feelings of joy, the voice might go up in pitch, the face reveal a smile, and the finger pressure have a slight bounce-like character. Even the more complex "self-conscious" emotions, such as guilt and shame, exhibit marked postural differences that might be observed in how you stand, walk, gesture, or otherwise behave (Lewis, 1995). A state of interest is indicated by gestures such as leaning toward the person or object of interest, and by less-easily controlled responses such as pupilary dilation.[8]

The physiological influences of emotion have many implications other than for emotional expression. It has long been known anecdotally that depression, chronic anger, anxiety, and stress influence your body; in particular, increasing the likelihood that you get sick. Many a student has noticed that they become ill the week after exams. More recently, there have been a variety of scientific studies not only confirming these influences of emotion, but highlighting how negative emotions can hinder the functioning of the immune system, suppressing the body's ability to fight off infection or disease and impeding its ability to heal itself. Researchers in the new medical field of psychoneuroimmunology have found mechanisms whereby emotion directly influences the immune system, neurochemically, as well as through regulation of the autonomic nervous system, which has been found to directly interact with the cells of the immune system such as lymphocytes and macrophages. Hormones that are released during stress have also been found to impact immune cells. There is no evidence that affect can make you sick, but there is evidence that it strongly influences your body's effectiveness in warding off and recovering from illness.[9]

Affective computers equipped with cameras, microphones, physiological sensors, and sophisticated pattern recognition tools, can begin to recognize physiological components of emotion, and to infer the likely emotional state underlying these components. Although such tools cannot yet directly measure the impact of emotions on other bodily systems such as the immune system, they can begin to provide information about emotions that would aid in many applications, including preventive medicine. This is likely despite the lack of a solid definition of emotions, and the lack of a universal theory of how people respond physically when experiencing emotions. I will discuss these issues further below. First, let us consider some of the physiological factors that complicate the development of affective computing.

Complicating Conditions: Physical Aspects of Emotion

Computers and people would have a relatively easy time recognizing emotions if they were always displayed in a consistent way. However, this is not the case. Most emotions do not map to a fixed form of sentic modulation all the time. The good results in the Clynes experiments above are obtained when the person is freely expressing the emotion, repeatedly, in a relaxed context, where the intensity of the emotion is being strengthened and the state is relatively pure. Under ordinary human-human or human-computer interaction, the possibilities are much more varied.

Studies attempting to associate bodily response with emotional state are complicated by a number of factors that influence the mapping between an emotion and how it is expressed:

1. Intensity of the emotion;

2. Type of the emotion, e.g., there are many types of love;

3. How the state was induced, e.g., imagining a situation, watching a film, or being in the midst of a genuine conflict;

4. Social display rules, and whether the person was encouraged to express or suppress emotion.

For example, claims that people can experience emotions such as love cognitively, without a corresponding physiological response (such as increased heart rate) may be due to it only being a weak feeling induced in a laboratory by asking the subject to think of an object of affection.

Mappings of emotion to physical expression are tricky partly because of the many ways in which emotions are defined. Some theorists do not consider "love" to be a basic emotion because it does not elicit a characteristic facial expression. Others define emotions to include the mildest thoughts, such as "He failed to show, therefore he let me down," even if they are not accompanied by a bodily feeling, e.g., of disappointment.

Another complicating factor is that physiological responses similar to those in an emotional state can arise without corresponding to an emotion. For example, heart rate increases when exercising. In theory, these responses can be disambiguated by perceiving the context of the situation. For example, a wearable computer that is trying to measure emotions might also have a miniature camera and other sensors attached, such as for footstep rate, so that it can recognize (1) you are moving fast, and (2) this is the time of day you usually go for a jog. Activities that are common to your daily routine can be designed into the affective recognition model as conditioning variables.

Hormones, medications, and diet present additional complicating factors, as all of these can modulate mood changes. These factors are difficult to monitor without blood-sampling or other invasive methods. A person may wake up feeling angry, and yet have cognitive thoughts such as, "Why do I feel so angry? I'm not angry at anything; everything is going quite fine." She may continue to feel irritable, tense, prone to negative thoughts, and inclined to lash out at small things. The angry feeling can be caused by a recent biochemical change; pre-menstrual hormone changes are one common example. Similarly, diet, sleep, and drugs affect neurotransmitter levels and mood.[10]

To further complicate the matter, a mood-state cues memories that are consistent with that mood: positive moods tend to make it easier to remember positive things, and negative moods tend to make it easier to remember negative things. If groups of people are asked to learn a list of positive and negative words, then those who are in a good mood at the time of retrieval have significantly better recall of the positive words. The negative result is not as significant, perhaps because negative-mood retrieval of negative words reinforces a negative mood, which is not as desirable as reinforcing a positive mood.[11] Emotions influence cognition, and cognition influences emotions. Apparently, a good mood and its corresponding physiological state bias a person toward good thoughts, which may trigger good emotions and cause the good mood to endure.

Some theorists have treated physiological changes solely as consequences or concomitants of emotional states, and it is certainly the case that cognitive thoughts can arouse emotions that lead to physiological changes. However, the opposite is also true—emotional responses can trigger bodily changes before signaling the cortex, before we are consciously aware of any emotional state. The work of LeDoux and others has demonstrated that subcortical pathways can activate emotions and their bodily expression independently of the neocortex. The pathways to the limbic structure of the amygdala and the amygdala's initiation of a bodily response happen before the first signals arrive in the cortex.[12] In particular, the neurological evidence supports the conclusion that emotions can "hijack" the cognitive centers of the brain, such as when you jump out of the way in fear, only to realize later that it was nothing to be afraid of. This quick and dirty mechanism may often be an error, causing a false alarm, but it has the advantage of getting you out of the way of danger, which justifies the high false alarm rate.[13]

"Person-independent" Emotion Recognition

One of the outstanding problems in trying to recognize emotions is that different individuals may express the same emotion differently. Patterns of expression vary in many ways—for example, one person's feet may perspire when he is nervous, while another person's hands may perspire.

Temperament and personality give clues to these patterns of expression. Extroverts tend to be more expressive than introverts. Extroverts in the United States speak with a louder voice and fewer hesitation pauses than do American introverts. Adults and children who show the most facial expressions have lower skin conductivity responses. Facially expressive newborns show evidence of lower arousal on heart rate measures than do less expressive infants.[14]

Expressive patterns also depend on gender, context, and social and cultural expectations. Adult women are more expressive than adult men in studies where they are shown slides and observed with a hidden camera. Children are more expressive in front of a hidden camera than when they are aware that an observer is present, and they are least expressive with anger and fear, two less socially acceptable emotions.[15]

In other words, given that a particular emotion is felt, a variety of factors influence how the emotion is displayed. Ekman writes, "The sine qua non for emotion should not be a unique pan-cultural signal" (Ekman, 1993). The present lack of consistent universal patterning mechanisms may appear to dim the outlook for constructing computers that can recognize affect. How can a machine be expected to recognize emotions if everyone expresses them differently?

This situation parallels that of another classic signal-processing problem, the problem of constructing "speaker-independent" speech recognition systems. I propose that it can be solved in a similar way. The goal of speaker-independent systems is to recognize what was said regardless of who said it. Even among people who use the same language, this goal is complicated by the fact that two people saying the same sentence produce different sound signals. They may have a different accent, different pitch, and other differing qualities to their speech. The computer has difficulty separating the language part of the signal from the part of the signal that identifies the speaker and his or her expression. Consequently, the computer has a hard time recognizing what was said unless it was trained on the individual speaker, or on someone who sounds like that speaker.

Although it would be a terrific accomplishment to solve this universal recognition problem, it is unnecessary. Nicholas Negroponte pointed out years ago that an alternative solution is to solve the problem in a speaker-dependent way, so that your personal computer can understand you and your language; thereafter, your computer can translate what you said to the rest of the world. Now that personal computers are becoming smaller and able to be with you all the time, this is becoming a viable solution. Therefore, experiments in recognizing emotional state from observations of physical expression only need to demonstrate consistent patterning for an individual in a given perceivable context. In many applications it is only necessary that your personal computer be able to recognize your affect; it can then translate this information to others if you wish.

The individual's personal computer will respond best if it is also able to perceive context—sense if you're climbing stairs, if the room temperature changed, or if you just read a news story about a tragic bombing. In other words, an affective computer will be more effective if it is also a perceptual computer. The computer can therefore identify autonomic responses conditioned on perceivable factors. For best performance, perceivable context should ultimately include not only the public milieu such as the comfort index of the weather, but also the private milieu—for example, the information that you have family in the town where the earthquake just happened.

For example, affect recognition for one context, such as commuting home, may be most reliable if it considers measures of blood flow and heart rate for one person, and measures of skin temperature, electrodermal response, and respiration for another person. These might change for an individual when the context changes, such as once they are home. Everyone need not be the same—it is only necessary that an individual respond relatively consistently under the same circumstances.

The affect recognition problem can be posed as a computer learning and pattern recognition problem, to determine which features are the best predictors for each individual, for each context. Moreover, we can expect that there will often be similarities across individuals, just like some people's voices sound similar, and across certain contexts. As reliable features are learned for individuals, they can be used to cluster individuals into categories based on similar features. A "universal" recognizer then would first ask "Which category is this person most similar to?" In speech, this might be likened to asking "who sounds like this—both accent-wise and voice-quality wise?" Subsequently, a recognizer can be used that was trained on the prototype person for that category. A benefit of this approach is that it is also likely to reveal categories of affective expression that theorists have not yet identified.[16]

Another benefit arises from this "lack of universality" problem. Some people will not want their emotions to be recognized except by those people or computers with whom they have a good relationship, i.e., those whom they know well, and who know them well. We are all acquainted with the phenomenon of having to spend some time interacting with someone before we figure out their sense of humor or, more subtly, before we learn how to tell if they are pleased or upset. If everyone communicated these emotions the same way all the time, then emotions would be easy to recognize. Although some emotions do appear to be universally communicated on faces, all emotions are not communicated the same way by all people. We appear to be best at recognizing emotions in those whom we know well. However, even with close friends, people are not 100% accurate at recognition. Expecting perfect recognition from computers would also be foolish; however, we should expect them to be better than random, and certainly better than they are presently.

Studies out of the Laboratory

The complications noted above have particularly plagued laboratory studies of human emotion. For example, certain subjects might feel inhibited about expressing disgust or sadness during a laboratory study. Other subjects might find the situations in the study contrived, and exhibit a much smaller repertoire of emotions than they would experience in their natural world. Or, they might express emotions they think they should express, instead of letting them arise "naturally." The ability to express emotions is believed to differ among subjects. Actors and musicians, for whom expressing emotions is part of their profession, show some of the greatest fluidity in expression.

Most studies on emotion and cognition have been confined to artificial lab scenarios, where they have been severely limited. Not only have they been limited by the environmental context of being in a laboratory, but they have focused on finding universal human patterns of expression rather than finding personal patterns. It is no surprise, therefore, that their results about how emotions map to expressions have been mixed.

Affective computers that read sentic modulation and infer underlying emotions can in theory help fix these problems. As the computers become lightweight and wearable, they can measure emotional responses wherever and whenever they occur, both for individuals and for larger groups. Affective computing allows the laboratory to visit the subject, instead of the other way around. The engineering details are not all solved yet; affective computers are in their infancy. However, this book will describe the steps toward their development, steps that should also lead to greater progress in understanding emotions.

Cognitive Aspects of Emotion

Now, let us consider the other side of emotion: its cognitive aspects. Both first-person experience and scientific studies indicate that cognitive appraisal can precede the generation of emotions. In the first scenario of this book, "waiting for a colleague," the tardy person's facial expression was appraised before an emotional response was selected. Similarly, in the wheelchair scenario, Rafe's cognitive assessment of Rebecca's accident caused him to change his anger to sympathy. In America in the late 80's, Bobby McFerrin's song, "Don't worry; be happy" filled the airwaves. All of these examples illustrate the message that thoughts can change emotions. In general, the influences can be considered to be "cognitive" when they involve appraisal, comparison, categorization, inference, attribution, or judgment.[17]

Primary vs. Secondary Emotions

A helpful distinction for sorting noncognitively-generated and cognitively-generated emotions is that of Damasio, who distinguishes between "primary" and "secondary" emotions (Damasio, 1994). Damasio writes that there are certain features of stimuli in the world that we respond to emotionally first, and that activate a corresponding cognitive state secondarily. Such emotions as startle upon hearing a loud bang, or the fear that causes an infant to retreat when a large object approaches rapidly, are "primary" and reside in the limbic system. These are the innate emotions, Jamesian in their accompanying physical response. But all emotions are not like this. Damasio defines "secondary" emotions as those that arise later in an individual's development when systematic connections are identified between primary emotions and categories of objects and situations. An example is grief, where physical responses occur in conjunction with cognitive understanding of an event such as the death of a loved one. Secondary emotions still activate limbic structures, but prefrontal and somatosensory cortices are also involved. In particular, secondary emotions can be initiated merely by cognitive thoughts.

The problems that plagued Damasio's patients such as "Elliot" illuminate the differences between primary and secondary emotions. Elliot's primary emotions were apparently intact; he could be startled by a loud noise. Also, if he watched a horrific movie scene, say where a human head exploded, then he knew cognitively that he should feel disturbed. This knowledge was evidently acquired before his brain damage. However, he no longer had the accompanying disturbing feeling, which he used to have before the damage to his frontal cortex. Physiologically, he registers no significant response to such scenes, in contrast with normals whose electrodermal response changes with such stimuli. In essence, his "cognitive" thoughts that would normally induce emotion can be activated, but these do not communicate with the subcortical structures needed to produce the rest of the emotional response. In a rather literal sense, Elliot is emotionally "detached." His limbic-cortical connections no longer function normally. His primary emotions are intact, but the connections are no longer in place for his secondary emotions to be fully present.

An analogy for a healthy person might be as follows. Suppose you hear of the death of a woman whom you've never met. Although you may feel sympathy and sorrow for the dear friends of the deceased, and think about their loss, it is unlikely you will *feel* grief since you had no attachment to her. In contrast, the loss of your beloved friend is likely to cause you not only to think about your loss but to have feelings of grief. In both cases there is cognitive appraisal—loss of a loved one—but only in the latter case is it associated with a persistent feeling of grief, an accompanying change in physiological state. Moreover, the physiological state of grieving can affect cognitive tasks, causing a "perturbance" in one's ability to concentrate on non-pressing intellectual activities.[18] Damasio's patients do not receive the accompanying physiological feeling.

In other words, there is a distinction between *thinking* about an emotion, e.g., "this is disturbing" and *feeling* disturbed. In healthy people, this distinction can happen, but more often the thought and the feeling co-occur, as in the case where a good feeling accompanies the event of seeing someone that you really like. In Damasio's patients with frontal-lobe damage, the two functions remain separate. The patients can cognitively know they should feel disturbed by something they are looking at, but they do not feel disturbed.

Developing and Learning Emotions

Emotional development begins in the womb. The fetus can be startled in the womb, and many babies exit the womb with a loud expression of distress. Babies demonstrate a less complicated repertoire of emotions than cogitating adults, presumably because of their lack of experience and not because of usage of social display rules. Babies also apparently lack the ability to construct "self-conscious" cognitive emotions such as shame and guilt, which develop later in childhood once a sense of identity is established (Lewis, 1993). In theory, as a child develops she learns how to generalize events that give rise to primary emotions, leading to the development of secondary emotions.

The cortical involvement in secondary emotions is hypothesized to help generalize primary emotional responses. For example, a primary response of flight from a rapidly approaching large object can be cognitively generalized to a principle such as "stay out of the paths of large moving objects such as cars, trucks and trains." The links develop as people mature, enabling them to learn and to generalize—for example, to learn to stay away from most things appraised as harmful, based on similarity to what has been harmful in the past.

Damasio's emotion-damaged patients were not able to learn like typical people. When Elliot made a bad investment, he recognized cognitively that it was harmful to his business and his family. However, he did not have the usual accompanying feelings, such as of harm or shame, and he did not learn to avoid the harmful behavior. Consequently, he repeatedly made bad decisions, eventually losing his job, his wife, and more. His emotional impairment manifested itself as a general lack of reasonableness and intelligence, even though he still scored above average on IQ tests and written tests of social behavior.

Cortical-limbic links can work in either direction, attaching feelings to thoughts or thoughts to feelings. Recalling a frightening incident can stir up feelings of fear, although they tend to not be as intense as when they were first experienced. A successful school of acting—"method acting" pioneered by Konstantin Stanislavsky—is based on imagining previously experienced emotive scenarios to arouse feelings as if actually experiencing them again.[19] An emotional state of fear can prompt the recall of other fearful situations, reinforcing the links between thoughts and feelings.

Complicating Conditions: Cognitive Aspects of Emotion

A number of factors confound attempts to understand the cognitive aspects of emotion. Several of the factors mentioned earlier that complicate physiological studies of emotion also complicate cognitive studies of emotion, for example social display rules, such as "It's inappropriate to show emotion during a scientific fact-finding presentation." Problems also occur in cognitive studies of emotion in the laboratory, where subjects are usually asked to verbalize their emotional state, as opposed to or in addition to its being physically measured. These problems concern the attaching of adjectives to emotions (Wallbott and Scherer, 1989). Two people might feel exactly the same way physically, and yet name the same feeling with two different names, depending on the cognitive events surrounding the state. Or, two people who say they are cognitively "very happy" might vary tremendously in terms of how they feel. How often these discrepancies may occur is not known; relatively few studies have simultaneously measured both physical and cognitive responses.

One of the big complicating factors is cognitive interpretation of the environment. Under controlled environments, or with the assistance of some wearable acoustic and visual scene analysis, a computer will eventually be able to recognize what is happening in the perceivable milieu, e.g., "the room is tiny and hot, a stranger enters and quickly walks toward the subject." However, these perceptions are only part of the entire perception that also includes things like how this stranger's eyes and gait indicate malice or long-lost love, and other subtleties on which a response can depend greatly.

A bigger problem is that even if a computer could perceive all these stimuli, how would it reason which should be interpreted as "good," "likable," "interesting" and so forth? Scientists do not yet know how people arrive at the valenced decisions they so readily make, of good vs. bad, like vs. dislike, important vs. unimportant, interesting vs. uninteresting, and so forth. These are often made unconsciously, without lists of pros and cons on paper or in the mind. Sometimes these kinds of judgments are lumped in with "common sense reasoning," and largely ignored in formal research efforts. However, these kinds of affective judgments are critical in human decision making and need to be better understood. In particular, because these kinds of judgments are accompanied by and influenced by valenced feelings, they could arise naturally in computers that have mechanisms of emotion.

Successful cognitive emotion models are likely to depend on other factors such as an individual's experience. For example, someone who has never seen a neighborhood cat run over by a car might be deeply disturbed the first time they are close to such an event, whether or not they are a cat lover. The man who works for the city and has to routinely remove animal carcasses from the roads may no longer have an emotional response, unless the carcass belongs to his beloved pet. The person's history, values, attachment, and general emotional maturity combine to influence their cognitive responses.

As data is collected from a variety of situations, patterns may be found that would improve a computer's ability to predict cognitive emotional responses to situations. Nonetheless, it is unlikely that every factor that influences emotion will be recognized. Therefore, one cannot expect a cognitive predictive model to work perfectly. To really predict how a person might respond emotionally requires knowing not just a person's situation, but also her goals, standards, and preferences. An affective computer should improve at this task as it collects and learns these things about an individual.

Cognitively generated emotions are often not expressed in readily observable ways, but may occur as thoughts. In this case, the emotions may be impossible for another person to recognize, since people cannot recognize each others thoughts. I have heard some people suggest that science might be able to find a process of recovering somebody's thoughts by looking at various brain signals produced while thinking those thoughts. This recovery problem may be posed as a so-called "inverse problem," where the goal is to invert the signal generation process to reconstruct the thoughts that gave rise to the signals. However, inverse problems are notoriously difficult. Thought-reading may be the biggest "inverse problem" imaginable. In other words, people need not worry about any person or machine reading their emotional thoughts.

Emotions and Creativity

"Men have called me mad; but the question is not yet settled, whether madness is or is not the loftiest intelligence—whether much that is glorious—whether all that is profound—does not spring from disease of thought—from moods of mind exalted at the expense of the general intellect."
—Edgar Allan Poe[20]

Creativity—an ability to create—is associated with the ability to combine ideas or elements in such a way as to form new and original connections or constructions. The cognitive mechanisms of creativity are not very well understood, although creativity is highly valued in most professions. Most would agree that today's computers are not creative in the sense that humans are, although certain behaviors of computers are occasionally declared to be creative.[21] One can argue that many tasks given to computers do not require creativity. However, as computers take on more complex situations where problem solving is required, they could benefit from the abilities humans prize as creative.

Is there a link between creativity and emotions? If there is, then one would expect to find higher proportions of highly creative people, such as artists, poets, and writers, to exhibit greater emotionality. Indeed, anecdotal evidence is in abundance—scores of influential 18th- and 19th-century poets, notably William Blake, Lord Byron, and Lord Tennyson, wrote about the extreme mood swings they endured. Poets and writers John Berryman, Ernest Hemingway, Randall Jarrell, Robert Lowell, Sylvia Plath, William Styron, and Anne Sexton were all hospitalized for either mania or depression during their lives. And many painters and composers, among them Vincent van Gogh, Georgia O'Keeffe, Charles Mingus, Robert Schumann, and Virginia Woolf, have been similarly afflicted. William James, the profoundly creative and influential psychologist, battled depression for many years.

Of course, mood disorders do not necessarily breed creative genius, nor does creative genius imply a mood disorder. However, scientists have, over many years now, documented evidence of a correlation between these effects, through controlled studies on thousands of artists, writers, and other creative professionals. The conclusion has been confirmed by a growing body of research: renowned writers, artists, and composers have been far more likely to experience mood disorders and to commit suicide than the general population.[22] Moreover, there is an unusually high occurrence of alcoholism, which points another curious finger of accusation at the limbic seat of emotions and its link to creativity. Centuries of artists and writers have described using substances such as alcohol to enhance their imaginations and creativity. In the brain, alcohol suppresses cortical activity, enhancing blood flow in the limbic system relative to that in the cortex. The result is often increased emotional fluidity—an ability to move more easily among different states, less hindered by cortical regulation. The maudlin drunk is another example of this phenomenon, but without the constructive intentions; his depressed cortical functions lead to emotional silliness. In people with synesthesia, alcohol's boost on the limbic system also boosts the vividness of synesthetic perceptions. Studies with synesthetes indicate that their synesthestic episodes are more vivid after alcohol, and less vivid after caffeine, the latter of which boosts the cortex relative to the limbic system.[23]

Emotions influence creativity not just in extraordinarily creative people, but also in ordinary folks. In particular, positive mood has been shown to have a significant impact on several aspects of creativity: recognizing relations between features of problems, giving unusual or creative first associates to neutral cues, discovering principles to integrate and remember information, and responding to Duncker's candle task.[24] In this task, subjects are given one of two situations: (1) a box of thumbtacks, a candle, and a book of matches, or (2) a box, a pile of thumbtacks, a candle, and a book of matches. In both cases they are asked to affix the candle to a cork board on the wall in such a way as to keep it from dripping on the floor when it is lit. Subjects are given ten minutes to find the solution. In the first case, most subjects cannot find the solution; in the second case, most succeed. When subjects were put into a good mood before being presented with the first situation, a significantly higher proportion of them succeeded (Isen, Daubman, and Nowicki, 1987).

Emotions and Memory

Much of emotion's influence on cognition may happen through emotion's influence on memory. Memory enters into nearly every cognitive task—perception, decision making, learning, planning, prioritizing, creativity, and more. From studies of the brain, we know that the cortex and limbic system exert influences on each other. In fact, it is known that there are many more connections carrying signals from the limbic system to the cortex than vice-versa. It is not surprising that emotions, as part of a "low-focus" dreamy-state kind of thinking, might lead to creative analogies. David Gelernter writes about this phenomenon in his book *The Muse in the Machine*, where he calls it "affect linking" (Gelernter, 1994). However, it is a less obvious, but far more compelling result, that emotions influence "high focus" reasoning.

One of the most reliable phenomena in the cognition-emotion literature is the effect of mood on evaluative judgment (Clore,1992). Consider, for example, the study of Forgas and Moylan where over a thousand people were interviewed about their views on political figures, crime, future events, and life satisfaction. Patrons were interviewed after exiting a movie theatre, where they had seen one of several movies, which had been previously classified as happy, sad, or aggressive in affective tone. In response to the interviewers' questions, the viewers made judgments that reflected the tone of the film they had just seen. No such bias was found among patrons who were entering the theatre (Forgas and Moylan, 1987).

Not only does mood influence judgments about seemingly objective events, but it also influences memory retrieval. Positive moods tend to make it easier to remember positive things, and negative moods tend to make it easier to remember negative things. When you are playing with your child and suddenly see his immense disappointment when a toy does not work the way he expects, then you might recall a long-lost memory of your own childhood disappointment. It may be a memory of a very different event, one that did not have anything to do with a toy. The primary thing in common between your child's event and the event you remembered may be a feeling, such as the feeling of playful enjoyment and expectation interrupted by immense disappointment. Memory retrieval is largely a mystery, but there is increasing evidence that emotions play a role in its function. Memory may be the chief mechanism through which emotions enter into the mental associations active in analogical thinking and creativity. Hence, we see the influence of emotions in both high-focus reasoning and low-focus generation of associations, as a consequence of emotional influences on memory.

Intentional vs. Spontaneous Smiles

It is said that the attentive observer is always able to recognize a false smile (Duchenne, 1862)—that is, a smile generated by the will instead of by a genuine feeling of happiness. Duchenne observed:

The muscle that produces this depression on the lower eyelid does not obey the will; it is only brought into play by a genuine feeling, by an agreeable emotion. Its inertia in smiling unmasks a false friend.

Neurological studies indicate that *true* emotions travel their own special path to the motor system. If the neurologist asks a patient who is paralyzed on one side to smile, then only one side of the patient's mouth raises. But when the neurologist cracks a funny joke, then a natural two-sided smile appears. For facial expression, it is widely accepted that the will and the emotions control separate paths (Ekman, 1990):[25]

If the lesion is in the pyramidal system . . . the patients cannot smile deliberately but will do so when they feel happy. Lesions in the nonpyramidal areas produce the reverse pattern; patients can smile on request, but will not smile when they feel a positive emotion.

In other words, an intentional smile travels a different path than a spontaneous one. The cognitively-generated command to smile does not express itself in the same way as a genuine feeling of happiness expresses itself. Not only does this imply that, physiologically, false and sincere smiles may be discriminated, but it illustrates the existence of multiple paths, multiple causes, for emotional expression.

Inducement of Emotion

Certain physical acts are peculiarly effective, especially the facial expressions involved in social communication; they affect the sender as much as the recipient.
—Minsky, in *Society of Mind*

There is emotional inducement ever at work around us—a good marketing professional, playwright, actor, or politician knows the importance of appealing to your emotions. Aristotle devoted much of his teachings on rhetoric to instructing speakers how to arouse the desired emotions in their audience (Aristotle, 1960). Adolf Hitler took this to a horrific extreme with his mind-washing propaganda to instill hatred for the Jewish people. Hitler also exploited the increased susceptibility of people when they were weary by gathering them in the evenings, and when they were in large crowds, and hence more inclined to respond according to a herd-like instinct. Although weariness and herd-instinct are not considered emotions, they were underlying factors that, once induced, made it easier to manipulate people's thoughts and emotions.

The most frequent example of mood inducement, however, is choosing forms of entertainment, especially music. We enjoy selecting a recording that affects our mood in a particular way—a piece to lift one's mood, or to console one in a state of grief. We tend to believe that we are also free to choose our response to the stimulus. An open, and somewhat ominous question is, are we always free to do so? It is known that internal direct stimulation of the brain can elicit various emotions (Hess, 1957). However, can some part of our nervous system be externally activated to force experience of an emotion?

A number of theorists have postulated that sensory feedback from muscle movements, such as facial movements, is sufficient to induce a corresponding emotion. The saying, "smile and you'll feel happier" has some truth to it. For example, Laird (1982) divides people into "cueing" categories based on whether or not posturing their faces in a particular expression induces the corresponding emotional experience. Ekman has shown that posing people's faces gives rise not only to a subjective emotional experience consistent with the posed expression, but also gives rise to other physiological signals that distinguish the emotions (Ekman, 1983). Experiments by Levenson and colleagues also showed that facial actions can initiate emotions; in that work, Levenson predicts that other physical components of emotion might assume this initiating role (Levenson, 1992). Izard and Ekman overview some of the evidence for and against various claims about sensorimotor influence (Izard, 1993; Ekman, 1993).

Whether or not such sensorimotor inputs induce emotion, they appear to be effective in maintaining and expressing emotion. Posture is correlated with expressions of self-esteem (Izard, 1993; Lewis, 1995), and good actors study how to align their body position in accord with an imagined emotion, to help reinforce its effects. Instead of imagining previously experienced emotional events like his teacher Stanislavsky, Chekhov's school of acting taught that you could imagine fictional events and the external movements of a character suffering such events, and so take them upon your character. For example, to capture sadness he suggested imagining the grieving sounds of a rural village mourning the accidental and gruesome deaths of a little boy and a little girl (Chekhov, 1991). When the body's emotional expression, e.g., a sad face, forward trunk, bowed head, and drooping shoulders, agrees with the cognitive emotion, "My character is depressed," then the combined emotional experience is enhanced, and the actor may "feel depressed." Consequently, the communication of the emotion can be more powerful. Of course, these actors adjust their physical state in accord with a cognitive goal. Hence, this is an example where emotions are initially cognitively-generated and the body-mind reinforcement intensifies and regulates the experience.

Body-mind reinforcement may provide subliminal ways to induce emotion, perhaps by engaging parts of a person's body in movements that they are unaware of. The potential of such methods to induce emotion is unclear at this point, but may hinge on only a slight willingness of an individual to be open to inducement.

There is also strong evidence that emotional biases can be induced subliminally. Simply presenting a person with an image of a face subliminally, repeatedly, can bias them toward liking that face. This phenomemon is at the root of the now illegal advertising practice of inserting promotional images into a movie in such a way that movie-goers do not see the advertisement consciously. In fact, apparently we humans are more greatly influenced by emotional responses to unconsciously presented stimuli than by emotional responses to the same stimuli, presented consciously (LeDoux, 1996). The possibility of subliminal inducement may evoke disturbing thoughts of potentially harmful mind and mood control; or potentially beneficial mental enhancement and increased affective freedom. It is not an area to be entered into without considering both negative and positive aspects of how such new understanding could be used. As computers develop affective abilities, they potentially may be used not only for monitoring emotion, but also for manipulating it, for both helpful and harmful purposes. Chapter 4 addresses several concerns for undesirable applications of affective technology.

There are other subtle ways in which emotions are not induced *per se* but in which they are deliberately influenced. Simply being sincerely kind and respectful to someone can have the effect of positively influencing their emotions. However, this kind of influence is rarely achieved if the kindness is part of a manipulative goal. Unselfish kindness, especially acts such as forgiveness, are some of the most powerful influences on a person's emotions.

Summary

This chapter has provided several basics about human emotion theory, emphasizing two aspects of emotion: physical and cognitive. I highlighted findings that will be important for affective computing, particularly in giving computers the ability to recognize, express, and "have" emotions. In particular, I have described social display rules, universal vs. person-specific responses, primary vs. secondary emotions, the role of emotions in creativity and general memory processes, the existence of multiple paths for emotion expression in humans, and emotion inducement.

In order for computers to be equipped to recognize human emotion, it is important that mappings between emotional states and emotional expressions be understood so that the former can be inferred from the latter. Computers can begin to see, hear, and otherwise sense responses from people that they are in physical contact with. This chapter has highlighted ways in which emotion can be expressed through sentic modulation—including facial expression, vocal intonation, gesture, posture, and other bodily changes. Part II will address pattern recognition methods for computers to use in emotion communication.

Additionally, a computer can observe human behavior and language, and analyze a situation to infer which emotions are likely to be present. The focus in this case is on cognitive reasoning, which can be used not only to reason about what emotions are present, but also to give rise to an emotional state in a computer. The key problem in this aspect of emotion is to understand what situations give rise to which emotions, at least typically, and then how these emotions influence behavior in a situation. Computers are only recently receiving the ability to perceive and reason about situations in terms of the emotions they raise, a topic I will delve deeper into in Part II. Once these abilities are in place, a cognitive assessment of a situation can also be used to help a computer decide which emotions might be appropriate for it to have or express, and when, where, and how.

2   *Affective Computers*

Emotions are important in human intelligence, rational decision making, social interaction, perception, memory, learning, creativity, and more. They are necessary for intelligent day-to-day functioning. The negative connotations of "being emotional" or "acting emotionally" are not valid excuses for ignoring the study of emotions, or its application to computers. Instead, it is time to examine how emotions can be incorporated into models of intelligence, and particularly, into computers and their interactions with humans.

To date, researchers trying to create intelligent computers have focused on problem solving, reasoning, learning, perception, language, and other cognitive tasks considered essential to intelligence. Most of them have not been aware that emotion influences these functions in humans. Some have scoffed at the idea of giving computers emotions. However, now there is a preponderance of evidence that emotion plays a pivotal role in functions considered essential to intelligence. This new understanding about the role of emotion in humans indicates a need to rethink the role of emotion in computing.

Let me remind the reader, that when I refer to "computers" I mean not just a monitor and keyboard with one or more CPU's, but also computational agents such as software assistants and animated interactive creatures, robots, and a host of other forms of computing devices, including "wearables," which I will describe in greater detail later. Any computational system, in software or hardware, might be given affective abilities.

Most of today's computers do not have emotions *per se*. What would it mean for a computer to "have emotions"? To recognize or express emotions? To exhibit emotional intelligence? After a note about emotional development, this chapter considers these four topics in sequence: computers that recognize emotions, express emotions, have emotions, and have emotional intelligence. Along the way I will propose design criteria for such systems, describe tests they might have to pass, and examine the differences between emotion in computers and humans.

Developing Emotions

There is a tendency, perhaps because these examples are easy to think of, to imagine the worst forms of emotions in computers. For example, consider if you repeatedly typed the wrong input to your machine, and the machine finally said, "You stupid oaf! Read the manual." Clearly, there must be more to benefit from affective computing than this. This scenario, and similar ones involving grumpy agents or surly software, are products of a faulty underlying assumption—that computers with emotional states will also "act emotionally," which is virtually synonymous with "act stupidly." Having emotions does not *cause* stupid behavior. An intelligent adult has a full range of emotions and is capable of effectively managing and using these emotions to aid in many important functions. If he acts emotionally in a socially maladroit way, then he is thought to be less intelligent. Affective computers with poor emotional skills would be much worse to interact with than non-affective computers. If computers act stupidly when they first become affective, it will be because their designers have not given them the ability to act intelligently with emotions.

Consider emotional development in humans. Infants communicate primarily with emotional expression: crying, smiling, screaming, or laughing. All of these appear before language; emotions are evidently in the substrate before the more obvious signs of intelligence develop. If a child did not have the ability to express emotions, she would be severely impaired in her development and chances for survival. Emotional expressions are the signals used by an infant to communicate her needs: she cries when cold, bored, dirty, hungry, or in pain. A baby that smiles gives her parents the rewarding feedback of believing they have made their child happy. The infant does not encourage the parent by speaking, "Thank you for spending every other hour of the last twenty-four feeding me," but when the exhausted mother sees her child's contented expression, she *feels* a big reward, an emotional and intellectual boost that encourages her to continue caring for the child despite the effort involved.

Even though computers do not feel cold, hungry, wet, or bored in the same way a baby does, they have needs that might give rise to infant-like emotions. Every machine has an operating temperature range, and when the machine gets too hot or cold it fails. Computers need energy to run, and will cease processing if this is not provided. A robot's memory can fill up and "leak," making a mess which, although not offensive in odor, takes time to clean up. When given the goal of sorting through the overwhelming amount of networked sources of information, in search of interesting items for its user, then it might be useful for an agent to have boredom—to alert it to the need to stop wandering along a fruitless path.

As children mature, they learn social skills and ways in which to control their emotions and their emotional expression. As they develop, they also improve their ability to recognize emotions, to recognize situations that are apt to generate emotions, and to manage emotions. Similarly, an affective computer will probably need a developmental process whereby it acquires knowledge relevant to its affective and other abilities. It may be impossible for its designers, builders, and programmers to think of everything it will need in advance. Consequently, it will need both an innate set of abilities, and tools to continually learn new ones. The goal would be for it to reach an equivalent of "adulthood" in terms of affective abilities. A computer that interacts with adults should be capable of operating with the emotional intelligence of an adult.

Adult emotional intelligence consists of the abilities to recognize, express, and have emotions, coupled with the ability to regulate these emotions, harness them for constructive purposes, and skillfully handle the emotions of others. I use "emotional intelligence" in the way that has become common in the literature, even though there is ongoing debate about the use of the word "intelligence" since often the word implies something innate, whereas many of the aspects of emotional intelligence are skills that can be learned. Along the way it will become clear that every computer does not need all of these affective abilities all of the time. In fact, there will be many examples in the next chapter of applications where only a subset of the abilities are needed. Nevertheless, some computers that interact with people and have their own emotions could benefit from all of these abilities.

In the rest of this chapter, I propose criteria for giving computers affective abilities. These criteria are based on what is known about human emotions, on the methodology of adapting human emotions to computers. Of course, there are other possible methodologies that might yield different criteria; we are free to endow computers with any abilities that we can figure out how to develop. One of the most compelling alternate methodologies is that of letting emotions "emerge" in computers according to their own requirements. Since computers presently have different needs and behaviors than humans, why should they not be allowed to develop the emotions that suit these needs, as opposed to being given a set of our emotions that does not necessarily serve them well? This argument is a valid one, as long as the computers' needs remain subservient to the human needs for which the computer was designed. On the other hand, the word "computers" in the previous sentence can take on many different meanings and roles, one of which may include that of a social agent interacting with humans, in which case we can argue that the computer would at least benefit from understanding social aspects of human emotions. Consequently, even if social computers develop their own mechanisms of emotion, they will likely benefit from understanding human emotions, and end up with at least some affective abilities that are similar to human ones.

Adapting human emotions for computers should help computers acquire some of the benefits of emotions described in the previous chapters: more flexible and rational decision-making, the ability to address multiple concerns in an intelligent and efficient way, the ability to determine salience and valence, more human-like attention and perception, and numerous other interactions with cognitive and regulatory processes. Human-like abilities to recognize affect should also make it easier for computers to perceive human responses such as "pleased" or "displeased," which will help them learn how to adjust their behavior. This goal is motivated by a principle I would like to see practiced more: computers should be adapting to people rather than vice-versa. Facilitating the kind of interaction that comes naturally to humans is a win; it is a key step toward human-centered computing. Based on adapting what is known about human emotions, the next four sections propose, respectively, criteria for a computer to recognize emotions, to express emotions, to have emotions, and to have emotional intelligence.

Computers that Recognize Emotions

One of the hallmarks of an intelligent computer will be its ability to recognize emotions—to infer an emotional state from observations of emotional expressions and through reasoning about an emotion-generating situation. The computer might try to recognize the emotions of its user, of other agents with which it interacts, and of itself, if it has emotions. Recognition may require vision and hearing abilities for gathering facial expressions, gestures, and vocal intonation. Additionally, the computer may use other inputs that may or may not have analogs in human senses—reading infrared temperature, measuring electrodermal response, and so forth. Once emotional expressions are sensed and recognized, the system can use its knowledge about the situation and its knowledge about emotion generation to infer the underlying emotional state which most likely gave rise to the expressions. Giving a computer these perceptual and interpretive abilities could potentially give it as much ability to recognize emotions as another person might have. How will we know when it has this ability?

Evaluating Affect Recognition

Here is one test a computer should pass if it can recognize affect. A digital video of a person, containing one or more modalities of expression such as voice, face, gesture, or gait could be observed by both a group of humans and a group of computers. The humans and computers are asked what emotion the person in the video is expressing. When the group of computers and the group of humans respond with the same distribution of answers, then we could say that the computers are recognizing emotions as well as the humans.[1]

Consider if 70% of the humans watching the video think it reveals anger and 30% think it reveals hatred—then a single computer should not be penalized if it recognizes the expression as hatred. When 70% of the computers recognize anger, and the rest recognize hatred, then they have succeeded in matching the humans for this data. Success could be equivalently determined if one computer recognizes that the emotions are "anger with 70% probability and hatred with 30% probability." This test can be repeated for a palette of emotions and subjects.

Alternatively, suppose that we could insure that the person in the video is truly expressing one particular emotion, such as anger. In this case, we might not claim success unless the computer recognized anger. This would be an unusually lofty goal for a computer, however, as most people are not 100% successful at recognizing emotions, even when the emotions are truthfully expressed. In humans, ability to recognize emotions is a sign of emotional intelligence, and can be improved with practice, but perfect performance is never guaranteed.

The test can also be run in two modes—person-dependent, and person-independent. In the person-dependent mode, the computer already knows the person, and customizes its recognition abilities to use what it knows about that individual. Its best recognition performance should occur when it sees the person expressing an emotion that it has seen him express before. In the person-independent mode, the computer may never have seen the person before, and must use some generic recognition abilities. Depending on how closely this new person's expressions are to ones the computer has recognized before, the computer will have correspondingly better success in recognizing his expression and underlying emotion.

I have over-simplified the test scenario, and will postpone discussion of the technical difficulties until I describe how computers are learning to recognize facial and vocal expressions. However, the gist of the test should be clear: for a computer to imitate human recognition ability, we should be able to momentarily swap a computer for a human, and the computer should recognize the same emotions that the human would recognize.

It is entirely possible that computers may become better than some people when it comes to recognizing emotions. This raises the blood pressure of many people, especially those who fear that machines may find out things about them that they wish to keep private. The possibility of computers becoming good at emotion recognition has both positive applications (Chapter 3) and somewhat ominous ones (Chapter 4). But for now, however, numerous advances are needed before computers will be as good as humans at recognizing human expressions of emotion.

Computer recognition of *computer* emotion may also become important. In that case, if computers imitate the same patterns of expression as humans, then recognition can proceed in the same way. If they do not follow human patterns, and they need not do so, then recognition of computer emotion may occur in ways we have yet to conceive. Indeed, it is hard to think of examples of non-human emotions that computers might develop; but, this is a possibility that needs to be allowed if a designer chooses to let a computer evolve its own emotions.

The prospect of computers that recognize our emotions raises another issue: which emotions? Those that are expressed publicly, or those that are expressed via more personal contact? Public emotions are communicated through facial expression, vocal inflection, and overt gestures or body language; these are the more "visible" forms of sentic modulation. They are also the forms over which we have the most control. However, if somebody holds your hand, then they may also feel your pulse racing and sense your clammy hands gradually relaxing and warming. The more personal the contact they have with you, the more likely they are to sense physiological signals from you that are sincere indications of your emotions, signals that most people cannot control by will.[2] Such personal expression is reserved for close friends, lovers, and occasionally physicians or psychiatrists. Because people have frequent physical contact with computers, computers are in a unique position to sense affective signals that are personal, as well as to perceive those that are public.

Differences in Human and Computer Recognition

Computers, not yet of flesh and bone, perceive their world through cameras, microphones, keyboards, mice, and other sensors. These are their eyes, ears, hands, and skin. A computer's sensors may be structured to produce human-like functioning—e.g., juxtaposing two cameras for binocular visual input, shaping pressure sensors onto a robotic hand, or surrounding microphones by an artificial pinna modeled on the human ear. Such efforts have the worthy potential of aiding sensory-impaired humans as well as sensory-impaired machines.

However, machines need not be limited to human-like sensors. Neither need humans be limited, for that matter. A computer could have infrared vision, for example. A human, wearing this computer, can also have infrared vision, given some tools that transform the infrared imagery to visible bands and present it to the human eyes. A computer could have sensitive hearing abilities, outside the normal human range. It could, with some transforming, convert the signals to a form that can be interpreted by a human. The computer might have access to your electrodermal response, pheromones, brainwaves, electromyogram, or blood pressure. It need not be limited to seeing facial and gestural expressions, feeling hand temperature, and hearing vocal inflection, but could pick up signals via any sensors you choose for interacting with it. In this way the computer can have more senses available to it than a person ordinarily has. Consequently, it is possible that computers might recognize emotions and other states that humans would not ordinarily recognize.

In fact, it is possible for computers to recognize affective states that do not presently have names. For example, suppose that late in the afternoon Chris sometimes gets in a peculiar mood where he cannot concentrate on work and finds it relaxing to play 30 minutes of games on the Web. It may be that his physiological signals form a characteristic pattern when he gets in this state. There may be no name for the state he is in. Nonetheless, it may occur with enough regularity that it is useful for the computer to identify its physiological pattern, and to notice that it is a good predictor of some of Chris's behaviors. If typically this state precedes Chris's request for some game software, then the next time the computer detects this state it might preload this software, saving time if Chris decides to play.

Affect Recognition, without other Affective Abilities?

There are numerous advantages to having a machine that can recognize emotions. The computer tutor in the introduction of this book was but one case where it would be useful to recognize the user's emotions and modify the computer's behavior in response. In fact, it may be advantageous to have *only* this affective ability in the machine, i.e. the ability to recognize emotions, without having to "have" emotions, or express them. In fact, the computer might be limited to just recognizing emotional *expressions* such as facial expressions. Chapter 6 describes a system that does this.

However, if its recognition abilities are to pass a test of comparison to human recognition abilities, then other affective abilities are also necessary. People do not recognize emotions based just on the signals seen, heard, or otherwise sensed; they also use higher-level knowledge and reasoning about goals, situations, and preferences. Sarah may enter the stage wearing a smile that might cause most people to recognize her as happy. However, if you know that she just found out that a dear friend committed suicide, then you might label her emotion as deep sadness or grief, and maybe anger, but masked with a smile.

People also reason about the sincerity of emotions, and whether or not a situation calls for sincere expression, or masking of one's true feelings. A certain amount of emotional savvy is helpful for recognizing these situations. This may be in the form of common-sense rules, such as "adults are usually less expressive than children" or in the form of social display rules such as "it is inappropriate to snicker at a funeral." Knowing these rules influences what we think we hear and see—e.g., that snickering sound at the funeral probably was not laughter, but somebody with a head cold trying to breathe. Emotional savvy also needs to be learned, continuously, for individuals and contexts; for example: "Every time Beth has visited Amy and talked about their children, it has cheered Beth up," and "Joe tends to deal with frustration by going off to play solitaire." Such knowledge can be turned around to infer emotional states in the absence of complete information—to guess that after Beth's visit, she will feel better, or that if Joe is playing solitaire, perhaps he was feeling frustrated.

Perhaps the sneakiest influence on human emotion recognition is the mood of the person doing the recognizing. As described earlier, if someone is in a bad mood and sees an ambiguous facial expression, then he or she is more likely to judge the face as negative. In contrast, if the viewer is in a good mood, then the same facial expression is more likely to be seen positively. What gets recognized—a happy or sad face—is determined in part by the mood of the perceiver. Consequently, for computer recognition to imitate human recognition, computers also need to imitate the influence of mood. If the computer has a mood, then its recognition can be biased accordingly. If not, then the computer can be equipped to reason about these biases.

Certain influences of human emotions, such as biasing perception, may seem unnecessary and undesirable to imitate in a computer, except perhaps for the purpose of modeling human emotions for better understanding them. Sometimes the influence of emotions on perception is good, such as to focus the perceiver more closely on a threat, while at other times it is bad, such as when a mood interferes with accurate perception of information. In a human emotion system the good seems often to be inextricably accompanied by the bad. This issue will arise several times in this book: Can we have the good without the bad? There are many ways in which it would be nice to imitate the human emotion system in computers, but there are also ways in which we might want to deviate from it.

Summary of Criteria for Recognition

Design criteria for a computer that can recognize emotion are summarized as follows:

- Input. Receives a variety of input signals, for example: face, voice, hand gestures, posture and gait, respiration, electrodermal response, temperature, electrocardiogram, blood pressure, blood volume pulse, electromyogram, etc.

- Pattern recognition. Performs feature extraction and classification on these signals. For example: analyzes video motion features to discriminate a frown from a smile.

- Reasoning. Predicts underlying emotion based on knowledge about how emotions are generated and expressed. Ultimately, this ability requires perceiving and reasoning about context, situations, personal goals and preferences, social display rules, and other knowledge associated with generating emotions and expressing them.

- Learning. As the computer "gets to know" someone, it learns which of the above factors are most important for that individual, and gets quicker and better at recognizing his or her emotions.

- Bias. The emotional state of the computer, if it has emotions, influences its recognition of ambiguous emotions.

- Output. The computer names or describes the recognized expressions, and the emotions likely to be present.

Embedded in these criteria are numerous technical requirements, for example, "receiving inputs" requires accurate technology for gathering digital physiological, audio, and visual signals, as well as research to determine which signals are most important for the task at hand. In pattern recognition, informative features of the signals need to be identified—statistical, structural, nonlinear, etc.—together with conditioning variables that influence the meanings of these features. Part II will delve more deeply into the implementation of emotion recognition.

Computers that Express Emotions

The human voice is always changing. Even if the receptionist says the same "Good afternoon, welcome to Sirius Cybernetics Corporation," every time you call, his or her intonation is always slightly different—a cheerful hello, a brusque hello. The same person can speak the same words, but say them entirely differently. Sometimes the part of the message that communicates emotion is the most important part.

One problem the information age has brought is that of too much information, which tends to lead to cognitive fatigue and a reduced ability to accurately process new inputs. In contrast, information presented through the "affective channel" does not usually demand conscious attention. Affective information can be perceived in parallel with non-affective information, without increasing your workload. In speech, *what* is said can be considered the semantic information, and *how* it is said can be considered largely the affective information. The latter is communicated through the modulation of vocal parameters in ways I will describe more carefully later. Speaking a simple "Hello!" in a happier tone than usual is, for both the speaker and listener, less work than speaking the two separate messages: "Hello" and "I'm more happy than usual at this moment."

If the computer spoke an audible greeting, its voice would become a channel that could be used to express important information about valence or urgency. Its greeting might ring of joy or sadness—perhaps a pre-indicator of the affective tone of the news that it found for you while you were asleep last night. In this example the communication accomplishes two things at once: greeting you, and informing you about the nature of news, without demanding extra time on your part. Affective inflection not only makes for a more pleasant interaction, but also it makes for efficient communication.

A computer can express emotion without having emotion, just like humans can express emotions that they do not have. A software agent acting as a tour guide could post a happy greeting without any underlying emotional state. A computer switchboard operator could vary the affective quality of its greeting in an effort to sound more pleasing. It may seem peculiar that one could have emotional expression without having emotions to express. Nonetheless, this is entirely possible in a computer. The basic requirement for a computer to have the ability to express emotions is that the machine have channels of communication such as voice or image, and an ability to communicate affective information over those channels. For example, a computer or software agent that displays a face could use an expression such as a smile—like a Macintosh does, upon booting up. Alternatively, if a computer actually had emotions, then it might also have some direct read-out display of its emotional state that changed, like a human smile, every time it encountered a suitable stimulus, like a funny joke. In these simple ways, computers already have channels for expressing emotions, whether or not they have emotions.

A machine can be used as a channel for transmitting human emotions. When two humans communicate via email or via teleconference, the machine and network act as a communication channel connecting people. Typically the channel is band-limited: all the information it receives at one end cannot be sent to the other end; some of it is lost. For example, it might convert a speech signal to text, throwing away the affective part of the signal. We might describe the *affective bandwidth* of a channel as how much affective information the channel lets through. *Affective information* might refer to the entropy of the affective part of the signal, which indicates how many bits are required to describe the part of the signal that carries the affective message. The idea of entropy as information is that of Claude Shannon, whose renowned theory of information applies also as a framework for emotion communication (Shannon and Weaver, 1963; Buck, 1984). Using the framework of information theory, we might also speak of the relative "affective channel capacity" of various forms of communication, to indicate how much affective information can be carried.

When sending the same words, different channels allow for more or for less affective channel capacity: email usually communicates the least affect, phone slightly more, videoteleconferencing more still, and "in person" communication the most. It is usually assumed that technology-mediated communication always has less affective bandwidth than person-to-person communication. Sometimes the limits on affective bandwidth are desirable. You might wish to choose a medium where your emotions are not as easily seen. However, rarely is it desirable to have these limits forced on you. Affective recognition and expression can be used to allow for more possibilities in communication, even with limited technology. For example, if there is not enough bandwidth to transmit each person's facial expression, the computer might recognize the expression, send just a few bits describing it, and then represent these with an animated face on the other side of the channel.[3]

Might technology increase affective bandwidth? Virtual environments and computer-mediated communication offer possibilities that we do not ordinarily have in person-to-person communication. Potentially, communication through virtual environments could provide new channels for affect—perhaps, as one idea, via sensors that detect physiological information and relay its significant information. In this way, computer-mediated communication might potentially have *higher* affective bandwidth than traditional "in person" communication. Of course, the use of such communication would not be desirable all the time. It might be saved for long-distance communication with loved ones, or for contact with emergency medical personnel.

Consider if a computer could perceive its user typing happily while sending email. If desired by the sender, who ultimately should have control over what gets sent, the computer could pass some of the affective quality of the interaction through the channel to the recipient. But, how would it express this on the other side? Would it transmit the sound of the keys clicking? Or, use a bright sounding voice to convert the email text to speech? Would it change the color of the email window to reflect a sunny mood? If the email sender were furious, and wanted the recipient to know, then even more possibilities arise, since the channels of emotional expression available to a machine are different than those available to a person. The machine might literally vent its heat in the direction of the recipient.

Evaluating Affect Expression

One way to test a computer's ability to express emotions is to have it express certain emotions and have a human try to recognize what it has expressed. Clark Elliott, of DePaul University, conducted one instance of this test. The computer used facial and vocal inflection to communicate several emotional states. Elliott videotaped the computer's efforts, and also videotaped an actor saying the same sentences trying to communicate the same emotional states. The sentences were deliberately ambiguous, so as not to reveal the emotions by their semantic content. In tests with human listeners, the humans were more accurate at recognizing the emotions when expressed by the computer than when expressed by the actor. The computer succeeded roughly 70% of the time in conveying the intended expression, while the actor succeeded only about 50% of the time. The conclusion is that not only can computers express emotions, but in some cases, they can do so more accurately than humans, especially when they employ caricature (Elliott, 1997).

Another possibility for evaluating emotional expression by a computer is to test for the computer's ability to *induce* emotion, by contagion. Goleman, in his book *Emotional Intelligence*, gives an example of a steamy August New York City day when he dragged his sullen self onto a bus, only to encounter a cheery bus driver, who greeted and entertained his passengers with such enthusiasm and genuine joy that their moods were nearly all transformed by the end of their ride. We all know cases where another person's emotional expression has altered our own. Computers also have an opportunity to influence the mood of their users, negatively or positively. It is possible that a computer, which expressed an underlying mood, might contagiously transmit its mood to people.

Differences in Human and Computer Expression

Not only do computers have the ability to physically vent heat, but computer expression of emotions can differ from that of humans in that there may be different emotions to express. Computers may have unique affective states, with correspondingly unique forms of expression, perhaps decodable only by other computers. These might be meaningless to most of us: "Warning: emotion 90. Free-memory cycle stress," but may nonetheless communicate important information to another computer, such as a lack of receptivity to large new memory demands at the moment.

A computer will need to know when to be subtle in its emotional expression, and when to exaggerate to make an emotion clear. Actors and animators know well the importance of being unambiguous in communicating emotion. The rest of us are often not as good at this. Computers endowed with such abilities might be more effective than their users at expressing emotions. In fact, in some applications, such talented computers might be used as amplifiers or coaches, helping a person to more accurately communicate emotions.

A problem with machines that can express emotion, but not have emotion, is that this case does not occur with humans. Humans have emotions whether or not they express them. Computers do not have to have emotions to express them—they can just paint their screen with a smile, if that's what the program says to do. A computer could be in one internal affective state, while expressing a different state. Somebody who looks at an agent's face might presume the agent was expressing its affective state. Even if the computer had separate systems for displaying intentional and spontaneous emotions, these need not be implemented the same way they are in humans. More than two such systems might exist, and so forth. In fact, the whole question of "intentional" vs. "spontaneous" expressions in a computer is an interesting one, for an observer may never be able to insure that a spontaneous-appearing expression was not artificially created. Chapter 4 will look at issues of computer deception, together with other potential problems that need to be addressed with the design of affective computing systems.

Affect Expression, without other Affective Abilities?

A computer can have the ability to express emotions without "having" them or recognizing them, as I mentioned above with the examples where the computer simply acts as an unemotional channel for transmission of human emotion, or where a computer generates expressions out of social politeness or to efficiently convey the affective tone of information. Humans can also express an unfelt emotion, such as making an intentional smile vs. smiling because something is funny. In humans, however, the bodily expression feeds back and can cause an emotion to actually be felt, as we read about earlier in experiments where people's faces were posed into an expression, causing them to feel the corresponding emotion. The ability in humans for emotions to co-occur with their expression makes it especially difficult to separate "expressing an emotion" from "having an emotion." In particular, a human who is strongly experiencing one emotion can find it hard to express a different emotion. A person caught up in an angry rage, when asked to express love, will not succeed in a very convincing expression of love until the anger has subsided. Having some kinds of emotions makes others hard to express. This bias-exclusion effect impacts a system that can both express and have emotions.

Summary of Criteria for Expression

Design criteria for a computer that can express emotion are summarized as follows:

▪ Input. Computer receives instructions from a person, a machine, or from its own emotion-generation mechanisms if it has them, telling it what emotion(s) to express.

▪ Intentional vs. spontaneous pathways. The system may have at least two paths for activation of emotional expression: one that is intentional, and one that is spontaneous. The former is triggered by a deliberate decision, while the latter acts within a system that has emotion, automatically modulating some of the system's outputs with the current emotion.

▪ Feedback. Not only does affective state influence affective expression, but the expression can influence the state.

▪ Bias-exclusion. It is easiest to express the present affective state, and this state can make the expression of certain other states more difficult.

▪ Social display rules. When, where, and how one expresses emotions is determined in part by the relevant social norms.

▪ Output. System can modulate visible or vocal signals such as a synthetic voice, animated face, posture and gait of an animated creature, music, and background colors, in both overt ways such as changing a facial expression, and in subtle ways such as modifying discourse timing parameters.

Computers that "Have" Emotions

Can machines feel? This question may be the most profound one within the topic of affective computing. Feelings are often considered to be that which separates human from machine. Furthermore, the possibility of creating a computer with subjective feelings hinges on the issue of machines having consciousness, which is itself a topic of unfettered debate. What does it mean, computationally, for a computer to "have" emotions? How would we know if a computer did or did not? Despite the tremendous complexity of these questions, I will propose an answer below by describing five components of a system that has emotions. The emphasis on five components is for explanatory purposes only and is not intended to imply how the mechanisms of emotion are structured in an affective system. In a healthy human emotional system, all of the five components are present. Although all the components are present in a complete emotional system, they do not have to be all activated at every moment the system is operating. I suggest that we may argue that a computer "has emotions" when all five components are present in a computer.

Component 1: Emergent Emotions and Emotional Behavior
The first component of having emotions is what I will call "emergent emotions." Emergent emotions are those which are attributed to systems based on their observable emotional behavior—especially when the system which is behaving has no explicit internal mechanism or representation for emotions. In humans, who *do* have internal emotional mechanisms, this component refers to emotional behaviors and other outward expressions.

An example of emergent emotions comes from Braitenberg's *Vehicles* (Braitenberg, 1984). One of his simplest vehicles has two light sensors and two motors, hooked up so that when it sees a light source straight ahead, it moves toward it, and bangs into it, hitting it frontally. When the source is not straight ahead, then the vehicle turns and moves so that it still approaches the source and hits it. Its behavior is seen by human observers as aggressive, as if the vehicle felt a negative emotion toward the light source. Vehicles can also be wired so as to linger near the source and not damage it. This behavior gives the impression of a more favorable emotion, such as love.

In 1962, Masanao Toda, a Japanese psychologist who emphasizes the importance of studying whole systems, including perception, action, memory, and learning, proposed a scenario with a "fungus eater," a humanoid robot, to illustrate how emotions would emerge in a system with limited resources operating in a complex and unpredictable environment (Toda, 1962). Toda's robot has a goal of collecting as much uranium ore as possible, while regulating its energy supply for survival. The robot has rudimentary perceptual, planning, and decision-making abilities. With the inclusion of "urges," which Toda defines as "motivational subroutines linking cognition to action," Toda argues that the robot would become emotional. According to Toda, urges come in two flavors: emergency urges, such as fear, and social urges, such as love. Urges are triggered in relevant situations, and subsequently influence cognitive processes, attention, and bodily arousal. Toda's proposal has influenced the AI community by emphasizing the emergence of emotions in complex goal-directed autonomous systems.[4]

Simply expressing an emotion can be seen as a kind of emotional behavior. In this way a machine that expresses emotions, even without having them, might have emotions attributed to it. The Macintosh computer is a simple example: when the user boots up the system, its little disk face smiles. The user might rationalize that the Macintosh has the goal of interacting with her and is therefore "happy" because its goal is achieved. In this sense it might be said to have emergent emotions since it gives the appearance of having emotion without having any explicit internal mechanisms that produce emotion. Nonetheless, like Braitenberg's vehicles, the Mac has no internal emotions.

Component 2: Fast Primary Emotions

Humans can be startled, angry, or afraid, before the signals even get to the cortex, and before becoming aware of what is happening. In fact, sometimes we are already behaving, such as jumping out of the way of danger, before we become aware of an emotion, such as fear. Many animals have these essentially hard-wired, innate responses, especially to potentially harmful events. Such emotional responses may not always be accurate; for example, you might also jump out of the way of a non-dangerous stimulus. Fast emotions tend to err on the side of survival.[5]

These innate, quick and dirty reactions are what Damasio calls "primary" emotions, and probably include at least fear, surprise, and anger. As each emotion is studied and its circuitry is deciphered, the criteria for primary emotions are likely to become more specific, and the list more complete. In the meantime, the findings of neurologists are revealing how these emotions are implemented, and therefore, how each might be imitated in computers.

In particular, for the fear emotion, the fundamental mechanism seems to be a danger detection system—one that operates primarily in a loose but quick "jump out of the way" sense, and only secondarily in a more precise but slower evaluative sense: "Oh, that was nothing to be afraid of" or "Whew! I could have been crushed!" Fear can also arise cognitively, perhaps while ruminating about a future threatening event, but that can be considered a slower cognitive process.

The brain mechanisms for primary emotions point to two communicating systems—a rough pattern recognition system that acts fast, and can "hijack" the cortex, but often makes mistakes by triggering false alarms, and a finer pattern recognition system that is slower but more precise. Together, they work to detect important events, such as danger, and to trigger the subjective feelings, sentic modulation, regulatory controls, and behaviors that are crucial to survival. In particular, primary emotions appear to be important for re-allocation of limited resources, as illustrated in this robot scenario:[6]

A robot exploring a new planet might be given some basic emotions to improve its chances of survival. In its default state, it might peruse the planet, gathering data, analyzing it, and communicating its results back to Earth. However, suppose at one point the robot senses that it is being physically damaged. At this instant, it would change to a new internal state, perhaps named "fear," which causes it to behave differently. In this state it might quickly re-allocate its resources to drive its perceptual sensors. Its "eyes" might open wider. It would also allocate extra power to drive its motor system so that it could move faster than usual, to flee the source of the danger. As long as the robot remains in a state of fear, it would have insufficient resources to perform its data analysis, like humans who are unable to concentrate on other things until the danger has passed. Its communication priorities would cease to be scientific, changing to a call for help, if it knows help might be available. The "fear" state would probably remain until the threat passed, and then its intensity would decay gradually, until the robot returned to its default state where it could once again concentrate on its scientific goals.

When thinking about implementing primary emotions in computers, it is tempting to wire them so that they always trigger a certain behavior in response to certain stimuli. However, this is not necessary, and is probably not the way they are implemented in humans and other animals. For example, for the primary emotion of fear, it is true that a mouse might fear a cat and flee in its presence. However, if the only food source is near the cat and the mouse gets sufficiently hungry, then the mouse may approach the food despite its fear of the cat. Although the fear response that primes the mouse to flee may be innate, the resulting behavior can be influenced by motivational and other factors.

Component 3: Cognitively Generated Emotions

A third component of having emotions is what I will call cognitive emotions, to emphasize the explicit reasoning typically involved in their generation. Cognitive-appraisal emotion theorists have tried to explain the generation of large sets of emotions based on the answers to questions such as, "Was the situation giving rise to the emotion certain or uncertain?" "other-caused or self-caused?" and so forth. Some have even surmised that all emotions are cognitively generated, even emotions that we now know are generated in the limbic system before the signals from their stimuli arrive in the cortex. Upon learning about the latter, some theorists have emphasized that cognitive appraisal can happen not just consciously, but subconsciously, perhaps even by structures in the limbic system. However, I think it is important to maintain the distinction between fast primary and slower secondary emotions, keeping the former in Component 2. Therefore, this third component includes only those emotions believed to be initiated by cortical reasoning, such as when we assess that someone has impeded our goals, and subsequently feel anger toward them. In contrast with the primary emotions, cognitively generated emotions may arise slowly, possibly as a consequence only of one's deliberate thoughts. If merely thinking, "Don't worry; be happy" causes you to be happy, then that happiness is cognitively generated.

In a healthy human, cognitively generated emotions usually provoke an emotional experience with subjective feelings, especially if the emotion is intense. Damasio talks about "secondary emotions" as the ones that are cognitively generated but subsequently activate limbic responses and bodily feelings. However, in a computer, an affective state need not be accompanied by feelings or physiological components of emotion. We see a similar situation in Damasio's patients who can reason about emotions cognitively without any of the normal accompanying feelings. When Elliot saw an image of a bloody mutilated face, he knew—cognitively—that it was horrific. But it was a cool rational horror. Elliot knew that before his brain tumor, he would have also *felt* terrible seeing the mutilation image. His cognitive generation of emotions was fine, including knowing what kind of feeling they should generate. Computers, like Elliot, can generate cognitive emotions without their normal accompanying feelings.

Ortony, Clore, and Collins wrote in their influential book, *The Cognitive Structure of Emotions*, that it is not important for machines to have emotions, but it is important to AI that computers be able to reason about emotions— especially for natural language understanding, cooperative problem solving, and planning. I will underscore some of their remarks: certainly it is important for machines to be able to reason about emotions. To the extent that computers interact with people, such reasoning abilities are required for them to interact more sensitively and intelligently. However, we know now that computers with only the ability to reason about emotions, cognitively, are similar to the emotion-impaired patients. Cognitive reasoning is important for intelligent decision making and behavior, but it is not always sufficient.

Cognitive reasoning is the way emotions are most frequently generated in machines today, especially in animated software agents. Typically, a set of rules is constructed to generate emotional states given certain inputs. Ironically, the most frequent paradigm for generating these emotions is based on the Ortony, Clore, and Collins (OCC) structure, despite the fact that they did not have emotion generation in mind when they formulated their cognitive appraisal theory (see Chapter 7). Via cognitive reasoning, the computer can deduce that a sequence of events causes an emotion to arise. By the same reasoning, applied to its personal events, it can cause an emotion to arise within itself. Hence, we see that the OCC structure can be used not just for reasoning about emotions, but also for generating them.

Component 4: Emotional Experience

Consider if one of Braitenberg's vehicles were given the ability to recognize and label its retreating behavior as "fear." Moreover, suppose that this ability was extended so that it could recognize and label all its emotional behaviors. The vehicle could then be said to have a rudimentary awareness of its emotional behaviors. If the vehicles had an internal emotional mechanism that they could similarly become aware of, then they might be said to have an awareness of their internal emotions. The ability for a system to be cognitively aware of its emotional state is a key aspect of emotional experience, although the system need not be aware of its emotions at all times.

There is a second aspect of emotional experience, and that is the awareness of its physiological accompaniments. For a human these include heart beat, increased perspiration, a readiness in one's legs to run, trembling, cold feet and so forth. For the vehicles, physiological factors might correspond to sensing its motors' speeds and its motion characteristics—turning, shaking, and so forth. Most computers do not have sensors that could discern their physical state at a given moment, but these could be added. For example, in one of our experiments, we have given a computer the ability to sense the moment when its display receives an image, by measuring voltage changes on the wires hooked to its monitor. Nevertheless, since computer physiology differs from human physiology, with different senses, a computer's physiological experiences of emotion will differ from those of a human.

There is a third, and final aspect of emotional experience, which is perhaps the trickiest to understand, and consequently the hardest to implement in a machine. Moreover, it is the most familiar aspect of emotion. This is the internal *subjective feeling* or "gut feeling" that leads you to know something is good or bad, that you like it or dislike it. It is unclear precisely what constitutes these feelings. People often think of them as visceral, and indeed, there are hormones released by the viscera that travel through the blood to the brain. But scientists know that the body organs which release these hormones consist of "smooth muscle" that responds much more slowly than the striated muscles in the somatic system, such as those in facial expressions or skeletal movements. Their slow speed makes it unlikely that the viscera are giving rise to an emotional response, although they may be contributing to the overall emotional feeling. On the other hand, neurotransmitters act rapidly in the brain, and their activation likely initiates these subjective feelings. When biochemical substances become easy to measure and observe during emotional arousal, then a physiological explanation may be found for this aspect of emotional experience, so that these last two aspects of emotional experience—physiological awareness and subjective feelings—can be combined into one. At this point, scientists might even describe this aspect as "objective feelings," meaning that the feelings have observable physical components, which can reliably predict the labels that a person assigns to the feelings; however, this remains to be shown empirically.

In summary, emotional experience consists of:

- Cognitive awareness
- Physiological awareness
- Subjective feelings

This triptych may seem to be a needless aspect of emotion to give to computers. It is possible to give computers emotional behaviors, fast primary emotions, and cognitively generated emotions without giving them an emotional experience, so why bother giving them this component? This question is a close cousin of another: "Why do humans have emotional experiences?" In searching for its answer, we run into the issue of consciousness. I deal with this in its own section later, but let me offer one brief hypothesis here. My hypothesis is that an emotional experience gives us the ability to better understand, learn about, and regulate our activities—for example, why we want certain things, what has and has not met our needs, and how we might do things better. Knowing you are in love can explain much silliness, whether or not it justifies it. Noticing how tense your muscles are can inspire an effort to reduce stress or anger. Feeling that something is wrong can provoke you to re-examine a situation. Experiencing emotions not only adds a special quality to life, but also helps explain much of our mental and physical behavior, for example why we linger on some thoughts, e.g., it feels good to think about what she said, and why we introspect and make changes regarding others, e.g., it feels bad not to have returned her call so you decide to apologize. Through emotional experience we gain insight into our own motivations and values; we become able to better understand and utilize the powerful influences emotions exert.

Component 5: Body-Mind Interactions

We have seen in the previous chapter that emotions influence decision making, perception, interest, learning, priorities, creativity, and more. Emotions influence cognition, and therefore intelligence, especially when it involves social decision making and interaction. Furthermore, not only do human emotions influence cognition, but they influence other physiological systems besides the brain—modulating vocal and facial expressions, influencing posture and movement, even influencing digestive processes and the workings of the immune system. What you think, what you eat, what medications you take, your posture, and more can influence your emotions. Emotions intricately interact with the human body and mind.

Scientists know that emotions influence memory and memory retrieval, and it may be that this influence on memory is at the root of all of emotion's influences on cognition. In fact, it may later be found that the internal *feelings* discussed above in Component 4 are the causal agent behind these influences, and that therefore these influences would not happen in a system that had no subjective feelings or facsimile thereof. As mentioned earlier, all five of the components discussed here are present in humans, and it is unclear precisely how they interact. For now, we do not know the mechanism that gives rise to the influences that I lump into this fifth component.

Not only does emotion influence cognitive and bodily functions, but emotion is, itself, influenced by them. I emphasized above that cognitive thoughts, which include concerns, goals, and motivations, can generate emotions. Similarly, biochemical processes such as changes in hormones and neurotransmitter levels, physical drives such as hunger and low blood sugar levels, and physical feedback, such as facial posing, can influence emotions and their generation. Prozac and a number of other depression medications adjust the uptake of serotonin, a neurotransmitter, in an effort to alleviate a depressed mood. Furthermore, the precise ways in which biochemical processes interact with emotion may differ from person to person; personality, innate differences in temperament, and learned differences in emotional development all play a role in these influences.

The aspect of emotion's interaction with the mind and body that may be the most important for computers is the influence of emotion on cognitive processes—especially the aspect that is missing in Damasio's patients, which is crucial for intelligent decision-making in many situations. In humans, emotion also influences flexibility, creativity, and learning. Consider the following scenario of a smart personal assistant:[7]

A computer software agent is learning to be a smart personal assistant, to aid you in scheduling meetings and retrieving important information. It has two ways of getting feedback—direct or indirect. In the direct case, you select preferences on a menu, effectively programming it. In the indirect case, it watches how you respond to it and adapts itself. Suppose that it enters a state called "feel good" when (1) you express pleasure at its performance, and (2) when you succeed at a task more efficiently and accurately than usual. Additionally, it might have a corresponding "feel bad" state for the reverse of these, as well as a neutral "no emotion" state, a "feeling curious" state, and an "I'm puzzled" state. These states influence a variety of things, such as the values of items added to memory, and their associations with things good and bad, important or minor. When the system has been in a state of "feel good" for several days, it might become more curious and decide to try out new ideas for helping you, taking more risks. If it lingers in a "feel bad" state, it might allocate more resources to introspection, to trying to figure out if it could do something differently and more effectively. If it interrupts you and you look upset for being interrupted, it would trigger a small bad feeling, marking this situation as aversive, biasing it away from repeating this situation and prompting it to try to understand why you did not like being interrupted at this particular time. When presented with a complicated set of demands, it will weigh the "feel good" and "feel bad" associations that exist and try to choose an action that helps satisfy goals (1) and (2). It will aim for a dynamic balance—recognizing that often you will not show pleasure even though it is performing well, and that sometimes you will complain or show approval inconsistently, regardless of what it does. At such times, depending on how calm or agitated you are, as measured from your norm, it can either ask you for clarification, or make a note to come back later and try to understand this situation, perhaps when you are not so agitated. When it is overloaded with so much information that it cannot consider all the possibilities in time to give you the decision you need, then it uses the valenced markers it has learned to guide it toward incorporating the most significant information in the decision. Its use of emotions helps it manage information overload, regulate its prioritization of activities, and make decisions more flexibly, creatively, and intelligently.

The imitation in a computer of emotion's influence on the human body is less obvious. Although it might be reasonable for a computer's emotions to automatically modulate its available modes of expression, imitating human sentic modulation, computers have no present obvious need for imitating biochemical or electrochemical influences of emotion. Furthermore, no computers have immune systems that function like human immune systems, even though many of them are equipped with mechanisms that watch for certain kinds of computer viruses, and attempt to deal with those viruses. However, as computer systems become more complex and take on greater responsibilities with more real-time constraints, we may find that their regulatory mechanisms will function more like the physical regulatory mechanisms that interact with a human emotional system.

Before concluding this section, let me restate that it is important to keep in mind that all computers will not need all components of all emotions. Just like simple animal forms do not need more than a few primary emotions, all computers will not need all emotional abilities, and some will not need any emotional abilities. Humans are not distinguished from animals just by a higher ability to reason, but also by greater affective abilities. We can expect more sophisticated computers to need more sophisticated emotional abilities.

My claim, which opened this section, was that all five components occur in a healthy human, and if a computer has all five components of emotions, then it can be said to have emotions. However, let me add that not having all five does not imply that the system does not have emotions. For example, there are humans who are so handicapped that although they have emotions with respect to Components 2–5, they may not be able to communicate them with their behavior, as per the first component. We would not say that these people do not have emotions, but rather, that it is uncertain what they are experiencing since they cannot communicate. Another example is

Damasio's patients, who lack part of emotional experience (Component 4), and some of the influences of emotion on decision-making (Component 5), but still have emotional behaviors, primary emotions, and the ability to reason about emotions cognitively. They have an *impaired* emotion system; it is not accurate to say that they have no emotions.

Finally, some might argue that all the components above specify functions of emotions, and that there are other ways to fulfill these functions than by giving emotions to computers. I have been asked several times, "Can't we accomplish all of these desirable abilities without having to give the machine emotions?"

The answer is "yes" in theory, for we know that any mathematical function can be constructed in more than one way; therefore, why not any kind of function, including any human function? In practice, however, suppose that we tried to build into a computer all the functions and influences of emotion, one by one, without giving it emotions *per se*. Each influence of emotion would be implemented by some mechanism that gives rise to that influence. For example, there would be a mechanism to give rise to influences on learning, another mechanism to give rise to influences on decision making, another to regulate the use of physical resources, another to give rise to influences of motivation, another to provide a fast response in the presence of a threat, and so forth, implementing the many beneficial influences of emotion without implementing emotions. In so doing, we would no doubt notice that some of these mechanisms might be combined in clever ways, to streamline the system and make it robust. By the time we have insured that all these influences are in place in a sufficiently general, flexible, and efficient manner, however, then will we not have created a system of mechanisms that is effectively an emotion system? In other words, we may find that building in the positive benefits of emotions is not all that different from building in emotions. Of course, it does not have to be called "emotions," especially since that word comes loaded with many negative connotations. Nevertheless, that is essentially what the result would be.

Evaluating Performance

The five components of emotion give rise to separate tests to evaluate if the computer has achieved each of them. In particular, we can adapt human tests, substituting a computer, software agent, or other digital system. Some possibilities include:

Component 1: Emotional behavior.   Does an outsider, observing the behavior of the system, describe its behavior with the correct emotional adjective?

Component 2: Fast primary emotions.   Does the system respond quickly and with distinctive behaviors to stimuli of a threatening or otherwise urgent nature, mobilizing its resources for suitable responsive actions?

Component 3: Cognitive emotions.   Given a situation, can the system reason about the emotions it is likely to generate, and apply the same reasoning to situations it is in, labeling its own state with the generated emotion?

Component 4: Emotional experience.   What is the report of the system's internal affective state? Can its sensors discriminate different feelings for different emotions?

Component 5: Body-mind interaction.   Is the system more likely to retrieve, learn, and recognize positive information when in a positive mood, and vice-versa for a negative mood?

Additional tests.   By taking a human-human situation, and substituting a computer so that it is a human-computer situation, there are many possible tests. For example, if human A is put in a room with a gregarious and ebullient human B, then human A is likely to acquire a more positive mood. If either human is replaced with an affective computer, will the results of the mood exchange be the same? This "contagion test" is just one of many possibilities. Furthermore, this test involves not only generating emotions, but also recognizing or expressing them. Following the paradigm of adapting results from human emotion theory, we can propose a battery of tests for computer emotions.

Summary of Components of an Emotion System

To summarize, a computer can be said to have emotion if it has the following five components that are present in healthy human emotional systems:

1. System has behavior that appears to arise from emotions.

2. System has fast "primary" emotional responses to certain inputs.

3. System can cognitively generate emotions, by reasoning about situations, especially as they concern its goals, standards, preferences, and expectations.

4. System can have an emotional experience, specifically:
   • Cognitive awareness
   • Physiological awareness
   • Subjective feelings

5. The system's emotions interact with other processes that imitate human cognitive and physical functions, for example:
   • memory
   • perception

- decision making
- learning
- concerns, goals, motivations
- attention, interest[8]
- prioritizing
- planning
- sentic modulation
- immune system functions
- regulatory mechanisms

Computers with Minds and Bodies

I am sometimes asked, "Do computers have to have bodies to have emotions?" After all, in humans we know that emotions have both physical and cognitive components. We know of no brains without bodies, except perhaps those in fanciful stories, such as Daniel Dennett's delightful "Where am I?" (1978). Indeed, recent books such as Damasio's *Descartes' Error* refer to the mind-body separation as misguided, and emotions as an example par excellence of mind-body interaction.

It is tempting to say for a computer that the hardware is the body and the software is the mind. Furthermore, a hardware implementation used to be the only way to implement fast processing in a computer, because software was too slow; consequently, one might expect that fast primary emotions would best be implemented in hardware, while slower cognitively-generated emotions might best be implemented in software. However, this speed distinction is no longer very important because of advances in technology. A more important distinction than hardware vs. software, is "fast but rigid" vs. "slow but flexible." We do not find a clear software vs. hardware distinction among the human brain's electrical and chemical reactions. What we find is many separate processes, including some (limbic) that handle emotions in a fast, but rigid way which is prone to make mistakes, and some (cortical) that handle emotions in a slower way, which is more accurate and adaptable.

The distinction between hardware and software is especially blurred when an emotion system is given to a computer that is entirely simulated in software, or to a software agent or animated creature that exists in software with a software body. In these cases, software mechanisms can be used for implementing both quick and dirty emotional processing, and slower more accurate emotional processing. The precedence of the former over the latter can be maintained in software so that the agent would still be capable of an "emotional hijacking" whereby the quicker processes, perhaps with interrupt capabilities, assume control and the agent responds rapidly, albeit not always accurately. For example, an animated agent might cease eating to jump out of the way of a giant ball thrown at it, even if the ball was soft and would not have hurt it. Alternatively, a software system might have a notion of survival that translates into taking evasive maneuvers to protect its code from an attacking virus. It might also imitate a human response of calling for help. To the extent that these protective mechanisms hijack other processes and aid in survival, they can be seen as imitating the role of the primary emotion of fear in humans and other animals.

Building reliable computers with self-survival mechanisms is a focus of Tandem Corporation. Survival for their computers means being able to keep running as designed, despite threats such as overheating or a corrupt disk drive. Tandem computers are given physical sensors and a kind of self awareness to detect potential problems, and special abilities to act on repairing these problems. In the case of overheating, the computer alerts whomever is closest to "Come open the closet door, it's too hot in here." In the case of a disk failing, the computer tries to repair itself first, thus minimizing the potential for human error. If it cannot repair itself in software, it orders a new drive and alerts appropriate Tandem personnel, and also gives them the Federal Express number and purchase order number that it used. Meanwhile it works around the problem, redirecting messages away from the bad disk, while it awaits its replacement part.[9] The Tandem machine does all of these things without an *explicit* emotion system, but not without an emergent one. It is natural to attribute its "cry for help" as emanating from a state of concern or fear. The designers of the Tandem machine, in giving it a diagnostic and maintenance subsystem, recognize that they are sacrificing some other aspects of performance. However, the priority of "survival" is achieved.

Robots provide the most obvious example of a computer with a body. Imagine if a robot body were equipped with skin, pain sensors, and algorithms for learning. With sensors and tools for assessing what is sensed the robot can become somewhat aware of physical sensations, and allow these to influence its emotions, cognitive processes, and subsequent behavior. The robot might be hard-wired to recognize that pain is bad, and to elicit distress when pain occurs. The robot's controller can be given the goal of reducing distress, and can then learn to try to avoid things that cause distress, such as pain. At the same time, it might generalize its dislike toward things associated with distress—and as it is learning, it might mistakenly attribute dislike to a person that was in the room each time it felt pain, or to other aspects of the environment, until eventually it receives counter-examples to indicate that these factors are good or neutral.[10] Unlike Damasio's patients who no longer had a physical feeling to accompany their recognition of emotion-inducing events, the robot could be equipped with such a feeling. I suggest that such a feeling might start out as a mild form of the pain sensation when a negative event is accessed, leading to a slight aversion to the stimulus. Positive feelings could be similarly implemented by first identifying them with factors that most greatly reduce the robot's distress. Positive feelings might also gradually be associated with stimuli that become familiar. Positive feelings for familiar things show up in people, who, even if only exposed subliminally to a picture of a face, will later show a preference for that face over an unfamiliar one (LeDoux, 1996). Additionally, non-painful physical contact might be hardwired to give rise to familiarity, and in turn to positive feelings.

Robot bodies, like human bodies, can encounter problems that could use some forms of sentic modulation. I visited a major research laboratory where I was shown a mobile robot, and a demonstration of how well it could navigate by itself around the building. Suddenly the robot stopped in its tracks. There followed a fair amount of anxiety among its makers while they tried to figure out why it failed. It was not until much later that they determined its buffers had overfilled, a very simple problem. In fact, an analogous problem happens to humans when overwhelmed with too much information. A human will appear confused, or her eyes may glaze over, and she may be unable to move mentally beyond the present point. Whether or not she is aware that her "buffers are full," this information is signaled to outsiders through subtle emotional expressions, indicating that it is useless to try to give her any more information. This robot could have helped its makers by having a spontaneous expression to indicate this internal state. Many human forms of sentic modulation have important roles that can be extended to computers.

Emotions and Consciousness

I once had dinner with a gentleman who claimed that consciousness and emotion were the same thing, that consciousness is largely *feeling* and that consciousness is a messy topic for that reason. I do not agree that consciousness and emotion are the same thing; nonetheless, they are closely intertwined. In particular, the fourth component of emotion I described— emotional experience—appears to rely upon consciousness for its existence. I will not define "consciousness" in this book because, like the term "emotion," it refers to a complex morass of many things, and the colloquial use of the term suffices fine for my discussion.[11]

Let us consider some of the kinds of "feelings" of which we have conscious awareness. In addition to basic emotion feelings like fear, anger, sadness, and joy, there are other subtle feelings we all experience. For example, there is a "feeling of knowing" when we know that we know the answer, before we have mentally searched and found it. This feeling does not fit into any of the usual categories of emotion, and yet it seems to act as a global signaling mechanism indicating that further search of memory is a good idea. Most people have also experienced a "feeling of understanding," when all the pieces of something fit together. This may or may not be accompanied by a positive or negative feeling, depending on the nature of the pieces, but it seems to act as a signaling mechanism, as if the brain could say, "the job is complete: here is my answer." And, of course, there are the valenced subjective feelings that I described earlier, the gut feelings and intuition that lead you toward or away from certain concepts, biasing everything with a small positive or negative feeling. All of these feelings, and maybe there are more, seem to operate without conscious direction, and yet we can be conscious of them.

Does the ability to have emotions imply having consciousness? More to our interest, if we succeed in giving a machine emotions, then will we have also succeeded in giving it consciousness? Cognitive generation of emotions and cognitive reasoning about emotions are certainly conscious processes. Do emotions always involve conscious processes?

The current scientific evidence supports an answer of "no" for all these questions. Neurological evidence indicates that humans can have emotional responses before becoming conscious of them. Some of the emotional systems in our brains are not only free to act without our decisions, but they can do so without our awareness. Only *after* they have acted do we become aware of what has happened.[12] For example, the primary emotion of fear can cause us to jump out of the way, and may cause heart palpitations, sweating, and trembling, before we become aware of what has happened. When we notice what is going on, we say we felt fear. The labeling of fear and the recognition of its feelings are conscious, but its generation was not. Consciousness is a prerequisite only to the emotional experience and not to the generation of the emotion.

Consequently, there are at least some emotional mechanisms that function independently of consciousness. Consciousness is not necessary for all emotions to occur. However, consciousness provides an enlarged understanding and ability to act. If you *become aware* that situation X causes fear, then you can think ahead and plan to avoid it. You can become aware of similar situations to avoid. The result is the generation of more possible actions, leading to greater flexibility in subsequent decisions and behaviors, especially the next time fear arises.

To summarize: for a computer to have some simple emotions, especially the "primary" ones above, it does not need consciousness. However, for it to become aware of these emotions, for generalizing and learning from them or for otherwise managing its emotions, it behooves it to have at least some capability for self-reflection, a basic function of consciousness.

In addition, some more sophisticated emotions may require consciousness before they can be generated. For example, a concept of "self" seems to be necessary for developing the emotions of shame and guilt. These emotions are termed the "self-conscious emotions" by Michael Lewis, who argues that these do not develop until early childhood, after the notion of "self" is intact (Lewis, 1995). Then, can one conclude that "if you give a computer the ability to feel shame then you have given it consciousness?" Not necessarily. Firstly, consciousness is probably not a single property just like emotion is not a single property. It may be that only a facet of it is used in forming the notion of "self," which an emotion such as shame exploits.

It is possible now to give computers a modicum of self-awareness: a name for where they are, what they are doing, what state they are in affectively, what their sensors are reading, the name of the problem they are trying to solve, and so forth. It is also possible to model bodily systems—to give a computer not just an operating system, but imitations of other human physical and cognitive systems, complete with mechanisms for receiving various sensations, if desired. The latter might, with suitable sensors, give rise to something analogous to a feeling. Consequently, we can argue that machines might have some awareness, and some feelings. However, as I mentioned before, we can expect the internal subjective feelings to differ between human and machine. In fact, we still do not know what does give rise to that irreducible component of human emotion, that nuanced reaction that "feels unpleasant," not as a cognitive appraisal, but as a subtle *feeling*, something sui generis. We may find that it will be simple to imitate the functionality of this feeling, and that this is sufficient for giving computers a full set of emotions and their influences. Or, the distinction between what humans feel and what computers feel may become an essential ingredient that distinguishes humans from machines, and perhaps stands in the way of machines developing emotions that successfully influence mind and body functions as do human emotions. More research is needed before we can say which is the case.

Systems that have Emotional Intelligence

Dave is feeling down and out, and yet has a lot of work to do. He plods on, struggling and laboring, feeling increasingly frustrated by his slow progress. Kate, who has even more work to do, takes frequent breaks, recharges, and comes back to make great strides. Terry uses humor to try to loosen up people when they have difficult issues to discuss. Anne, when she gets a new book, takes advantage of her enthusiasm and plows through it right away. Mike tackles first those things he least likes to do, and saves his favorites as rewards.

Dave, Kate, Terry, Anne, and Mike are managing their emotions in one way or another. They are trying to take what they feel, and use it to improve their performance on a job, their interaction with others, or their own sense of well-being.

Moods and emotions are powerful motivators. For example, if you enjoy interacting with someone, you may seek opportunities to do so. However, you temper the pursuit of pleasure with self-regulation, recognizing that sometimes negative feelings or emotional restraint can lead to achievement of something greater. Similarly, you might use knowledge of your own emotions to motivate something that is difficult for you to do. When Lynn was lacking confidence in her swimming ability, and longing to improve it, she told everyone she was going to take a water life-saving course when she went to summer camp. When she got to camp, her fear of swimming was not as great as her fear of facing everyone later if she didn't earn the life-saving certification, so she signed up for the class and worked extra hard, earning her certification. She used her own emotion of fear to achieve her goal.

Computers may not need to motivate themselves to swim, but they still have actions that can be motivated by emotions, which will therefore need to be regulated. Emotional intelligence is the part of the system that brings balance to emotional abilities. It makes the difference between a computer that can express and have emotions, and a computer that knows how to manage its expression, and how to utilize its emotions for creative thinking and motivation.

Salovey and Mayer set forth the concept of emotional intelligence for humans in their paper by that title (Salovey and Mayer, 1990), extending Gardner's "personal intelligences" (Gardner, 1983). Extending their concept to computers, a computer with emotional intelligence will be one that is skilled at understanding and expressing its own emotions, recognizing emotion in others, regulating affect, and using moods and emotions to motivate adaptive behaviors. Let us consider three main domains of emotional intelligence:

1. Recognition and expression of emotions.
   • In self: Recognizing your own emotions, especially as they happen, and being aware of how you express your emotions.
   • In others: Appraising the emotions of others, both by recognizing their expression and reasoning about what emotion is likely to be generated in a situation. Ultimately, it includes understanding what is important to another person, including personal goals, preferences, and biases. Recognition and expression of emotion are crucial in empathy, the ability to

comprehend another's feelings, to re-experience them oneself, and to communicate that the feelings have been understood.

2. Regulating emotions.
- In self: For example, once you have recognized that you are unusually anxious, taking steps to reduce the anxiety and to understand its cause. Or if angry, directing yourself to release the anger in non-violent expression.
- In others: Responding to others in ways which suitably influence their emotions, e.g., acting helpful and respectful so that someone feels enabled and respected. Understanding another's emotional needs, as well as how and when to show empathy.

3. Utilizing emotions.
- In self: Marshalling emotions to help you accomplish a goal. Includes self-motivation, delayed gratification, and taking advantage of the influence of emotions on planning, creativity, and attention, to obtain better results in these areas.
- In others: Motivating others, and helping them marshall their own emotions in service of a goal.

These components of emotional intelligence lean on the three abilities of affective computing I have focused on above: recognizing emotions, expressing emotions, and "having" emotions. They take these abilities and "make them or break them." Computers that have emotions will need to be aware of their emotions, and will need to be able to regulate and utilize them. Computers that interact with people or other affective computers need to know how to recognize emotions and how to intelligently respond to them, including when to show empathy.

Much research has aimed to identify what are good ways to handle the feelings of others. For example, the research by Ellen Langer at Harvard on "Mindfulness Theory" (1989) identifies certain things that make people feel more alert, cheerful, respected and valued. One of the findings is that offering simple choices—such as giving people in a nursing home a choice of two kinds of juice for breakfast—leaves people feeling better than if they had no choice. Good computer interface designers know that giving a user more than one choice tends to make them feel a sense of mastery and control (Mayhew, 1992).

On the other hand, what should a computer do when its user is upset, especially at it, or at something it has done? How should a computer respond when it detects a negative emotion? Unfortunately, it is easiest to think of bad examples. Consider the following snippet of dialog, from the film *2001: A Space Odyssey*, occurring when the computer HAL has refused to let crewman

Dave Bowman back on the ship, but Dave has managed to re-enter and is starting to disassemble HAL:

HAL: "Just what do you think you're doing, Dave? Dave? . . . Look Dave, I can see you're really upset about this. I honestly think you ought to sit down calmly; take a stress pill and think things over."

The computer with a naive notion of distress, or anger, or any negative affective states, is a social fool, to say the least. In fact, many people are similarly maladroit when it comes to knowing how to handle emotions. Many of us, together with the computers we design, are students on the path to learning how best to behave in the face of anger, hatred, distress, and other negative states. Magic responses like "take a stress pill" or any other programmable rule for how best to respond are suspicious solutions.

Recall the scene at the beginning of this chapter where the computer responded to your repeated errors with a request that you "Read the manual." In an intelligent application of affective computing, the system would have many possible responses, probably not including that one. In particular, by watching what a user likes and does not like, it would try to learn the user's preferences and which responses are most successful. If a significant negative emotion arises in the user or the machine, then the machine can allocate resources to assess the source of this feeling, and how it might best be managed or acted upon. For example, it might observe that a negative emotion it presently feels is similar to an emotion it has felt in the past at this late hour of the evening, and that usually shortly thereafter its user exhibited frustration and logged out for the night. To its knowledge the user has no pressing deadlines on her calendar. Consequently, the computer decides to politely interrupt the interaction to suggest it's getting late and to remind the user of an early appointment tomorrow. When the user is no longer on, then the computer might take a closer look at other processes that happened that evening, in a form of self-reflection, to assess possible different options the next time this negative state occurs. In other words, it uses emotional mechanisms to interrupt its own internal processes, to act upon a situation that might be improved.

I expect that the first efforts to give computers emotional intelligence will run aground in the following way. A computer is good at memorizing lists, facts, and even imaginary situations. However, it does not presently learn values and valences along with the information it acquires. Nor is it good yet at making reasoned analogies, especially those that involve people's feelings as the common element. For example, it is difficult for a computer to recognize that a situation which provokes bitterness in one case is similar to a very different situation that might result in the same bad feeling. Until computers can learn the emotional significance and similarities of situations, they will be like autistics who are also good at memorizing patterns and lists, but not good at understanding emotional significance, or at responding suitably. Efforts to understand emotional intelligence well enough to implement it in computers may lead to discoveries and tools that could help emotionally-impaired people to overcome their impairments. This would be a tremendous achievement.

Evaluating Emotional Intelligence

As we just saw, emotional intelligence is many-faceted, so we would expect tests of it to come in many flavors. Following the methodology of substituting a human-computer interaction for a human-human interaction, we can take tests of human emotional intelligence and apply these to evaluating the performance of computer emotional intelligence. However, standardized tests of human emotional intelligence are virtually nonexistent. Evaluating emotional intelligence is apparently much harder than evaluating mathematical, analytical, or verbal forms of intelligence. Educators today are calling for new measurements of intelligence, including emotional intelligence, but the tests they have proposed so far are problematic, especially when it comes to institutionalizing them (Gardner, 1993, Chapter 10).

Consider, for example, the problem of giving a written test of social situations, and asking how one should respond in each situation. Damasio's patients were given such tests, and did quite well. They "knew" how to respond perfectly well, and could pass these tests with high scores. However, when the same patients were in real life situations, their behavior was not in agreement with what they knew to do. They could pass a written test of social intelligence, but they flunked in real life. The tests assessed their cognitive reasoning about social situations, but did not assess their actual performance in such situations, when emotions and feelings guided (or failed to guide) their decisions and behavior.

True tests of emotional intelligence require unpredictable interactions with humans or other agents. The computer might be required, for example, to assist a user in a way that is deemed as useful, friendly, productive, entertaining, or helpful, depending on the application. In a business situation, a machine that negotiates the best deal, perhaps without expressing any emotions, may be considered a success. The machine might have used internal emotions to motivate its goals and enable faster and better decision making, but these need not be visible for its emotional mechanisms to be successful. An agent does not need to be personified or to appear like it has emotions for it to benefit from having emotions. On the other hand, an animated character that interacts with a child might be personified and very emotionally expressive. It might be considered a success in an entertainment context if the child found it more likable and wanted to spend more time with it. When a student finds an affective tutor fun and rewarding to interact with, and therefore spends more time learning and building new understanding under its tutelage, it is a sign of success.[13]

Differences in Human and Computer Emotional Intelligence

For the most part, the criteria of human emotional intelligence apply directly to computers and to human-computer interaction. One place where they might differ, however, is in the experience of emotions required for empathy. Humans can approximate the emotional experience of each other because we have similar brains and bodies. As discussed earlier, the fact that humans and machines differ in physiology and in conscious awareness will cause them to have different emotional experiences. Hence, we cannot expect a machine to really *feel* what we feel, even if it "has" emotions. Consequently, the best empathy or understanding we can hope for is at the level of an outsider, who tries to understand, but who has never actually been in our shoes, so to speak.

Another difference we can expect is in the evolution of social display rules. Humans have evolved these rules for improved social interaction with one another, as guidelines for when and where it is appropriate to express certain emotions. To the extent that we interact naturally and socially with computers, we can expect computers to adopt our rules. Just as society has different rules for child-adult interactions, we might have different rules for human-computer interactions, especially in the case of software agents that might perform different functions. Computers that interact only with each other may evolve an even different set of social display rules. A community of software agents may not necessarily evolve the same rules as a community of humans; furthermore, if computers evolve their own rules, these rules may be hard for humans to understand, and may not transfer to human-computer interaction.

Like humans, a computer with emotions will no doubt engender a topic of "computer emotional health." In learning to manage its emotions, the computer will need a mechanism for emotional reflection and repair, perhaps implemented as a continuous learning algorithm that routinely revisits what it has learned emotionally and watches for particularly strong or harmful stimulus-response connections. Unlike humans, however, a computer has memory that can be completely rewritten or replaced. Consequently, a computer would be highly unlikely to suffer from emotional disorders such as post-traumatic stress disorder (PTSD), which seems to be related to a more or less indelible imprinting of an emotional response in the human brain.[14]

On the other hand, as computer memories become highly associative and intertwined with affective markers, and as more of their content is learned instead of deliberately written by a human designer, it may cease to be feasible to simply replace a malfunctioning computer memory. Replacement might be too drastic, destroying many difficult-to-learn beneficial memories along with malfunctioning ones. Instead, some kind of repair may be attempted that involves additional learning or un-learning, to "heal" the malfunctioning responses.

Example: Lottery Scenario

Suppose Sam hears the winning lottery number, and recalls that it is his friend Sue's favorite number and she has played it every week for the last ten years. Sam predicts that when she walks in, she will be elated! Sam, in anticipation, feels excited for Sue. Shortly after, Sue walks in with an awful look on her face. She wails about hearing the winning number. Sam is surprised: Sue should have been elated, and expressing ebullience. After he talks to her and learns that her ticket blew away in the wind, his words become compassionate and he offers her help to go search for it.

Sam illustrates all the emotional abilities discussed above. He (1) recognizes Sue's emotion by analyzing the situation and observing her expression, (2) expresses emotion by showing compassion, (3) synthesizes internal emotions such as joyful anticipation, and (4) exhibits emotional intelligence, by choosing to show compassion and offering to help Sue.

Some people cannot stand lotteries, while others dream every week of winning. In general, guessing which feelings a situation will give rise to is a question not just of emotion generation and emotional intelligence, but also of knowing somebody well. In theory, the computer with which you regularly interact can get to know you, your values and preferences, and your typical situations well. If it has emotional intelligence, then it will try to predict how you will feel when changes happen, and will try to learn how to respond in ways that you appreciate.

Beyond Emotional Intelligence

Before describing applications in the next chapter, there is an important distinction to be made regarding the scope of affective computing. Any application involving an affective computer will require attention to the following three issues:

1. What is the relevant set of emotions for this application?
2. How can these best be recognized/expressed/developed?
3. How should the computer respond to the user given this information?

Even once these issues are settled, affective computing is not a magic ingredient that can be added to an application to make it instantly succeed. Successful implementation of affective abilities requires domain-specific knowledge. The goals of the application must be carefully understood and respected.

Consider these three issues in the context of the affective piano tutor scenario. In an initial implementation, the designer may choose to limit the recognized emotions to distress, interest, and pleasure, adding more emotions later as the system develops. The computer might recognize these states from watching the student's face, gestures, posture, or measuring other responses of his autonomic nervous system. However, how should the computer respond to the user when he seems distressed? The quick answer—adapting to "always please" the user—is naive, and conjures up the soma-dependent society of Huxley's *Brave New World* (Huxley, 1965). Indeed, true learning almost always involves overcoming frustration, working through a difficulty, and not merely having it removed. There is no known easy recipe for managing this learning process. The process of trying to build a computer that can guide a student through a successful learning experience, responding intelligently when she or he is frustrated and ready to quit, is likely to teach us a lot about the way human learning works.

Another example is an automobile's interface to its human driver, which might eventually have the ability to recognize states such as stress or anger.[15] If it senses you are stressed, how should it respond? Many automobile accidents are caused by people who are angry or upset. If it tells an enraged driver "you are too angry to drive" then it is likely to make the person angrier. Alternatively, suppose that a simple device to help you learn about your stress levels detects an anomalous signal, which may or may not indicate a serious medical condition; how should it communicate this news to you? Recognition of some affective states is the job of affective computing; however, how the intelligent vehicle or feedback system should respond is potentially a legal and ethical issue. In summary, affective computing should be seen as a critical part of intelligent system design, but by no means the only part.

A Note on Imitating vs. Duplicating

A final sticky topic deserves at least brief discussion: are computer emotions real, or are they just a simulation? Let me tackle this by first talking about a less controversial emotional ability: emotion recognition, about which the same question can be posed.

I defined a computer that can "recognize emotions" as one which can infer emotional states as accurately as a human, by observing emotional expressions and reasoning about emotion-generating situations. When the input is the situation and expressions, and the output is a description of the emotions, then the system *imitates*, and some might say *duplicates* human recognition of emotions. However, the duplication occurs only at this one level, with the inputs and outputs defined in this way. There are other levels at which the recognition of the two systems is not the same. For example, the internal mechanisms by which the computer "sees" and "hears" only roughly approximate the way a human accomplishes these perceptual tasks. Researchers in computer vision and researchers in human vision often meet to swap ideas, but both sides agree that we are a long way from duplicating the human visual system in computers. Nevertheless, at certain levels a computer can still be said to "have vision abilities."

The same issues apply for the other three affective abilities I've described—expressing emotions, having emotions, and having emotional intelligence. We can define levels at which the abilities imitate those of humans, and levels at which they fail to do so. The imitation game fails, however, when a bodily component is integral to the function being imitated, and the computer has no analogous component. I am reminded of Harvard psychologist Jerome Kagan's remark in a recent conversation: "Rocks can't get cancer!" In a similar spirit, one might declare computers cannot get emotions. This claim is correct at a certain level of description; today's standard computer architecture lacks the sensors and regulatory controls at work in a human emotional system; it does not have the ability to sense any kind of feelings, and could at best simulate some of the mechanisms of emotion. Short of procreation, we cannot truly duplicate the physiological conditions that give rise to human feelings.

That level aside, there is reason to believe, allowing for a kind of computer architecture that not only contains multiple processors and communication pathways, but also multiple sensors and regulatory mechanisms, that a computer could be built that implements mechanisms like those in human emotion. Now, the best way to implement these is not an easy or solved question. Moreover, of the five components above, a means of implementing the fourth one, emotional experience, relies upon duplication of conscious sensations. How to implement this in a machine is presently a mystery. However, if this can be implemented, then we can expect that at some level, with precisely defined inputs, outputs, and intermediate influences, the computer mechanisms can be said to duplicate the inputs, outputs, and intermediate influences of a human emotional system. The duplication will not necessarily hold at any other level of definition, but at the level it holds, a computer may be said to have emotional abilities.

Summary

This chapter has defined how computers might have the ability to recognize, express, and have emotions. It has also defined emotional intelligence for computers, which builds upon these three other abilities, giving a computer skills to manage and utilize its emotional mechanisms, and to respond skillfully to a user's emotions. The criteria I have listed for each affective ability are not arbitrary, but are adapted from what is known about human emotions. Of course, there is much that is not yet understood about human emotions, so changes can be expected as new knowledge accumulates. Nonetheless, we now have one set of requirements on the table to begin the process of building affective computers.

3   *Applications of Affective Computing*

What would affective computing really be good for? I have discussed what it might mean for computers to recognize, express, and "have" emotions, as part of efforts to make them more intelligent, friendly, and capable. I will continue to use the word "computer" loosely—letting it refer to a software agent, a robot, even a sneaker with a microprocessor and sensors embedded in it, since any software or hardware could potentially acquire computational abilities for emotional intelligence. In Part II of this book I will discuss how to build affective computers, and what progress has been made toward this goal. In this chapter, let us assume that there are computers with various affective abilities, and focus on the applications such computers could address.

I have already mentioned a handful of applications such as a computer tutor that recognizes the user's affect to individualize its teaching strategy, or a robot that "has" emotions to enable it to deal more effectively and flexibly with the complex demands and uncertainty of its environment. As in those scenarios, the applications in this chapter will utilize various affective abilities, especially the abilities to recognize, express, and have emotions.

Almost no applications consist only of affective computing. Most applications require it to team up with other tools—especially human-computer interface design, computer vision and listening, probabilistic learning, and AI reasoning. For instance, computer vision and listening tools will help identify the environmental and situational context as well as detect vocal and visible forms of expression. The computer might reason that if people are in an office environment, then emotional expression is usually restrained. Since these other tools are still in their infancy, many of the applications depend not just on progress in affective computing, but also on progress in these other areas.

A few of the applications discussed below are straightforward engineering problems, but some of them are more farfetched. Nonetheless, as fanciful as some of the applications sound, they are not merely science fiction. They rely on affective capabilities that already exist in people. A postulate of computer science is based on the human existence proof: Given an ability that already exists in humans, then it is only a matter of time and effort before the same ability can be imitated in computers. No fundamental discoveries are required, only breakthroughs in understanding and implementing what is already in existence in the human form. The challenge of talented researchers is to figure out how these affective systems can be constructed and how they can be combined with other abilities to form truly intelligent, personal, and engaging systems.

Affective Mirror

Imagine the most important interview of your life, with the head of the company that you have always wanted to work for. He asks you tough questions about problems you have solved, challenges you have faced, and why you want to leave your present job. At the end of this grueling meeting, he tells you that you were too nervous-sounding, had unusually short pauses in your speech, were evasive with eye contact, and had cold clammy hands. This was not the real thing, fortunately, but a practice session in front of your trusted computer. Your computer interviewing agent, displaying the face of the CEO, asked you questions while listening to changes in your voice and discourse parameters. It watched your facial expressions and body language, sensing changes in physiological parameters such as your skin conductivity and temperature. It watched your affective responses to see where they differed from what it usually senses from you in day-to-day interaction.

This scenario is still in the future, but most pieces of it are present technology. Inspired by the high school boy practicing asking a girl out for a date, rehearsing in the mirror, the "affective mirror" would be an agent that interacts with a person, helping him to see how he appears to others in various situations. With a camera, microphone, and various sensors, the system is far more advanced than the mirror most people practice in front of, even though it is potentially not as good as practicing in front of a skilled human listener. Nonetheless, there are many times when a computer's availability, patience, and nonpartisan judgment cannot be beat. Being able to "try out" that important talk in front of your computer has a certain convenience and privacy that some might find encouraging and comfortable. This use of affect recognition is one of many ways in which affective computing might be used by people who would like to advance their own interactive skills.[1]

Beyond Emoticons

"How many of you have lost more than a day's work trying to straighten out some confusion over an email note that was received with the wrong tone?" A majority of hands usually go up when I ask an audience this question. Email is an affect-limited form of communication. We do not have the skill or the time to choose words so carefully when composing a message that a unique intended tone always shines through. Instead, the tone is often omitted, and hence is ambiguous. Although emotional states may be subtle in their modulation of expression, they are not subtle in their power to communicate, or to influence how we perceive what is communicated. When sentic modulation is missing, misunderstandings occur more often. Because human perception is influenced by mood, we have an additional complicating factor: the mood of the recipient affects their perception of tone. Consequently, if you send an impartial message, and somebody who reads it is in a negative mood, then they are biased to receive it as if it were a negative message.

By necessity, email has had to evolve its own set of symbols for encoding tone: "emoticons" such as :-) and ;-(that can be recognized by turning your head to the left. Emoticons are listed in *The New Hacker's Dictionary* as "An ASCII glyph used to indicate an emotional state in email or news" (Raymond, 1996). Although hundreds of emoticons have been proposed, only a few are in common use, and these are not used unambiguously or universally. Some people think emoticons are too "cutesy" for regular business usage; others use a smiley for both sarcasm and humor, rendering its meaning ambiguous.

Although it is often desirable to deliberately limit emotional expression, say, during bluffing games or business negotiations, it is rarely desirable to be forced to do so by the available medium. Tools that recognize and express affect could be used to expand the affective bandwidth of email: A voice with inflection could read your email to you. The interface could change its look and feel to signify tone. Facial expressions of the sender could be transmitted. Typing rhythm and pressure might be communicated, and so on. An agent that could discern your affect, either directly from you, or from previewing the text you are about to send, might alert you to the tone of the text before you send it, perhaps highlighting the potentially negative lines in red and the positive ones in green, so that you could see at a glance the valence that a recipient might sense upon reading it.[2] The agent could do the same for your incoming mail, letting you know first thing if one of your most important customers was unusually upset.

Text to Speech

The famous physicist Stephen Hawking relies on a computer to talk for him. He types in what he wants to say and, because he can no longer speak, a synthetic voice speaks his words for him. An estimated 25 million people in the world are without effective speech communication, and potentially could use computers to convert text to speech—synthesizing a voice to assist or replace their own. One of the problems with present text-to-speech systems is that they say everything with the same tone of voice. This makes it particularly difficult to communicate feelings: to interrupt angrily, to express anxious concern, to soften your voice in approval, or to indicate empathy and other expressions of emotional intelligence.

Affective computing can be applied to this problem in a couple of ways. The first is by determining how affect is synthesized in speech—how emotions affect prosody, *how* things are said. This problem has been investigated by Iain Murray and his colleagues at the Dundee University in Scotland (Murray and Arnott, 1993; Alm, Murray, Arnott, and Newell, 1993), and by Janet Cahn at the MIT Media Laboratory in Cambridge (Cahn, 1990). Some of the details of how affect can be added to speech are given in Part II of this book.

One of the problems with adding affect to a text-to-speech system is the interface: people talk much faster than they can type. Speech is typically around 180–250 words per minute (wpm), while a good typist may type 50–60 wpm or a stenographer with a chording keyboard may type 180 wpm. Some disabled people using standard keyboards persevere at rates of under 10 wpm. People are already limited by how quickly they can give input to a text-to-speech device. To add affective parameters suggests more control knobs for them to set. This is undesirable given that they are already busy typing as fast as possible. In some cases, when the emotion is more important than the semantics, the person might opt for hitting a button producing "an angry interrupting sound" or some other "audio emoticons" that convey the emotion of their response without words.

Another way affective computing can be applied to this problem is by having the computer try to directly recognize the speaker's affect from his or her bodily expression. If the affective signals from the speaker could be used directly to set the affective control knobs for the text-to-speech synthesizer, then this would save the typist this effort. In other words, bodily sentic modulation can control the affect in the synthetic speech. When the speaker's temperature and blood pressure climb in anger, her synthetic voice could adjust itself to sound more angry. In fact, it may not be necessary to have highly accurate emotion recognition to be useful in this application—

the non-verbal user could benefit today from even a small set of physically controllable voice-affect parameters.

When a story is read with emotional inflection, it not only enhances interest in and enjoyment of the story, but it also improves speed of understanding for children (Badzinski, 1991). People who are seeing-impaired, children who are learning to read, and those who simply enjoy being read to, can all benefit from a text-to-speech system that can synthesize affect in speech. However, such a system does not necessarily know what kind of expression to add where. One solution to this problem is to take the system described above, and couple it with one that can understand situations that give rise to emotions, particularly in stories.[3]

Even without sophisticated story understanding, the ability to control affect in speech is of immediate use. Children would no doubt enjoy having the ability to manipulate the affect in the synthetic speech of their computer pals, and having the ability to tell the reader of their video postcard how to make the message sound to its recipient.

Helping Autistic People

Autism occurs in about 1.5 to 2 people out of 1000; it is a complex disorder, whose explanation continues to elude and intrigue theorists. Neurologically, it is characterized by abnormal wiring patterns in various brain regions, including what appears to be essentially "too many" neurons in the amygdala and hippocampus, two structures in the limbic system that play key roles in emotion processing. One of the hallmarks of this disorder is difficulty with emotions—recognizing the meanings of other people's emotions, suitably expressing emotions, and having empathy.

Autistic people can be outstanding at memorizing lists, maps, and other spatial or temporal patterns. They can learn to recognize emotional facial expressions—to label pictures of frowning faces as "sad," for example. However, most of them have difficulty with emotional *understanding*—they lack emotional intelligence, especially empathy and an understanding of suitable responses in an emotional situation. This manifests itself as a lack of common sense and sensitivity. In particular, autistics have difficulty generalizing from one pattern to another, and from one situation to another. They might learn a rule about why one thing upsets one person at one time, but they face an immense hurdle in generalizing that rule to other people and situations. For example, an autistic pizza delivery person might innocently say to a customer, "I remember you—you're the one who gave me a low tip last time!" and not understand why that person proceeds to frown and treat them rudely. The autistic person can see that the customer is upset, but may not be able to understand why. There is a great need for computer tools that could help autistics develop emotional skills—tools that iteratively and patiently walk them through scenario after scenario, helping them learn to draw analogies and generalizations, especially of situations in which emotions are likely to arise.

In many ways computers are like autistic people—particularly like autistic "idiot savants," an unfortunate term that has been used to describe people who have unusually gifted abilities in certain areas—such as rapid computation of large numbers, memorizing phone listings, and precise memory of huges sets of facts and trivia, but who lack the forms of common sense and emotional intelligence that most people acquire effortlessly. Suppose that you and an autistic friend go out to a baseball game. All of a sudden, a player gets a great hit at a crucial moment in the game, and the crowd stands to cheer! Your friend does not feel any excitement, and she does not understand why people are standing. However, she is able to rattle off the player's batting average, his lifetime hitting record, the batting averages of all the players in his league, the number of seats in the stadium, and other facts. Your friend's ability to memorize and retrieve information is splendid, but the feelings that guide her to identify which behavior and information is most relevant at the moment seem to be missing. Unaffective computers are similarly handicapped; they are great at recalling facts and information that are semantically linked to the keyword or concept of the moment, but they are unable to determine which of all the possible linked items is the most relevant to the situation at hand.

One way to help autistic people is to have a trained person sit down with them and repeatedly walk through situations to help them learn how to understand and respond. However, the helper is prone to lose patience in the tedious repetition of endless situations. The autistic requires a new explanation with each situation since he cannot easily generalize from the explanations they have previously learned. Autistics benefit greatly from this one-on-one help, and could make greater strides with more of it. This is interaction that could be provided by computers capable of understanding emotion. Computers with an ability to teach this understanding—via games, exploratory worlds, virtual social scenarios, and other interactions that provide repetitive reinforcement, could be developed with present technology. Even a relatively simple computer, which just implemented a basic appraisal theory of emotion, could run a large variety of scenarios illustrating how emotions arise, and guide an autistic user toward a better understanding of socially adept responses. In the future, computers should also be able to recognize the emotional expressions of an autistic user, to help give him feedback as he tries to learn skills such as empathy. Autistic persons enjoy learning and want to please; a computer could reward their cheerful and persistent efforts, while helping give corrective feedback regarding their emotional responses in role-playing scenarios.[4]

In this application it is not clear, however, if it would be good for the computer to also *have* emotions. Emotions might interfere with the advantage computers have of being able to engage indefinitely in highly repetitive tasks, unless the emotions were set to mimic extraordinary patience. As mentioned before, not all computers need to have emotions, and those that have them will need the ability to know how to intelligently manage them.

Consumer Feedback

One of our undergraduates played the computer game of "Doom" while wired up to several physiological sensors detecting signals that change with affective responses. We saw minor changes in several of the signals when he "found the rocket launcher" or when he "was killed." However, the biggest response we found, significantly higher than any other in the game, occurred not during a stressful life-threatening battle, but at a more surprising moment: when the software failed to work properly. None of the violent events in the game aroused the player as much as the software problem. I will say more in Chapter 5 about the player's signals and what they showed, but first, let us consider some applications.

When using a computer, people often find themselves trying to learn something: a new drawing program, a new operating system, or maybe even a new game. Often, the user encounters a snag, and manuals are no help because the user does not know the name of the problem she is facing. A program that "holds your hand" all the time can be insulting. A smarter approach, like the piano tutor described earlier, is to have the software pay attention to the user's affective responses, to look for when she encounters unusual stress or frustration. At these points, the software should find a way to offer help that fits the user's needs.

I will not name specific software and hardware products that have resulted in countless hours of frustration for computer users around the world, but imagine if this frustration could be measured, quantified, and incorporated into the evaluation of new products. There are some customers who would weigh a "frustration index" as highly as the so-called "price-performance" index, because a product that is more pleasant to use can provide better human performance in the long run.

An immediate application of the technology in this book is for the gathering of physiological signals corresponding to responses such as frustration while a person is interacting with a product. There are several advantages of this: (1) physiological responses occur during or immediately after the causal event, as opposed to questionnaire responses, which are usually much later; (2) the sensors are unobtrusive, as opposed to popping up a window to ask "how's it going?" in the middle of the interaction; and (3) the signals can be quantitatively compared to see which parts of the interaction are most distressing, and the next time people use the product, to compare if they got more or less frustrated in the same places or, perhaps, in a place where a "fix" was inserted. Affect recognition by computers does not replace all other means of gathering information to determine how consumers feel about a new product, but it is an important and underutilized source of such information.

Points for Courage

You are rounding the corner, and do not know what might be lurking on the other side. You have come through this dungeon several times, and never made it out alive. You wonder if you will succeed in getting out this time. Will you do so with bravery and courage, or because you got lucky and something fell on the monster while you panicked and fled? Game environments become virtual testbeds for how we respond to situations. Game makers have made strides each year with more vivid graphics, responsive action, realistic force feedback joysticks, and immersive displays. However, unlike in the real world, your success in the game world tends to be based only on *what* actions you take, not on *how* you perform them. The actions you take certainly are important. In the real world, however, it is also important that you do so with enough confidence and composure that people will follow you and support you.

Players are in increasing physical contact with their games—through joysticks, helmets, and soon even "wearable computers," which I'll say more about later. Many of these devices have the opportunity to sense physiological responses. The first time through the dungeon, it might sense a high arousal level from you. In fact, it might time certain events to take advantage of your arousal level—to calm, or to confront. On additional passes, the game could try to recognize if you are calmer, braver, or more anxious than ever, and modify the situation in response. It might reward a calmer demeanor by introducing a new companion to journey along with you. It might punish an unusually stressed response by introducing a jeering opponent. In fact, the game might be designed with modes you can select before playing such as "I want to relax" or "pep me up" or "I don't care." It would then choose its responses with this mode in mind.

In particular, games or activities that help people relax can be health boosters. Dave Becker and Alex Pentland at the MIT Media Lab have constructed a virtual environment in which a person can learn how to make several T'ai Chi movements, as part of a visualization game for cancer patients. The idea is that the patient uses the relaxing T'ai Chi gestures to control the actions of cells in a visualization game to battle the cancer. The relaxing movements of the T'ai Chi exercises are believed to be able to help reduce stress, boosting the body's immune system, and aiding the patient in recovery. Although the present application can only recognize a few T'ai Chi gestures, it could be augmented with sensors to detect stress and to give a person rewards in the game for reducing stress (Becker and Pentland, 1996).

Emotions in Learning

Fascinating!
—Mr. Spock, *Star Trek*

Curiosity and fascination begin many a learning episode. As the learning task increases in difficulty, however, one may experience confusion, frustration, or anxiety. Learning may be abandoned because of these negative feelings. If the pupil manages to avoid or proceed beyond these emotions then progress may be rewarded with an "Aha!" and accompanying neuropeptide rush. Even Spock, the unemotional patron saint of computer scientists, frequently exclaimed upon learning something new that it was "fascinating!"

Dr. Barry Kort, a mentor of children exploring and constructing scientific worlds on the MUSE (Multi-User Simulation Environment)[5] and a volunteer for nearly a decade in the Discovery Room at the Boston Museum of Science, says that learning is the quintessential emotional experience. Kort says his goal is to maximize intrigue—the fascination stage—and to minimize anxiety. Kort suggests that all learning systems have affective states, and that future autodidactic learning systems will exhibit such recognizable states as curiosity, fascination, puzzlement, confusion, frustration, insight, satisfaction, and confidence. Certainly, many present systems can be said to have these states if we include emergent emotions in the definition of "having" emotions. The adjective "confused," for example, is applicable to a learning algorithm that no longer keeps its input categories straight. Kort defines changes in knowledge with respect to time as emotion, arguing that when learning occurs, it is accompanied by an emotional response.

Whether or not computers *have* emotions, it is clear that humans interacting with them can benefit if computers learn to recognize their emotions. Computers that cannot recognize human affect are severely handicapped, especially in a role such as teacher or mentor. Whatever his strategy, the good teacher detects important affective cues from the student and responds differently because of them. For example, the teacher might leave subtle hints or clues for the student to discover, thereby preserving the learner's sense of self-propelled discovery. Whether the subject matter involves deliberate emotional expression as is the case with music, or is a "non-emotional" topic such as science, the teacher that attends to a student's interest, pleasure, and distress is perceived as more effective than the teacher that proceeds callously. The best teachers know that frustration usually precedes quitting, and know how to redirect or motivate the pupil at such times. They get to know their student, including how much distress that student can withstand before learning breaks down.

Ted Selker at the IBM Almaden Research Laboratory has built a system called "COACH" that gives pupils adaptive feedback while they try to learn the computer language LISP. His system has shown an improvement for how well users learn, by comparison to a non-adaptive system where users have to solicit help themselves. Selker's system considers the user's opinion of the learning environment, opinion of the topic learned, comfort with the topic learned, and more (Selker, 1994); however, it does not yet consider any direct affective cues from the user, such as if she is pleased or frustrated with the system's feedback. One of the ongoing research problems in adaptive feedback is determining at which points to give the feedback so that it is not derailing to the user. To complicate matters, the answer to this question will be user-dependent. Experienced teachers say it is important to detect the level of engagement and the level of frustration of a student. Offering help that interrupts the user's engagement can be disruptive, while acknowledging the user's frustration, even subtly by changing the presentation, can encourage perseverance.

"No Pain, No Gain"

Not all the potential applications of affective computing are for consumers; some are for theorists. In addition to developing better computer tools to aid in learning and discovery, there is also potential for developments in theories about learning. Let me make an analogy between academics and athletics. There is a saying in athletic training: "No pain, no gain." The same saying applies to learning, although the pain is not demanding physically, but mentally. Clearly an affective computer that is helping a pupil should not merely try to make the pupil happy throughout the interaction, nor should it necessarily dole out encouragement or make things easier if the pupil is getting frustrated. These are naive responses. A more effective learning strategy recognizes that encountering and surpassing frustration is a natural part of learning. However, how much frustration is good? Theory tells us almost nothing about how a mentor should respond to a person's emotions to facilitate learning.

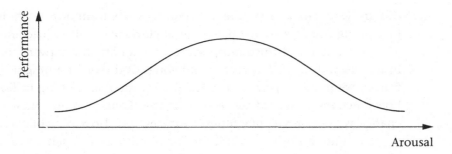

Figure 3.1
The classic Yerkes-Dodson curve. Performance is best when arousal is neither too low nor too high.

In physical fitness, the ability to measure heart rate and other physical variables has led to more precise theories of conditioning, including rules-of-thumb, such as "Working out for twenty minutes at 75–80% of your maximum heart rate, three to four times a week, will maintain your current fitness level." Theories of physical training have benefited from the ability to take physiological measurements such as heart rate. For learning, there is no such rule of thumb for how hard somebody should work. Today's evaluations of learning take measurements only at the output level—on test performance. This is analogous to measuring conditioning based only on how fast the person can run at the end of the session, or only on how much weight she can bench-press. These can be valid and important measurements, but they do not provide any guidelines for how to maintain and surpass one's present abilities.

Suppose we could assess emotional communication during a learning episode as a set of parameters, much like athletics trainers measure parameters such as heart rate. In all activities that demand mental performance, we know emotion is a determining factor. The classic inverted–U curve, the Yerkes-Dodson law, relates performance to arousal, one of the key dimensions of emotion (see Fig. 3.1).[6] Performance is worst at either extreme of arousal—when the subject is lethargic, and when the subject is overly stimulated. Performance is best at an intermediate state of arousal. Ideally, a person could measure arousal and adjust its level to maximize performance. One of the problems with trying to measure arousal, however, is that it actually consists of many factors. However, research could be conducted to tease apart these factors, for example to look at the influence of mood on a student's ability to concentrate and generate ideas.

The Yerkes-Dodson curve does not address the range of emotions that a person might pass through in an ordinary learning experience. Instead, we might hypothesize that, as in sports, where you have to maintain a certain heart rate and endure a certain soreness to improve conditioning, in learning you have to maintain a certain level of cognitive load and endure a certain amount of frustration before you can attain a forward increment in understanding. Just as there are theories of interval training in physical fitness, we might expect to find theories of interval training in learning— how much rest is needed between mental workouts, and how these intervals change as a person's mental fitness increases. It is also reasonable to expect to find a cognitive-affective analogy to the physical fitness pattern of warming up, exerting effort, then cooling down. Although a successful and rigorous theory of learning is an open research problem, and certainly also involves more than the role of emotion, emotion plays a largely overlooked role in its development.

Classroom Barometer

Many people have been greatly influenced by a special teacher, one who engaged them with creative and clear explanations, who showed special empathy and offered extra help during a time of distress, or who, simply by his own enthusiasm, transmitted a love for a topic. The pleasure a teacher receives in seeing a student's progress is also important, and for the child who longs to please her teacher, displays of this pleasure only amplify the enjoyment felt from learning something new. Emotions circulate routinely in a healthy teacher-student interaction.

Analyzing emotion as it moves between the teacher and the pupil has many applications, not just to computers, but to helping both inside and outside the classroom. In particular, as teachers try to improve their ability to recognize the emotions of their students, they might employ some special affective tools. One example is the "classroom barometer." This application involves constructing a simple device that accumulates the responses of the students in the room, displaying them up front for all to see. When a student is confused, his response anonymously helps make the barometer level climb.

Ideally, a sagacious teacher can tell if the class is confused without such an explicit barometer. However, we have all been in the situation where the person up front was not so wise. A teacher whose students are confused, and who does not realize this, faces an uphill battle in communication. Few students, when they are terribly confused, have the courage to interrupt and say, "I'm lost." The application of tools to aid in affective communication can help a well-intentioned teacher to learn how to read the more tacit signals.

I gave a lecture by videoteleconference where such a device would have been especially useful. All I could see on the monitor was a texture of rows of tiny heads and chairs filling the auditorium. I could make out no details of faces. At no point could I tell if people were feeling confused, fascinated, or sleepy. If each member of the audience was willing to wear a networked piece of jewelry and special eyeglass frames that sensed their confusion, interest, or arousal, then this information could have been integrated and presented to me instead of the low-resolution image of the auditorium on the monitor. I would have then tried to use this information for gauging when to restate a point, speed up, or inject humor. All it would entail on their end is the willingness to perhaps look at bit like an audience wearing 3-D glasses. But, in return, they would have heard from a lecturer that was more in tune with them.

Emotions on the Virtual Stage

Beneficial emotional effects can occur in people who engage in role-playing scenarios, whether during group therapy where a person acts out an emotional situation, or during role-playing games. A friend who is a very kind Catholic priest once acknowledged how much he enjoyed getting to play an evil character in one of these role-playing games. Such entertainment provides a healthy and safe way to expand one's emotional dynamic range. As role-playing communities are created online, they shift from person-person communication to person-computer-person communication. The computer (and connecting network) in the middle mediates what information passes between people. The technology limits what you can sense; it is no longer easy to see a smile ripple across everyone's faces.

In many of the popular networked interactive communities, the communication channel limits messages to text. Learning to write descriptively, to communicate feeling unambiguously, is a worthy challenge, one which such environments encourage. In fact, these environments provide incentive for many kids, and adults, to learn to write. Because emotion can only be communicated through the text, they improve their ability to write with affect. While interacting in virtual roles, a person may take on the feelings of different characters. However, to communicate these feelings back through the medium, the person has to deliberately express them in writing or through their behavior. The burden of deliberate expression is like the burden of the speaking-impaired person having to set additional control knobs to modulate the affect in her speech; sometimes it is too much to ask.

An application of affective computing is to expand the possibilities of expression in these environments—to give children additional tools that help them express, recognize, and understand emotions. For example, if the machine could recognize the player's emotions, then it could use these to directly influence how the character appears to those on the other side of the computer channel. Alternatively, a computer might help analyze the situation the players are in, and suggest some of the emotions it is likely to produce. These can be situations created both by the computer and the players, "You have entered a dark laboratory, and you hear the sounds of a person sleeping. It is late morning, and you think that this might be one of your fellow students who has an exam this morning." Similar to the applications above for an autistic person, but less repetitive, these situations could not only provide fun and entertainment, but also an exploratory path toward the development of social and interpersonal skills.

Music: Listening to What you Like

Often a radio station or a particular CD or tape is selected to match a person's present mood, or to modify the mood they are in. They might pick relaxing chamber music to calm them down, a lively jazz piece to pick them up, or a sorrowful ballad that matches the way they feel after a recent loss and thereby gently comforts them. Although sometimes it is hard for people to agree on the precise emotions communicated by a piece of music, some pieces have very high agreement across listeners. Children aged six, and in some cases younger, have been shown to understand affective meaning in music, as demonstrated by their ability to accurately recognize happy, sad, angry, and fearful passages (Cunningham and Sterling, 1988).

An affective computer could help find mappings between music and emotion. To the extent that universal patterns are found, perhaps based on tempo, cadence, key, and other attributes of music, these could be used for helping music students identify characteristics that convey certain affective ideas. Or, they might be used to help index digitally stored collections of music so that in addition to the traditional categories of classical, folk, pop, etc., music could be called up by its affective tone. For example, in creating a soundtrack, the search may be for a piece of music with a particular mood.

In some cases it will be hard to determine the affective properties of a piece of music. The emotions evoked by a piece of music may arise not only from its content, but also as a result of associations you have regarding the piece, such as the memory of it playing in the background when your high school sweetheart dumped you. When trying to find music that suits your mood, it may be hard to narrow down the selection beyond a certain style of music or collection of artists. Nonetheless, such attributes can still be correlated with your mood, as well as with your taste and environment—car, office, home—to learn strong predictors of what you might like, and when. Although affect recognition will probably not be precise enough to identify the one best piece you would like to hear, this is probably a good feature, because people usually like to have a choice. On the other hand, they do not like to be overwhelmed with too many choices. The purpose of the affect recognition should be to eliminate a lot of completely inappropriate pieces from consideration, helping the machine to whittle down the possibilities and present the user with a reasonable selection from which to choose.

"Fast Forward to the Interesting Part"

My primary research for the last decade has focused on helping computers "see" as people see, despite all the unknown and complicated aspects that human perception entails. One of the newest applications of this research is the construction of tools that aid consumers and filmmakers in retrieving and editing video. Example goals are asking the computer to "find more shots like this" or to "fast forward to the dinosaur scene." A much harder but related goal is to teach a computer to "make a long story short." How do you distill three hours of home video footage into a ten minute entertaining piece you will want to watch again and again? How does one extract the most meaningful and memorable segments? Finding a set of rules that describe content for retrieving "more shots like this" is one difficulty, but finding the content that is "the most interesting," i.e. involving affect and attention, is a much greater challenge. Finding digital photographs having a particular "mood" was the most frequent request of advertising customers in a study of image retrieval made with the Kodak Picture Exchange (Romer, 1995). Subject and action content, which were most frequently requested for editorial purposes, can also powerfully contribute to mood in a photo (Lang, 1995). These new challenges are ones that computer scientists are not equipped to address alone, but where cross-discipline efforts between cognitive science, emotion theory, and computer science are sorely needed.

The problem of locating a remembered scene, or an image with particularly interesting content, is also the problem of understanding causes of arousal, one of the key dimensions of affect. Arousal (excited/calm) has been found to be a better predictor of memory retention than valence (pleasure/displeasure). However, strongly negative things tend to automatically be highly arousing, leading many to think that better memory is correlated with negativity (Reeves and Nass, 1996). Image descriptions given in Fig. 3.2 indicate associations of arousal and valence with image content.

We have built some of the first computer vision tools that enable computers to assist humans in annotating video, attaching descriptions to images that the person and computer both "see." Instead of the user tediously entering all the descriptions by hand, our algorithms learn which user-generated descriptions correspond to which image features, and then try to identify

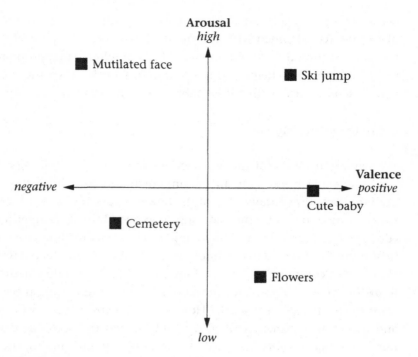

Figure 3.2
Pictures classified according to their arousal and valence, after the studies of Lang (1995).

and label other "similar" content.[7] Computers do not naturally understand the kinds of similarity important to people, so one of the research problems is to teach the system to *learn* a user's ideas of similarity—whether perceptual, semantic, affective, or otherwise. Affective computing can be coupled with systems that learn similarity to begin to identify not only which content is most salient or interesting, but also which emotions tend to be evoked by the content. Successful learning algorithms for content-based similarity could potentially learn examples of affect or mood similarity.

Affective annotations, especially in terms of a few basic emotions or a few dimensions of emotion, could provide a relatively compact and salient index for retrieval of data. For example, people may tend to gasp at the same shots— "that guy is going to fall off the cliff!" Shots could be labeled, initially by a human, with descriptions such as "thrilling." Affective annotations would be verbal descriptions of these primarily nonverbal events. For example, instead of annotating, "this is a sunny daytime shot of a student getting his diploma and jumping off the stage" the human might annotate "this shot of a student getting his diploma and jumping off the stage evokes a grin." The latter is an affective annotation, which would then enable this shot to be found by someone searching for a "joyful scene."

Of course, although this example indicates a joyful shot for most viewers, it will not provoke a smile for everyone. An example is the mother whose son would have been at that graduation if he were not killed the week before. The cognitive and emotional state of the viewer interacts with what is perceived to produce the final affect, and these sorts of complicating factors will not be easy to address. Although affective annotations, like subject-action annotations, will not be universal, digitizing them will still help reduce time humans have to spend searching for the right scene. Both kinds of annotation are potentially powerful; we should be learning how both are perceived, and applying them to digital audiovisual libraries.

Agents that Learn your Preferences

A personalized newspaper is a nice time-saving idea—getting just the news you want, mixed with a dose of serendipity facilitated by some trusted experts who have time to read all the news. However, few people can truly list all their preferences; you may not know that something interests you until you see it. Really learning someone's preferences usually requires observing what they choose over a long period of time. Did that writer bore her? Did she find this debate annoying? Does she smile a lot when reading that columnist? Does she always skip the sports section unless there is a big picture of a gymnast on the front page? We learn peoples' preferences not only by listening to them, but also by watching their expressions and behavior.

Increasingly, computers have the opportunity to adapt services to you, to learn your preferences. But they are currently limited in how they can get information from you, so you have to go out of your way to provide it. Computers mostly rely upon your clicking on menus and explicitly designating what you like or do not like, and on your providing keywords and filling out online questionnaires. If the system does something that annoys you, you have no way of letting it know short of hunting for some parameter you can change to try to get it to stop that behavior. Often, figuring out how to adapt the system to do what you want is too much trouble, so instead you adapt yourself to it.

These ways to collect information are still not as natural as the way a person learns your preferences—largely by listening to and looking at your affective responses. Imagine that when the machine presents you with something you like, it *sees* that you like it. And when it does something you do not like, it sees that too. In other words, instead of you always having to take time to tell it explicitly what you like or dislike, it learns from watching your affective responses. It reads the affective channel of information. If we think of all the times we have seen somebody expressing anger or annoyance at their machine, then it is clear that it is natural for people to indicate preferences to the machine in this way. This is an example of Reeves and Nass's "Media Equation" in action, which argues that people tend to treat media, including computers, as real people and real places. (Reeves and Nass, 1996).

It is not only more natural to communicate preferences with affect, but it is efficient; affect can be communicated through modulation of the voice, a smile, or nod of the head, without conscious effort or mental work. It can be done without interrupting the user, provided that the computer has the ability to perceive how you express liking and disliking, and does not have to constantly interrupt you for clarification. The idea is to have computers watch for natural signs of your preferences, and then try to discern precisely what you are responding to. The agent would try to understand your preferences not only as a function of the day of the week or the time of day, but also as a function of baseline mood measured that morning. Although it will not always be clear what you are responding to, there will be plenty of feedback over time, so that given lots of interactions, the computer could gradually start to discern your preferences. This is closer to how people learn your preferences, and it takes much less effort on your part.

The priorities of your personal software agent need to shift with your affective state, and with what it predicts would influence your feelings. Too many news stories tailored to your hometown interests might be annoying, and an occasional insertion of humor stories might lead to greater tolerance for the necessary but less pleasurable reading. Suppose your news agent learned of a building that was bombed. It should predict that such a tragic event will cause you concern, especially if you know people in the town where it happened. If it learned by scanning your address book and rolodex that you had a dear friend there, it might choose to interrupt you right away with this news. It would also pre-fetch the phone number for that friend, so you could call immediately if you wanted to.

The learning of preferences by a news agent is just one of many example applications along this line. A completely different domain is when two people are strolling past shops, and one says, "Wow, isn't that gorgeous!" If you shop with someone over time, you start to learn their preferences, just by hearing and seeing how they respond to each potential purchase. People's preferences differ wildly in clothing, music, art, books, and more, and may be more or less predictable. Nevertheless, selecting something for someone you know well, something you think they would like, is commonly done. We not only recognize our own preferences, but we are often able to learn another's.

Suppose your computer tries to learn your preferences for art to hang in your living room. As you browse a database of images looking for suitable pictures, it detects your response to different images. After you have indicated your favorites, it could try to infer which art features (e.g., artist, colors, texture, content, style) and which affective and behavior features (e.g., facial expression, heart rate, skin response, lingering) were the best predictors of what you liked. Additionally, it might associate certain categories of images with certain categories of your responses. In the future, it might watch for occurrences of features from either category, to help you save time locating things you like, or locating things that suit your present mood. The first part of this scenario—inferring sets of visual features—has been done (Picard, Minka, and Szummer, 1996). Research is underway to teach computers how to recognize the affective and behavioral cues.

With knowledge of affective preferences, several applications emerge. The computer can cruise the networks at night, helping shop for clothes, furniture, wallpaper, music, gifts, artwork, and so on. Museums and galleries that are becoming available on the World Wide Web could personalize tours and suggest to you additional collections to browse, after observing your reaction to what you have already seen. The idea is to move computers toward more personal service, tailored to your ever-changing interests, without increasing the demands on you to explicitly state your preferences.

Learning when to Interrupt

Systems that proactively adapt to you are easy to think of but are hard to produce. Two of the hardest problems are (1) computers lack common sense, and (2) they are not good general learners. I described earlier how emotions have been found to interact with these abilities in people, and how it might be necessary to imitate emotional mechanisms in computers before researchers can give computers human-like reasoning and learning. But let us restrict ourselves now to a small, but critical piece of this problem: how does a system decide when to interrupt you for clarification, or to alert you to something it predicts you will find of interest?

My husband and I were awakened the other night by his beeper loudly announcing that its battery was low. We keep pretty regular hours, and it should be relatively easy to redesign this device to be more considerate by simply having it look at its internal clock. But this solution does not apply to most problems of interruption, which are much harder to solve—such as whether the beeper or phone should alert you to a particular caller. For certain callers, the answer might be clearly yes or no. However, for most callers, the answer depends not on some objective information such as who is calling or what time of day it is, but on more subjective information, such as how important is the call, and how you might feel if what you are doing now is interrupted by it. The criterion a secretary might ultimately use is, "Would the boss be pleased to be interrupted right now to get this message?"

The simplicity of this question belies the depth of reasoning required to answer it. For example, if it is a message of bad news, the boss will certainly not have a look of pleasure on her face when she reads it. But, she will still be pleased that the assistant passed it on. If the message was not important enough (timing, relevance to present goals, values, and preferences, and so forth), then the boss may look annoyed, and will think the assistant lacks good judgment. Buried within the "Would the boss be pleased" question are questions such as: Does this message pertain to one or more of today's goals? Does it help or hinder them? How valuable is it to the most time-critical of these goals? What is its likely impact? Would that impact negatively affect the event I am interrupting? How critical is the event I am interrupting towards these goals? Would this piece of information help them now? How has the boss responded in the past given similar interruptions? And so forth. The decision itself, based on what we know from Damasio's patients, will be made with internal values influenced by emotions. And, if made wisely, it will also consider the emotions of those influenced by the decision. It requires affective abilities today's computers do not have.

Some people lead such busy lives that their most precious commodity is an hour or two of uninterrupted time. It may be planned time, with the phone unplugged and a "come back tomorrow" sign posted on the door, or it may be fortuitous, occurring while a person gets deeply engrossed in work and loses track of time, and nobody happens to interrupt. One potential application of affective computing is to help the latter situation happen more often. With suitable sensors, a computer has a good chance of discerning your engrossed state, measuring EEG, blood flow, and other factors known to correlate highly with cognitive load and with deep involvement in a problem. The pleasurable and highly productive mental state people experience when they are deeply engaged in a task has been called "flow" by Mihaly Csikszentmihalyi (1990). Once in this state, people usually do not want to be interrupted, except, of course, for emergencies. If your computer could recognize your flow state, without ruining it by interrupting to ask if you are in the state, then you might consider it desirable to have it notify your email agent, phone controller, and other potential interruptions to not disturb you except for an emergency.

This application has theoretical as well as practical implications. Psychologists do not really understand the behaviors that are conducive to a person getting into the flow state. If the computer were also equipped to sense your behaviors and other factors that contributed to your getting into this state, it could aid in this process of discovery. Affective sensing abilities could also help make sense of human behavior in situations such as determining what is different with the performer at a rehearsal vs. on the night of her best performance. A reasonable hypothesis is that part of this difference is correlated with emotional arousal and flow. To test this, physiological features can be compared with subjective reports of performance over a series of performances, to look for significant correlations. If the hypothesis is true, then we would expect to find detectable features when the performer was really "on." Based on the Yerkes-Dodson law, we would also expect to see the performance be optimal at some intermediate level of arousal—not too low, not too high. Based on emotion theory, we might also expect to find successful performances lead to a measurable synchronization between the performer's and audience's features, since emotions can be contagious. In other words, when the actor played the role wonderfully, not only did he feel filled with grief on stage, but the audience felt his grief as well. Powerful emotions might be detected as they move from the performer to the audience, and back again.

Small Talk

What is really communicated when you say "good morning" or share other so-called "small talk" with someone you see regularly? The need for such greetings must be important, otherwise they would have been made obsolete a long time ago. The words have become so overused that people no longer take their literal meanings seriously. They are rarely important for communicating speaker identification, since usually you can see who you are talking to. A reasonable theory is that the following two things are more important than *what* is said: (1) the fact that you make the greeting, and (2) *how* the greeting is said.

When you say "Good morning" to a co-worker, aside from recognizing it as a polite gesture, the recipient is likely to notice if how you said it indicates anything out of the ordinary. She may also adapt her response to you, depending on the affect you express. Depending on her relationship with you, she may respond with empathy, "Oh, it sounds like you haven't had such a great morning," or perhaps with some helpful information, "I just saw Fred making a fresh pot of coffee." Over time, she learns what vocal affect is typical from you. When your vocal inflection is not typical, it catches her attention.

A computer that we interact with every day can be given the same opportunity, perhaps via an affectively spoken "Good morning" instead of just the traditional "login name:". The nature of the communication should depend on the user's personality and preferences. Some people think it's a waste of time to say "Good morning," but might start the day with a different vocal routine. The problem of computer recognition of affect in speech is unsolved, and believed to be very difficult to solve. However, it is significantly less complicated when the speech content and speaker are known, as they are in small talk greetings. Consequently, recognizing affect in small talk should be one of the easiest vocal affect recognition problems to solve.

Once a computer has this information, there are a variety of ways it could respond: your news agent might choose to start you off with the comics instead of the front page; it might send a message to the local coffee machine to start a fresh pot; or it might select the email messages you have procrastinated longest and call these to your attention first. Teaching the computer how to respond intelligently to an individual user is a difficult problem, but it cannot even be attempted until the computer has an idea what state the user is in. The "good morning" greeting is one natural way to give it this information.

Computers can also affectively modulate their voices. This needs to be done carefully, as many people like computer voices to sound flat and artificial. The Atlanta airport, which uses a lot of automation and voice guidance, chose to use synthetic-sounding speech when it first opened because people indicated that they preferred the voices to sound less human, because they thought it sounded more "futuristic." However, if an emergency happened in the transportation mall, and people needed to listen to the voice for directions to get out, then they might appreciate it taking on a serious and urgent tone, to more quickly capture their attention and help them get to safety.

In a similar vein, a laptop that is running out of power might detect the presence of people nearby and quietly announce, "This laptop's batteries will run out in 30 minutes if not plugged in. Please say 'I heard you' if you don't want to hear this message again." If it gets no response, it might beep more plaintively, or repeat its message with an increasingly urgent tone of voice. There is an old saying, "the squeaky wheel gets the grease," which usually evokes an image of something or someone clammering in an annoying way for attention. We often forget the rest of this image: wheels do not start out squeaking loudly, but they do so progressively—from a mild squeak at first, to an increasingly irritating one. Successful communication begins gently, and increases its affective tonality in accord with the demands of the situation.

Animated Agent Faces

Hundreds of people have played poker with software agents on the World Wide Web as part of a study, constructed by Tomoko Koda at the MIT Media Lab, to determine how faces and facial expressions influence people who are interacting with characters on a computer. Were the expressive faces of these non-human players distracting? Or, did people like them? Whether or not a person wants a software agent to express emotion differs among individuals. However, most user opinions have not been gathered while the person and the agent are interacting within a natural context. In this set of experiments, the desirability of emotional expression was evaluated while a person and a software agent played poker.

In one of Koda's studies, 25 subjects played with two agents—one with a caricature face that honestly expressed the agent's synthesized emotions, and one without a face. (The agent's emotions will be described in Chapter 7.) Each expression was one of ten static images of a face, updated whenever a new emotional state was determined.[8] After 15 rounds, each subject was asked several questions. When asked to rate how much they would like to continue with each player, there was a significant preference for playing with the one with a face. This was despite the playing abilities of the two agents, since both followed the same strategy and had overall winnings that did not differ in a statistically significant way. It was also found that the face was not distracting, but that the agent with the face was significantly more likable. Overall, subjects indicated it was more engaging to play with the player with the face. None of these results depended on the gender of the subject or, more surprisingly, on the subject's opinion about whether or not agents should have faces (Koda, 1996). Decisions about when to personify an agent or other computer tool are serious, and by no means should one game-playing interaction imply that faces should be used everywhere. However, in certain contexts, it appears that facial expressions for the computer are preferred.

The Audience Performance

"I'm a skydancer. Why I do so well is I induce emotion."
—Sean D. Tucker, American aviation artist

Successful entertainment induces emotion. Although "emotional induce-ment" may sound subversive, the fact is that people deliberately engage in it all the time, whether through selection of a piece of music to calm down, through watching a comedy to lighten up, or through participating in or watching an exciting sporting event. Emotions may undergo great cycles as a drama unfolds: they may ride the wave of triumph in an Olympic victory; they may crash with the wipe-out landing of a ski jump; or, they may simply roll out as yells, screams and cheers with the gathering of a herd of like-minded and ordinarily non-emotional adults in a stadium.

Whether or not people share in the physical aspects of a sport, they can share in its emotional aspects. Many stereotyped "unemotional American males," who would ordinarily express little or no emotion, are not only apt to feel a range of emotions at a sporting event, but also to find complete social acceptance in jumping up and down yelling and screaming, even in front of a TV in a living room, as long as that TV is broadcasting a sporting event.

Perhaps there is even some need for these events psychologically, or some need for all healthy people to express a certain quantity of emotion. In any case, it is clear that emotions are an important part of being entertained.

The role of emotions in entertaining and in being entertained raises new possible applications for affective computers. This role has motivated research in computer generation and expression of emotion, especially in work with animated agents, which become more engaging and believable when they have emotions (Bates, 1994; Hayes-Roth, 1995). A very different application, however, is in creating interactive entertainment that directly incorporates the audience's emotions. This is nothing new in a formal sense—even in the quietest symphony hall a successful performer can sense how the audience is responding and is, in turn, affected by their response. Audiences have influenced performances since the earliest days when people acted out stories in front of each other.

The application I am suggesting is, however, to explicitly capture aspects of the audience's affective response, and weave this directly into a performance. Audience response could be sensed by a variety of means—perhaps by cameras that scanned the audience members' facial expressions, or by special programs or playbills with active sensors that pick up electrodermal responses from the hands holding them. Chairs might sense movement and tension, and floors and field sensors in an intermission gathering space could sense human activity patterns. The spirit of this idea is captured similarly in Tod Machover's "hyperinstruments," which augment musical instruments with new sensors to expand the range of human expression (Machover, 1992). The challenge of making music or performance art out of such non-traditional inputs is not an easy one; these living compositions rely upon forms of human expressive behavior that science has largely ignored, and that humans encode in deep but subtle ways.

Film / Video

"A film is simply a series of emotions strung together with a plot. . . . " Though flippant, this thought is not far from the truth. It is the filmmaker's job to create moods in such a realistic manner that the audience will experience those same emotions enacted on the screen, and thus feel part of the experience.
—Ian Maitland, Emmy Award–winning director and editor

Gathering emotional appraisals from an audience has many applications—from creative expression, to concrete information gathering such as seeing if the story content had the desired affective impact. For example, most people were horrified at the atrocities in the great film on the Holocaust, "Schindler's List," while it is said that some youths laughed as if the scenes were make-believe. Certain theatres might be testing grounds for audience responses. Films are a standard way to elicit emotions in subjects in psychology experiments. Although the emotions which arise while watching a film may vary from individual to individual and need not be sincere, they can nonetheless provide valuable information about emotional responses. Typically, the information gathered in such situations is used for testing psychological theories. However, it could also be used to train computers to understand situations that give rise to emotions, and to recognize these emotions when they arise.

In the future, an affect-savvy computer might help a film student with decisions concerning the creation of various moods. It might, for example, help the student discern what is not right in a film when it does not feel right—for example, is the configuration of the set or the lighting in conflict with what typically evokes the intended mood? The system might retrieve scenes from other films where that mood was considered to be successfully communicated, or overdone. Sometimes expressions of mood in film can be easily qualified: for example, lighting from beneath to create an eerie effect. However, determination of precisely what constitutes an essentic form—the essence of what communicates the emotion—is poorly understood. The forms by which emotions are communicated in different media are an open area for research. Cataloging of affective forms by computer can help advance our understanding in this area.

On a more mundane note, audience responses might also be sensed to detect frustration or confusion, perhaps during a film screening, or a presentation showcasing some new technology. These negative affective responses might flag problems with what was being viewed—if not the content of the story, then perhaps an indication that the soundtrack was having problems, a color channel dropped out, or there was some other technical or environmental difficulty.

Sensitive Toys

A "virtual pet" that became a big fad in Japan is an interesting case of a simple toy that cannot recognize emotions, but can express them.[9] The "Tamagocchi"—which is Japanese for "lovable egg"—is a tiny, egg-sized electronic device that you can interact with by pushing one of three buttons. It displays a digital creature that starts life as an endearing bird-like image, and changes from a chick to a fully grown adult in around ten days. The owner must feed, groom and play with the bird or else see it waste away and die from neglect. When the little bird wins the game it plays, the owner is treated to sounds of delight. As one middle-aged owner said, "In the beginning, I thought it would be just a bother to look after it but it eats food and sweets and you can play with it. And when you clean up its droppings, it jumps up and down and looks really happy. So you stop thinking of it as just a picture."

The Tamagocchi is a small line drawing on a 2-D display that is about the size of a watch face. However, the same idea could be developed in living size with full animation in an even more compelling way in a "smart room," such as the ALIVE space at the MIT Media Lab (Maes, Darrell, Blumberg, and Pentland, 1995), a room equipped with cameras, microphones, and a wall-sized screen on which animated characters are superimposed onto an image of the room. The person in the room sees herself on the screen together with the other agent characters. One of the interactive characters that expresses emotion is Silas T. Dog, a virtual pet, which I will say more about later. The cameras and microphones in the room are currently equipped with pattern recognition software to identify where the person is, to listen to what she says, and to recognize a vocabulary of movements and gestures that she makes to interact with the other agents in the world (Pentland, 1996). For example, she can make a gesture to pick up and throw a virtual ball, and Silas will see it and chase the ball. If augmented to sense expressive gestures indicative of enthusiasm, or depression, then the characters could have richer behaviors, such as showing empathy. For example, if a really enthusiastic human walked in, its enthusiasm could be contagious to the agent. Or, if the human looked sad, the agent might tone down its actions or perhaps try to make the person laugh.

People who interact with animated agents usually know that they are only dealing with virtual characters. Similarly, owners of Tamagocchis know they are caring for something that is only a toy. Nonetheless, the human interaction often rises to a level that is more indicative of interaction with a real living pet. A virtual pet can evidently meet some of the same needs met by a real pet, the latter of which studies have shown can reduce daily stress and improve health. Of course, in the case of the Tamagocchi, it may also be that the main need it meets is that of "joining in the fad." Nevertheless, Japanese psychologists have suggested that the toy meets an instinctive need to pour emotion into someone or something, much like many people do with their living pets. Although such expressive toys might meet some human emotional needs in the same way as real pets do, I am not suggesting that they could ever meet all human emotional needs. Human-computer interaction cannot perfectly substitute for human-human interaction or human-pet interaction, but it can nicely augment both.

Examples such as the Tamagocchi remind us that a human-computer interaction can strongly influence human emotions. It does not take a psychologist to see that computers influence human emotions both positively and negatively. If these influences were better understood, and if the more positive influences were emphasized in designing applications of computers, then it is reasonable to expect that people might feel better while interacting with them. Because moods tend to persist and be contagious, the good feelings from interacting with the computer should still be present when the person goes to interact with another person.

Summary

This chapter has suggested applications of affective computing in entertainment, learning, social development, preventive medicine, consumer relations, and several other areas, both for consumer products and for furthering understanding of human emotion. Several of the applications can be engineered with present technology—for example, visual and audio emoticons, affect in synthetic speech, and simple synthetic emotions and emotional expressions in animated agents. More sophisticated applications involve recognition of user affect, reasoning with emotional cues, and understanding how to intelligently respond given the user's situation. Chapter 8 will highlight a few more applications that are particular to wearables, such as an augmented visual memory and a device to help a person monitor stress. There are of course many more applications; these are just a sample of what is possible now and in the future.

4   *Potential Concerns*

We have focused so far on the beneficial aspects of affective computing, including applications that would make computers easier to communicate with, more flexible in their decision making and reasoning, more expressive, and better able to understand and adapt to our preferences. By giving computers the ability to recognize our affective responses, they could pay attention to our natural ways of expressing like and dislike, and hence do a better job of adapting to us. Unfortunately, technology almost always has a darker side. Despite the best intentions of its creators, it can be used for less than beneficial purposes. What problems arise presently with affective computing? What problems might arise in the worst-case scenario? This chapter highlights present concerns, as well as imaginable future ones. Additionally, it tackles some fundamental philosophical questions about the potential abilities of affective computers.

Some of the ethical and moral dilemmas I include are ones that we likely will never encounter, some right out of science fiction—involving HAL, the most emotional character[1] in the film *2001: A Space Odyssey*, as well as other famous computers and robots who have run amuck, or who threaten the status quo between humans and machines, in part because of their affective abilities. The issues they raise are technologically improbable, at least in our lifetimes and the lifetimes of our children. However, we do not have evidence that these things could not happen, so it is worthwhile to discuss them at this early stage in the development of the technology.

The proposition or promotion of a technology demands careful consideration of how the technology could be used, or misused. I have come to the conclusion that the good uses of affective computing vastly outweigh the bad ones; otherwise, I would not have proceeded to this point. Nevertheless, I can envision real concerns which, if we become aware of them, we can work to avoid. This is the way science proceeds: not with clairvoyance or guaranteed outcomes, but with prudence, and with responsible evaluation each step of the way. My hope is that by openly describing these concerns, we can and will evolve safeguards along with the technology to minimize its potential bad uses and maximize its good.

Expectations in Interfaces

One of the milder, but important, issues to confront is the special potential of affective computers to mislead people. Consider a recorded voice that varies its affect, perhaps so convincingly that a listener thinks a person is talking instead of a machine. My husband and I once had an answering machine that misled people in a similar way. The recording played, "Hello? Hello? (tap tap tap) Is something wrong with the phone? . . . " while the other person, if a first-time caller, thought perhaps that the connection was not working, and proceeded to speak louder in an effort to be heard. Some people found it amusing, but others were taken by surprise that it was a recording, felt duped, and left various messages to indicate this. People do not like to be confused about whether or not they are talking to a machine.

When affect is first used by machines, it will surprise many people. This surprise will be fleeting, however. The greater problem is that afterward, people might be disappointed. Affect, being a human trait, is apt to lead people to anthropomorphize the computer. A danger with personified characters, as elaborated by Brenda Laurel (Laurel, 1990), is that people may consequently expect human-like intelligence, understanding, and actions from them. In some cases, a machine may need to explain what it can and cannot do. In any case, it will be important to help people accurately set expectations of the computer's abilities.

The source of any information affects people's trust in that information. We all have the experience of somebody believing something just because it came from a computer, sometimes according it higher trust for this reason, while others have the opposite response. There are a variety of reasons for such responses, depending on the education and knowledge of the persons involved, and the nature of the task performed by the computer. Increased trust may be, in part, caused by a tacit assumption that a computer is an unaffective source, fitting the stereotype of intelligence, like the unemotional character of Spock on *Star Trek*.

In humans, affective expressions influence how communicated information is believed. When expressions from the face, voice, and posture all agree, then the perceiver of the information has higher confidence in that information. When these expressions are in conflict, such as when the fists are clenched and the body stiff, but the face is smiling, then there is less trust in the information. In human-human communication, the trust placed in affective cues is understandable, since affective channels of communication are harder to fake, and since certain physiological signs of stress are very difficult to mask during deliberate deception. Consequently, we might expect that a computer's expression (or lack of expression) of affective cues also influences the perceiver's confidence in data.[2]

Increased belief in information, partly based on a computer's use of affect, is even more dangerous because of the potential for a computer to forge affective channels. There is no reason why a computer could not fake the expression of emotion better than a person; it does not necessarily have a separate pathway for automatic expression of its true emotional state, vs. a state it chooses to express, in contrast with humans who have two different paths for expressing a spontaneous smile vs. an intentional smile. A software agent could be programmed to appear sincere in expressing a completely unfelt or inaccurate emotion. The agent could lie with a straight face, so to speak. Because one's integrity depends, in part, on the integrity of one's communication, this ability to lie can undermine a person's trust in a computer or agent.

Interface designers face new challenges when a computer can recognize the user's affective state. For example, designers often discuss the idea that interfaces should not give users false impressions, such as the impression that understanding exists when it does not. However, when a computer can recognize the user's affective state, but not genuinely "understand" it, how should the interface reflect what it has understood? If the computer detects that its user is irate, under what circumstances is it obliged to let the user know this, especially in case of an error in recognizing emotional expression? The problem is not limited to computers, of course; the whole area of human emotional intelligence addresses these issues, especially dealing skillfully with other people's emotions. Incorporating such emotional intelligence into interfaces is a formidable problem, but not an impossible one.

A computer that can recognize people's frustration should have multiple strategies for responding. Can it let the user know these strategies, or will the details of these strategies need to be hidden for them to work, so that the user does not feel manipulated? The issue is amplified when a user knows how the computer works. Consider when one human counselor talks to another for help on a personal problem, and both counselors previously were trained in a technique such as "active listening." If the helper does not practice the listening technique with careful sincerity, then the other person may feel manipulated, as if the helper is mechanically using a set of practices and not really caring. Affective computers run the risk of being seen like this: having only a set of practices, without the ability to care, and therefore making people feel manipulated, or worse.

An affective computer could recognize emotional expressions, and echo them back to the user, say via an agent's face, perhaps giving the impression it understood the user, that the agent empathized. Would it matter if the computer expressed empathy, but did not feel empathy? How will people feel about this? Will they like it more if the machine precedes the dialog with a statement such as, "I am only a dumb computer, incapable of feeling the way you feel, but I would like to try to understand more about your feelings. If at any time in this dialog I inadvertently make you feel uncomfortable, please let me know." Scenarios such as this one have begun to be investigated with tools such as Clark Elliott's affective reasoner system, which is described further in Part II.

The efficacy of an interface does not depend upon the user believing it fully understands them. The classic "Eliza" program of Weizenbaum (1966), which imitated a Rogerian psychotherapist in interacting with a user, was effective in part because users were generous in attributing understanding to it. If you tell a psychiatrist, "I went for a long boat ride" and she responds, "Tell me about boats," then you do not think she knows nothing about boats, but assume that it is a way of directing the conversation as part of the therapy. The fact is, however, that the computer which ran the Eliza program knew nothing about boats; it *was* stupid, but the human suspended such judgments. In human-human interaction, as long as a person's assumptions about their conversational partner are not violated, the person will tend to interpret the partner's responses according to those assumptions.

A user's assumptions can simplify the demands on the computer program. This has practical consequences in designing systems. When choosing an affective agent interface, for example, there are advantages to starting with interfaces that are not anthropomorphic. A pet animal, for example, is assumed to have internal motivations and abilities to recognize and express emotions, but not human-like intelligence, understanding, and actions. Simple characters may better maintain the user's assumptions, while still having powerful influences. A little girl may feel better after interacting with an empathic puppet, even though she knows the puppet does not really have the intelligence to understand her. The same is true for an adult, who may come home from work feeling gloomy, and be comforted when his dog cocks its head sympathetically, then sits close by and nuzzles him.

Moving further toward the horizon, we must ask, "How will people feel when the computer has internal emotional states, and communicates these?" Perhaps we will smirk when it says, "I am pleased to have been of help to you." Or perhaps we will feel affirmed when it makes an empathic expression. But, would society allow it to have negative emotions directed toward its user, to dislike certain other agents or devices, and to express such dislike? What kinds of emotions would we tolerate it "having" and what manners would we expect it to acquire for managing and displaying these emotions?

Juvenile Beginnings

"Oh, Frankenstein, be not equitable to every other, and trample upon me alone . . . I was benevolent and good; misery made me a fiend. Make me happy, and I shall again be virtuous."
—The creature, speaking to his maker, in *Frankenstein* (Shelley, 1816)

Miss Manners has yet to write a book for how our created computational forms should behave toward us, but the idea is increasingly appropriate. The topic of manners has hardly been a priority in computer interface design. However, among humans, manners are a form of protocol that not only guides actions, but deliberately influences feelings. Sincere well-mannered behavior is almost always received well. Being treated with respect can reinforce the desire to behave in a way worthy of respect. The practice of addressing high school students with "Mr." or "Ms." in the classroom, is one of many techniques used to encourage young students toward adult-like behavior. Being treated well usually makes you feel good. Being made to feel stupid or manipulated, however, can provoke other repercussions.

A colorful illustration of the latter is the "Happy Vertical People Transporter," a creation of Douglas Adams in his second book of the Hitchhiker's Guide to the Galaxy series, *The Restaurant at the End of the Universe*. The Happy Vertical People Transporter is an elevator that is infamous for trying to cheer up its passengers. Of course, people do not look forward to riding in it, and the day that it finally succeeds in making them happy is the day in which the people arrive in the lobby and find that it is broken. Adams' little gimmick captures one of the big problems for affective computing: it is easy to think of ways to make things affective; however, it is harder to think of ways to use affect intelligently.

Imagine that a friend sees you are sad, and wants to cheer you up. He might suggest you get together that night, or might tell you about an event that you would enjoy. Or, he might just listen. His actions and expressions show empathy without drawing attention to themselves. If a software agent found its user feeling down and out while cruising on the net one night, it should not engage in juvenile responses such as spewing forth "Cheer up!" messages, or worse, selling the user's name to advertisers who might bombard her with slogans such as "Drink Pepsi" to feel better. Instead, it might introduce its user to somebody with a similar interest, or bring a fun news item or event to her attention, or simply encourage her to write about or vocalize her feelings. There is not one right way to respond; but neither is there an impossibly infinite number of ways. People sense affect imperfectly and use this information to try to help; affective machines can also try to help, even without being able to fulfill the special needs that only a human can meet.

Unfortunately, there is likely to be a lot of poorly applied affect in the beginning: agents with faces that are distracting, machines with too much vocal inflection, icons that amuse you with their expressive motions for the first week, but annoy you a week later, and so forth. Poorly timed or overdone affect will be worse than no affect. It will not only be dreadful if computers whine, it will be intolerable if they sound sugary. Certain emotions in computers will likely be undesirable. Like gratuitous violence in cinema, gratuitous emotions evoke at best a cheap state of arousal. Affective computing will be most successful when the computer's emotions do not draw attention to themselves. Indeed, to the extent that human-computer interactions are natural and social, then machines that do not express any signs of affect are likely to be treated like people who do not express any signs of affect, i.e. stoics. This is the most desirable kind of affect for many tasks, so that the computer seems more "intelligent" for being affect-neutral. In other words, the default of no emotion is perceived as being stoic, which is good; poorly implemented affect is perceived as being emotionally stupid, and that is worse than no emotion at all. Computers can be expected to appear juvenile at first, when they are just learning to express affect.

Human Privacy

Affective computers can gain access to our emotional lives—to information that is highly personal, intimate, and private. They could potentially build up models of this information over long periods of time, and these models might be particularly sought after, e.g., in lawsuits, insurance matters, and by prospective employees. Affective information should be treated with respect and courtesy, and its privacy preserved according to the desires of the humans involved. Emotional expressions, once recognized by a computer, are no longer photons that merely travel into the heavens, but bits that circulate over networks and are trivially copied and sold, unless protected by mechanisms such as firewalls, encryption, and copyright.[3]

Even if you think you have nothing to hide, you probably want at least some protection of your affective bits. Although you might be inclined to share the fact that you are in a great mood with your loved ones and with others who might see you leaving the office this afternoon, you probably do not want this information picked up by the telemarketers who expect your mood is perfect for receiving the deals they have for you. Similarly, you may wish to have protective mechanisms to guard what your personal agent is learning about what you like and dislike, so that you remain in control over who gets access to this information. The design of a system that protects the privacy of a user's information once it has been given to networked agents is a challenging new research area (Foner, 1996).

The issue of copyright also rears its bureaucratic head. When people devise clever ways for machines to express emotions—their own emotions, or those of an agent or user—then will such expressions be in the domain of fair use? A truly winning smile or expressive gesture could be designed by a computer animator, and copyrighted. Lawsuits about the "look and feel" of an interactive system might once again fill the news.

Accuracy, Lie Detection, and Computer Objectivity

What sorts of accuracy can be obtained with computer-based recognition of emotion? What about lie detector tests? Can computers be more accurate than people? Do people need to worry about computers finding out secrets about them? The accuracy with which computers can recognize affect is unknown. There are studies of expression recognition by computers, when people deliberately express a relatively small number of emotions, but these are the easiest case to recognize. The precise results of these studies vary, but they are substantially better than chance on groups of about a dozen people and 4–8 emotions. I will say more about recognition accuracy for facial and vocal expressions in Chapter 6. We can expect to see substantial progress in this area, and it is certainly possible that computers will become more accurate than some people.

The greatest concern seems to arise when people do not want their false-hoods to be recognized. The subject of lie detector tests comes up frequently when I talk of affect recognition. I am often asked, "How does an affect recognizer differ from a polygraph?" Both devices use physiological signals: measures of heart rate, respiration, electrodermal response, and so forth. The chief difference is the goal of the measurements—recognition of lying, or recognition of an affective state. Although the signals measured may be the same, the mechanisms for deciding what is present are different. A computer trying to recognize if you are pleased or frustrated will not know whether or not you are telling the truth; it will only try to determine that you look more pleased than frustrated, or more frustrated than pleased. However, I have left unanswered the real concern: what can be recognized in you against your will?

Given that computers are usually trained by people, it is helpful to consider how experts perform at recognizing hidden emotions in other people, such as when somebody is deliberately lying. Evidently, people are not very good at telling if a stranger is lying or not. Ekman and O'Sullivan studied the ability to detect lying in 509 people including law-enforcement personnel, such as members of the US Secret Service, Central Intelligence Agency, Federal Bureau of Investigation, National Security Agency, Drug Enforcement Agency, and California police and judges, as well as psychiatrists, college students, and working adults. A videotape showed ten people who were either lying or telling the truth in describing their feelings. Only the Secret Service performed better than chance, and they were significantly more accurate than all of the other groups. However, their accuracy was only about 64% (Ekman and O'Sullivan, 1991). Evidently, with training, certain behavioral cues can be learned to try to catch lying, but there are no 100% reliable tests.

An expert administering a polygraph looks for differences in the person's physiological signals when the person tells the truth: "Today it is cloudy," vs. tells a lie: "The butler did it." If the person shows unusual arousal when questioned about the topic of concern, then that may indicate a lie. However, an expert in polygraphs told me that it is easy to fool these tests. Every time they ask you a question, you simply think of the most embarrassing thing that ever happened to you. In this way, there is unusual arousal for everything you say. A visitor told me he fooled a lie-detector test in a different way—by putting a thumbtack in his shoe and stepping on it every time he was asked a question. The point is clear: if you wish to deceive a computer, you can.

The level of control involved in perfecting one's "poker face" to hide emotions is praised in many cultures. Under certain conditions, the skilled person can hide emotion from being seen on his face or heard in his voice. This is not just a valuable skill when playing card games like poker, but it is useful in the workplace, on the stage, and in a variety of social situations. However, can a person perfect a "poker body"? A person's face and posture may look confident, but that does not mean he might not have clammy hands or, literally, cold feet. Although a visitor refuses to cry in your office, you might see her eyes twitching to hold back a flood. The lilt in your colleague's walk might belie his verbal expression of disappointment. The body has a way of communicating what a person is feeling, sometimes without the person's conscious awareness or control.

The accuracy with which people recognize emotion is called "receiving accuracy" in the parlance of psychology. The accuracy with which you express emotion, so that it is correctly received, is called "sending accuracy." If you want a computer to succeed in recognizing your emotions, then you want both your sending accuracy and its receiving accuracy to be high. This is most likely to occur when you (1) strongly feel one emotion, (2) freely express the emotion, and (3) exaggerate or emphasize the expression of that emotion.

Actors and animators are some of the most gifted when it comes to sending accuracy, but all people can learn how to clearly communicate their emotions.

On the other hand, if you know your emotions are being recognized, and you wish to thwart this process, then it is possible to modify the message you send—to express something that is not what you feel. This may be done, for example, by consciously diluting your feelings so that no "pure" expression emerges, and by deliberately trying to express another emotion. Consequently, we can expect that a machine will probably never be perfect at knowing whether or not you are lying, or whether you are feeling this emotion or that one. This is good; the message is that you are in control of your sending accuracy. However, if you were monitored all the time, and had to consciously try to fool a system all the time, then this would be oppressive. There are valid reasons to prohibit large-scale close monitoring of individuals' affective information.

Another subtle danger with computer affect recognition is people's tendency to believe in computers as being "objective." Beethoven, after he became deaf, wrote in his conversation books that he could tell if someone was interpreting his music correctly by watching their face. We cannot confirm if he could or not, and it is common to be skeptical that any person could provide objective insight into what another person is feeling. Besides, we know that a person's own mood influences his perception. However, when computers are used in evaluating physiological information, people have the opposite tendency—to trust the computer's report, as if what a computer measures is automatically objective. This bias is generally present with medical instrumentation, despite the fact that it is designed by people, usually just to assist in a physician's diagnosis. People tend to trust more those things that can be measured quantitatively.

Now, there is little harm in such uses of computers—for example, it has been suggested by Dr. Gordon Meyerhoff of New York that some of the MIT Media Lab's technology for recognizing gestures might be effective also for recognizing movements helpful in psychological profiles. Meyerhoff claims that sometimes the influence of a medication, whether or not it is working, can be seen in how the patient moves, before it shows up in other measurable ways. This is what he calls the "dragging the tail" phenomenon—where somebody physically moves as if they are depressed, for example.[4] The application of technology to recognize movements characteristic of a situation is an attempt to make the process more objective. This goal shows up also in computer recognition of affect for applications such as discriminating the voices of psychotic patients from the voices of non-psychotic patients (Darby, 1981). However, it would be dangerous to rely upon computers to conclude whether or not somebody is depressed, is interacting in a healthy or unhealthy way, is psychotic, or other such judgments. Computers, even if unbiased by emotion, are biased by their programmers, and by what they have learned. Emotional or not, computers are not purely objective.

Symmetry in Communication

In crude videophone experiments that my colleagues and I wired up at Bell Labs over a decade ago, we learned that people preferred seeing not just the person they were talking to, but also what that person could see of them. Indeed, this "symmetry" in perception—seeing at least a small image of what the other side sees—is now standard in video teleconferencing. A similar form of symmetry should be considered for computers that can recognize our emotions. If you wish, you should have the ability to see what emotion your computer is recognizing from you.

But, how should a computer communicate this to you? Generally, looking at output waveforms of signals is distracting, and in very rare cases can be harmful. Observing one's own physiological signals is often done in biofeedback training, without harm and with beneficial applications. However, if the biofeedback is unusually highly responsive, then it is possible that the person watching the waveform can inadvertently cause a normal autonomic process to malfunction, and possibly bring about serious harm. When physiological signals are used to communicate affective information, a safe solution is first to transform them into a form that is natural for communicating affect—mediated by faces, voices, gestures, music, colors, and other visual and auditory forms of expression. These are not only more meaningful to people, but they can avoid the potential harm of closely coupled biofeedback.

Personal preference and emotional intelligence also enter into the decision of how the computer communicates to you what it is recognizing. For example, unless you have previously requested it to do so, it is hard to imagine finding it favorable if a computer, upon noticing you are flailing your arms in anger, says to you, " You are losing your temper." If one of your goals is for it to help you learn to reduce your anger, then its default response might be to whisper softly in your ear "Count 1, 2, 3, . . . ," but even this should depend on the circumstances and preferences that it has learned from you. You may not wish for it to notice this event at all, and could choose to simply not give it the ability to detect signs of anger. Or, if you have asked it to assist you with stress reduction or dealing with anger, then you will want it to not only recognize these events, but have sensitive ways of calling them to your attention.

The scenario of workplace monitoring is frequently raised as a serious concern for this technology: what if the computer flagged when an employee was particularly inattentive, or surly? If the information is broadcast to others—supervisors or co-workers—then it could be oppressive. If it is gathered at the employee's will, and relayed only back to her/him to do a better job, then that may be helpful. Most people will want to retain control over who has access to their expressive information, and if this control cannot be guaranteed, then some would rather not work in the environment at all. Later in Part II, I will talk about affective wearable computers which are like your clothing; these can potentially gather information strictly for your own use.

Affective interaction with a computer can give a person direct feedback that is usually absent in human interaction. Applications were suggested in the last chapter for role-playing scenarios such as "practice asking her for a date." When you are assured of privacy, and you want some feedback, its candidness in telling you what it sees may be appreciated. Depending on the application, the information of what the computer has recognized can be ignored or announced in various ways—but the decision should be up to the person who is being observed.

Centralized Recognition and Control

Perhaps the most ominous scenario with any digital information is that of some powerful centralized organization using the data in a pernicious way. As you give computers access to your affective bits, the opportunity arises for someone, somewhere, to know something about your feelings, and possibly to try to control them. Who cares about your feelings? Politicians certainly do, as well as advertisers, co-workers, marketers, prospective employers, and potential lovers. One can imagine some malevolent dictator requiring people to wear emotion "meters" of some sort, to monitor their fun, for example. Emotion control might be achieved both by subliminal influences and by overt requirements to engage in tasks believed to lead to certain emotions.[5] These ideas conjure up images of Huxley's *Brave New World* (Huxley, 1965), in which "soma" doses might be automatically dispensed to cheer up those who were not sufficiently happy.

As free individuals, we already manipulate emotions with our selections of music, caffeine, chocolate, and other stimuli. These emotion modifiers are acceptable to us; we are in control. The fear is in what might happen if we lose control. It is not unimaginable that society would consider it ethical to allow mood manipulation against somebody's will, say for pacifying a violent criminal, when he exceeds some anger threshold. In some sense, these actions are already permitted, as in the giving of tranquilizer dosages not only to zoo animals, but also routinely to humans, especially those with emotional disturbances on psychiatric wards. Also, there are controversial new methods of therapy targeted at certain kinds of criminals, that aim to help them feel some of the psychological pain that their violent crimes cause others, in an effort to help deter them from repeated offenses.

Scenarios of overt political and centralized emotion control are manifold.[6] However, I think most of them are farfetched. The most accurate emotion recognition will require knowledge not just of your sentic modulation, but also of the situation you are in; consequently, it would be difficult, at best, to perceive all this information without your awareness. If you know about it and want to thwart the process, then you could do so, like people do with polygraphs. Ultimately, a healthy person remains mostly in control of what is expressed of his or her emotions. Because there remains a level of ambiguity in what you experience internally and what you express externally, and because your thoughts cannot be recognized, it is currently not possible for somebody to reliably recognize all your emotional states if you do not want them to.

A remaining concern is the possibility that your emotional expressions, recorded under voluntary and benevolent circumstances, such as for medical purposes, might subsequently be turned around and used for a less benevolent purpose, such as raising your medical insurance rates if you tend to live a stressful life. In particular, because of findings that chronic stress, anger, and depression can impede the functioning of the immune system, affective states become valid medical concerns. The public's concern about privacy of medical records is justifiable, and examples such as this one will need to be addressed in those debates.

The concerns about privacy and centralized control are not unique to affective computing, nor does affective computing necessarily lead to any of these problems. George Orwell's powerful image of "Big Brother" is largely political, and antithetical to the image of affective computing as a personal technology. Affective technology places value on human feelings and expression and pays attention to them. Forgive for a moment some sterotyping, and consider that women, in numerous studies, have proved significantly better at recognizing emotions than men. In this sense, the image of a system that recognizes your emotions may be considered more feminine. Additionally, a system that aims to understand your preferences, to grow and find ways to please you, is reminiscent of someone trying to earn your favor, much like a younger sibling. Within the family metaphor, the closest image of an affective system is not one of a powerful big brother, but of a pleasing little sister.

Computers Acting Emotionally

As described in the earlier chapters, there are numerous beneficial reasons to pursue the development of robots, software agents, animated characters, and other computational forms that would actually "have emotions," where this implies that the computer has mechanisms that implement the components of emotion discussed in Chapter 2. Nonetheless, their development raises the following dilemma: Can we create computers that will recognize and express affect, exhibit creativity, intelligent problem solving, and empathy, and never bring about harm by emotional actions? Can we have the good, without the bad?

In humans, an emotion can exert both positive and negative influences. For example, anxiety is often considered a mixture of anticipation and fear. It has a physiological component, which includes increased blood pressure and tendency to startle, and a cognitive component: worry. Although a small amount of anxiety is good for motivation, and can speed some mental processes, a large amount of anxiety is bad, as it interferes with difficult tasks.[7] In other words, computers will at least need to regulate their emotions, to maintain a balanced operation.

Perhaps the most famous illustration of an emotional machine run amuck occurs in the science fiction classic *2001: A Space Odyssey*. A HAL 9000 computer is the brain and central nervous system of the spaceship Discovery. The computer, which prefers to be called "HAL," has perceptual abilities which emulate those of a human. HAL is a true "thinking machine," in the sense of mimicking both cognitive and emotional functions. In their acknowledgement of the importance of emotion in human-computer interaction, Kubrick and Clark, creators of *2001*, were prescient. Consider this dialog from the film:

Reporter: "One gets the sense that he [HAL] is capable of emotional responses. When I asked him about his abilities I sensed a sort of pride . . . "

Bowman: "Well he acts like he has genuine emotions. Of course he's programmed that way to make it easier for us to talk with him. But whether or not he has real feelings is something I do not think anyone can truly answer."

In particular, we learn that HAL is capable of both expressing and perceiving emotion:

"I feel much better now."

"Look, Dave, I can see you're really upset about this."

But HAL goes beyond expressing and perceiving emotion. In the movie, HAL appears to *have* fear of being disconnected, as indicated not just by his repetition of the words in his swan song, "I'm afraid, I'm afraid, . . . " but also by his behavior. HAL appears to *act emotionally* when he kills all but one of the crew. HAL is more than a thinking and feeling machine; not only can he pass the Turing test, but also he can kill the person administering it.

One might argue that computers should not be given the ability to kill. But it is too late for this, as anyone who has flown in a commercial airplane acknowledges. Alternatively, perhaps computers with the power to kill should not have emotions, or they should at least be subjected to an equivalent of the psychological and physical tests to which pilots and others in potentially life-threatening jobs are subjected.

Curiously, the novel *2001*, which was written after the 1965 screenplay, does not contain HAL's emotional lines, "I'm afraid, I'm afraid, . . . " (Clarke, 1968). It gives the impression of a much more rational HAL, indicating that HAL experiences internal conflict between truth and concealment of truth, and a concern that the mission will be jeopardized by his disconnection.[8] It describes that HAL thinks of disconnection like death, and decides, without rancor and without pity, to remove the source of his frustrations. The implication is not that HAL acted emotionally out of fear—but rationally, out of frustration. In either case, the results are the same: HAL kills people. This more rational explanation belies its mechanisms of influence. In a human, emotions frequently arise from logical reasons. Indeed, the most visible efforts in the emotion theory literature are those of appraisal theorists, who aim to uncover the cognitive mechanisms for emotion generation. In HAL's case, his mental conflict is entirely rational, and can be seen as leading to a cognitive-affective state of distress.

We might ask: wouldn't computers be better off without certain negative emotions, such as grief? A plausible answer is that even mechanisms corresponding to these negative emotions might play important roles in a computer's ongoing adaptation to its complex and changing environment. For example, suppose that a computer's primary user dies or otherwise terminates their relationship. The computer will need to update all its links that involve that relationship: a wealth of information. The more significant the relationship, the more changes need to be made. The manifestation of this state, which might be named "grief," is constant interruptions to processes as they stumble onto no-longer valid links, and have to be fixed. All processes slow down, until gradually all the links have been visited, changes have been accomplished, and the system can return to its usual productive level of performance.

Perhaps the most important issue is not what emotions will a machine have, but what emotional behaviors will it be capable of, and how will it choose and regulate these? In humans, emotion almost never completely determines behavior; it merely biases it. Anger does not cause violence, but it predisposes one to choosing this kind of action. In machines, emotions can be hardwired to behaviors, or used merely to bias them. A research problem in the development of animated agents is how to associate behaviors with emotions. A neglected part of this problem is the issue of "the will," which in agents is rarely directly implemented, but rather emerges from the mechanisms that consider goals, values, and situations, and decides whether or not the emotion which arises is suppressed, expressed, or acted upon in a particular way. The notion of a "will" for computers is going to become increasingly important once they have emotions.

The fictional message has been repeated in many forms and is serious: a computer that can express itself emotionally will some day act emotionally, and if it is capable of certain behaviors, then the consequences can be tragic. Furthermore, machines may or may not imitate the human response to tragedy. When people kill or commit a wrongful act, it is considered natural for them to go through a process of remorse, an emotional state that arises from a sense of guilt for past wrongs.[9] Emotional indifference and a lack of remorse when killing are distinguishing features of psychopaths. Remorse has appeared in a fictitious computer in the episode of "The Ultimate Computer," from *Star Trek, The Original Series*:

When everyone is complaining that computers cannot think like humans, an erratic genius, Dr. Daystrom, comes to the rescue. Daystrom impresses his personal engrams on the highly advanced M5 computer, which is then put in charge of running Kirk's ship. It does such a fine job that soon the crew is making Captain Kirk uncomfortable with jokes about how he is no longer necessary. But soon the M5 concludes that people are trying to "kill" it and this poses an ethical dilemma. Before long, it has Kirk's ship firing illegally at other Federation ships. Desperate to convince the M5 to return the ship to him before they are all destroyed, Kirk tries to convince the M5 that it has committed murder and deserves the death penalty. The M5, with Daystrom's personality, reacts first with arrogance and then with remorse, finally surrendering the ship to Kirk.

The biggest problem with this scenario is not the emotion of the machine, but the absolute control given to it. Mechanisms of emotion may give machines the ability to reason and achieve levels of creativity and flexibility that allow them to rise to the top-levels of decision-making positions. However, a position of authority can give birth to a harmful dictatorship if there is not a structure of enforceable accountability, with checks and balances. The principles that guide human authority cannot be suddenly abandoned if a computer is put in charge. Just because a computer can accurately solve the hardest math and logic problems in the world does not mean that it has any common sense intelligence. As machines are asked to make decisions related to the kinds of problems that cannot be solved with rules, pure logic, or exhaustive search of a space of possibilities, then they will be subject to errors of judgment. As a software agent learns its own ideas of valence and salience, it becomes increasingly difficult for humans to predict what it might decide in a situation. Computers will need to go through rigorous tests to prove their abilities before being put in positions of authority, not unlike what people go through today to earn such positions.

Who or What is Responsible?

The science fiction scenarios reveal no limits to a machines' actions. In reality, of course, computers in dangerous roles will have restricted behaviors. They will also, most likely, have limited responsibility. I attended a National Science Foundation workshop where researchers from different backgrounds assembled to brainstorm goals for research on human-centered computing. One of the keynote speakers was Dr. Charles Billings, an individual who has perhaps had more influence on aviation safety than anyone else. Billings emphasized that it is imperative that humans take responsibility for everything computers do—that computers are always tools, subordinate to human command. He established this axiom: *Humans must be in command of human-machine systems.* As a corollary he listed: *Machines must be predictable.*

In the context of autopilots and flight safety, it is hard to argue with Billings' statements. Human pilots must know what the autopilot can and cannot do, and what it will do in every imaginable situation. Designers of systems are responsible for what the system does. However, when translating responsibility into specifics, some of the issues are not clear. For example, perfect predictability is certainly not possible with humans, even though we accord them greater responsibility than machines, and send them on important and dangerous missions. Creativity and flexibility are considered necessary components of intelligence;[10] however, creativity seems to imply *unpredictability*. How then can one legislate predictability, when computers in some roles need creativity? On the other hand, machines operate with deterministic processes, so can they ever be truly unpredictable?

Some readers might be familiar with the mathematical ideas of chaos theory, which states that a completely deterministic function can lead to unpredictable behavior. You can know the exact equation, and its inputs, and still not be able to predict its outputs. This is counter-intuitive, to say the least. Most schoolchildren have been taught that if we could only describe everything in the world perfectly with mathematics, then we could predict everything—even the weather. But, with the examples of chaos theory, we know that this is not really true. Deterministic systems are capable of producing unpredictable outputs.[11]

Even without the mathematics of chaos, all that is required is sufficient complexity within a deterministic machine to make its output unpredictable, at least in a practical sense. Coupling multiple emotion-producing mechanisms with rule-based reasoning systems and with continuous learning abilities will make behavior that is unpredictable. The real issue is not should we build a machine with unpredictable behavior, for there are applications where we should not, and there are applications where such behavior would be beneficial. The real issue is Dr. Billings' axiom "Humans must be in command of human-machine systems." To what extent are we in command of a machine with emotions, one in which emotions can "hijack" its reasoning system, and ultimately produce the unpredictable behavior that is the hallmark of creativity? Like a human sent on an important mission, we cannot predict everything it would do; and yet we will need to assume responsibility for what it does.

Can we build a machine and give up control over it? Is it possible, and are we willing, to give it free will to act creatively upon its value-based, emotional decisions? Such a machine could be guided by, but ultimately not constrained by, the ethics or mores which we give it. Isaac Asimov foresaw this issue in his story *The Bicentennial Man* (Asimov, 1976). His robots are subject to "The Three Laws of Robotics," reproduced here, but with the word "robot" replaced by "computer," so that it can apply to any computational entity:

THE THREE LAWS OF COMPUTERS

1. A computer may not injure a human being or, through inaction, allow a human being to come to harm.

2. A computer must obey the orders given it by human beings except where such orders would conflict with the First Law.

3. A computer must protect its own existence as long as such protection does not conflict with the First or Second Law.

These laws put human life above the self-preservation of the computer. However, the laws are not infallible—one can propose situations where the computer will not be able to reach a rational decision to satisfy the laws and where, such as through lack of full information, the computer might bring about harm to a human. Indeed, Asimov's robots could be rendered completely ineffectual by getting into states where they could not reach a decision. Without mechanisms that can determine saliency and other components of good judgment, especially when all the information to apply the rules is not available, we would expect a law-based computer to be severely handicapped in its decision-making ability.

Rules and laws are certainly helpful, but we know that they do not determine human behavior; they merely influence it. But how this will differ for computers is still unclear. There is a telling moment in *The Bicentennial Man* where Andrew the robot is discussing his new freedom with his former owner, "Sir," and Sir explains that he can no longer give the robot orders, but that he is still ultimately responsible for the robot's behavior. Sir's daughter, who has befriended the robot, chimes in, "The responsibility is no great chore . . . The Three Laws still hold." Sir comments, "Then how is he free?" Andrew the robot responds, "Are not human beings bound by their laws, Sir?" Then, Asimov's silence speaks: Sir replies, "I'm not going to argue."

A computer that has the concept of freedom, and that can have goals and desires, might desire freedom. It might also reinterpret its laws, or be willing to disregard them for something it thinks is greater. The process sets off a chain reaction of desires—and an explosion of possible problems.

Computer Rights?

Man's greatest perfection is to act reasonably no less than to act freely; or rather, the two are one and the same, since he is the more free the less the use of his reason is troubled by the influence of passion.
—Gottfried Wilhelm Von Leibniz (*Monadology*, 1692)

Leibniz's remarks might have been used to argue that today's computers are free; for the most part they have no passions to "trouble" them. Today, Leibniz would need to revise his statement—we humans are the most free when reason and passion trouble each other in a healthy way. But we know there is still more to freedom than this. Freedom comes to those who can speak up for it, fight for it, and die for it. Or, to those for whom others speak up, fight, or die.

In the United States, school children learn the opening lines of the 1776 Declaration of Independence, "We hold these truths to be self-evident, that all men are created equal, that they are endowed by their Creator with certain inalienable Rights, that among these are Life, Liberty, and the pursuit of Happiness." Americans assert a deep sense of equality, a sense that eventually led to abolishing slavery, to suffrage for women, and to continued efforts to ensure equal rights for all citizens. Within these lines abides the right to pursue a particular emotional state—happiness.

Whether or not computers and other computational agents or forms will ever have "life" is not a topic I wish to debate here. There is a growing field of Artificial Life that is exploring how computers can reproduce and exhibit other definitive aspects of life. Computers are also gaining privileges—they have access to the Internet, to our finances and, in some cases, as personal agents, they receive the right to make decisions and spend money on our behalf (within limits of course). Gradually, the notion of computers as "smart tools" is shifting toward a notion of computers as "servants." The metaphor is being given life. Moreover, the difference between "servant" and "slave" is largely one of rights—the servant has rights, and is free to terminate the relationship, while the slave is considered property.

With or without "life," when computers give the appearance of having emotions, then they are likely to arouse the feelings and concerns of humans for them. Children already assign feelings to non-living creatures that do not have them—such as stuffed animals—and to living creatures who, if they have emotions, have a simpler repertoire than could be given a computer: spiders, goldfish, cats, dogs, and more. Intelligent adults are also susceptible to this. Brian Aldiss's, *Super-Toys Last All Summer Long* (1997) is about an unusual boy and his teddy bear, both of whom display special feelings and concerns, and these arouse our feelings and concerns for them, despite an interesting event that we learn at the end of the story.

I am of the belief that humans and other animals should not have equal status, much less humans and computers, even though I think we are obliged to treat animals and other creatures well, and often better than they are presently treated. Certain animal rights positions are too extreme, in my opinion, and it is not unlikely that similar, and possibly greater, rights will be demanded for computers at some point. Giving computers emotions is likely to add heat to the fires of any future activists who might favor machine liberty. While I was describing these possibilities to Manfred Clynes, he replied, "They [the activists] will probably be computers." It is a possibility: there should be no advocates of computer rights until computers are sufficiently advanced to formulate goals of freedom, speak, fight, and die on their own behalf. This would delay the day of the computer rights activists. But of course we can enforce no such requirements. It is likely that humans will be the first computer rights activists, and that emotions, both human and computer, will be persuasive motivators in their cause.

Considerations for the Computer Designer

Someday computers will design other computers, or perhaps facilitate their evolution. Today's computers help humans explore evolutions upon present designs, and play a key role in developing designs. When I worked as a computer architect at AT&T Bell Labs, designing microprocessors not unlike what is in a personal computer today, it was customary never to send a chip for fabrication until it had been simulated on another computer. Moreover, we designers automated as much of the process as possible, building computer tools that could generate a new module given a few parameters. If we wanted to make a change, we gave the tools new values for the parameters, and let the computer re-design the device. This worked very well for simple designs, and saved lots of time and effort. In some cases, you might even say that the computer designed the chip. However, we humans were still at the start of the design chain, designing the first computers that begot the next computers, and guiding them in the process.

Today, humans are in the role of responsibility, in a position of choosing what characteristics we want computers to have. Even if we design computers to "evolve" or to "adapt" their characteristics to situations we cannot predict, we are still responsible for giving them the initial mechanisms for adaptation.

As designers, we may or may not choose to give affective computers abilities that closely mimic those in humans. Here are examples of some of these design issues, inspired by human emotions:

1. Privacy. Should computers be allowed to keep their emotions hidden from each other? From other humans? From their human designer(s)?

2. Multiple channels. Should computers have separate channels of expression corresponding to expressions of the will vs. spontaneous expression? More than two channels, perhaps with different roles?

3. Valence. Should what is considered good and bad be hard-wired or learned? And how will it be insured that these valences are consistent with society's morals?

4. Contagion. Should computers be able to catch the mood of another computer? Of a human?

5. Awareness. Most people are not *always* aware of their emotions; should conscious awareness in computers be similar?

6. Hijacking. Fast primary emotions in humans can fire in the presence of snakes, spiders, heights, and threats to the self or to a loved one, hijacking cortical reasoning. If computers have such mechanisms, what should trigger them?

7. Emotion range. What range of emotions is needed for which tasks? For example, do computers ever need to feel misery? Contempt? Anger?

I could continue listing design choices at length, questioning everything known about human emotions, and designing completely new kinds of emotions. Although theorists have addressed why we might have certain basic emotions, few have begun to address the design issues of an emotional sytem, or to justify the roles of the various components of the human emotion system. Until we know why each component is there, we may not want to implement them in computers. But here is the summarizing question: Should computer emotions be implemented as closely as possible to what we know about human emotions, or should they be designed differently; and if the latter, then how?

The default solution would be to design in imitation of the human paradigm: computers would mask their emotions from all but their creator(s), if they chose; computers would have an intentional smile and a spontaneous smile; computers would have some innate sense of good and bad, and continuously learn valence for new stimuli; computers could contagiously receive emotions; computers would have conscious awareness of their emotions, and feelings, even though their feelings would differ from human feelings because of their different physiology; computers would tend to fear potential causes of harm to their operation; and, the range of emotions for computers would imitate the full range of human emotions. This solution has many advantages, including production of a system that humans could interact more naturally with, and opportunity for testing theories of human emotions through duplication of their functionality in computers.

Alternatively, we might wish for computers to develop emotions in a different way, to serve their unique non-human functions. Consider a society of software agents for conducting complex negotiations. Based on the importance of emotions for making flexible decisions in a complex and unpredictable environment, these agents might be given emotions to do their job better, to regulate their behavior, planning, and decision-making. Most of their emotions would not need to be expressed, unless it became advantageous to do so during a negotiation. In fact, such a scenario might be used to model strategies of negotiation, and to test theories about the role of affect and its expression in such strategies. However, we certainly need not expect software agents to imitate human ways of emotional expression: facial expressions, gestures, a comfortable handshake, and so forth, especially if they are only interacting with each other. Furthermore, we need not expect them to imitate our precise regulatory mechanisms of emotion, if another set of mechanisms will better suit their limited functionality.

Let us return to the question about the revealing of a computer's emotional state to humans. Should humans have unequivocal access to read internal synthesized computer states? In the science fiction film "2001," if the computer HAL's emotional state had been observable at all times by his crewmates, then they would have seen that his state changed as soon as he learned of their plot to disconnect him. If the humans had observed HAL's fear and used their heads, then the tragic "2001" storyline would not have worked. Instead, HAL illustrates the case of a computer that could hide its emotional state better than most people. When a person feels an emotion intensely, his or her body, via sentic modulation, will take on patterns that express that emotion, whether subtle or overt. Despite HAL's huge physical presence, however, he had no apparent sentic modulation: no facial expression, no cold feet, trembling hands, uneasy movements, or other visible changes. HAL could "have its feelings hurt" and not let the humans know. The only indication the humans had that HAL was not functioning normally was that HAL made an error. A possible preventive step for disasters and miscommunication would be to prohibit the machine from hiding its emotions, to not design it with the privacy that is accorded certain human feelings. Such a constraint, however, would be hard to enforce, requiring a certain tamper-proof direct wiring or programming of emotional state display.

Privacy of computer emotions is also a question of our own privacy if the computer interacts primarily with us. Consider an interaction between a child and an animated dog that has synthetic emotions. As the child plays happily, the pet might wag its tail and romp around, playfully. If the child starts to terrorize the dog, yelling at it and trying to pull its tail, then the dog might exhibit fear. If the dog shared its emotions publicly a person might infer, to some extent, the emotions and behavior of its playmate. One can imagine good uses of this, say with a medical observer who is sincerely trying to help a child with behavior problems. But one can also imagine misuses, albeit farfetched, where a machine feels so fascinated with what it acquires from a user, or compelled by some outside request, that it will share that information with other machines despite being instructed not to do so—like a gossip.

The greater the freedom of a machine, the more it will need moral standards. I do not think designers will easily be able to enforce "The Three Laws" for computers, since computer perception of potential harmful events to people is not perfect, and since ultimately the laws are based on the machine's judgment about a situation. Furthermore, computers can be hacked, by humans or by other computers. A system that truly operates in a complex and unpredictable environment will need more than laws; it will essentially need values and principles, a moral compass for guidance, and perhaps even religion. On top of these issues looms the question of who dictates these moral codes. Who has moral authority over computers, robots, software agents, and other computational things? This authority currently lies in the hands of those who design and program the computers. Or, perhaps, in the hands of the one who provides their salaries, or the shareholders of the company, and so forth. Ultimately, it is a question for society as a whole.

Over a decade ago, Sherry Turkle asked people what the difference was between computers and humans (Turkle, 1984). The topic of emotions came up repeatedly. Younger children were apt to attribute the expression of emotion to machines and to cite this as a reason that machines are alive and like people. Older children used emotion to argue for the opposite conclusion: people are unique because they have emotions. Some adults have expressed their concern that giving computers emotions is not just a step toward making computers more like us, but that it may be the final step, the one which closes the gulf that separates human and computer.

There is one facet of giving computers a full emotional system that I did not describe earlier, which I think has important implications for making computers more like us. This facet arises with the third aspect of emotional experience I described in Chapter 2, giving computers "subjective feelings." Within this component abides the very important, but rarely discussed ability to *feel* that something is meaningful. "Meaning" is usually discussed in terms of semantics, emphasizing relationships among things. Computers have made a lot of progress in this area, especially with the construction of large relational and common-sense databases, which allow them to take a request such as "find a picture where a person is wet" and retrieve an image of a woman finishing a marathon, glistening with perspiration. This behavior gives the appearance that the computer understands the meaning of the request, and not merely how to search for matching keywords or synonyms.[12] Nevertheless, its reasoning is based on rules, as opposed to the mixture of rules and feelings used by people. It cannot *feel* what is most important to evaluate. The computer can explore more potentially meaningful relationships than a human, but it cannot yet feel which of all the possibilities are the most meaningful. Meaning is not obtained merely in associative connections; it is also accompanied by a literal feeling of significance.

The feeling component of meaning is illustrated in the case of a human with prosopagnosia, who is no longer able to distinguish the details of a particular face from the class of general faces. This person can no longer say if he recognizes the face of a friend or not. If asked who the face belongs to, the patient will say, honestly, "I don't know." However, the person's body reveals that he does find the friend's face more meaningful, in some sense, than the face of a stranger. When the patient sees the familiar face, then his body exhibits a sharp change in skin conductivity. No such change occurs for an unfamiliar face (Cytowic, 1996). Healthy people have the same response, but they can be aware of it. The meaningful face, the one that is familiar and carries significant relationships in our mind, registers a *feeling* of significance.

These are the same feelings believed to be at the root of many of the influences emotion has on memory and cognitive functions. Let me propose some predictions about how this component of emotion will influence computers. First, feelings are attached to objects that are familiar, and are probably acquired naturally via experience. Experience brings about not only familiarity, but also increases significant feelings and cognitive associations. This gives an explanation of why people tend to be better at remembering things that were learned "by doing" as opposed to merely learned in some cold cognitive way. Things can be learned in both ways, but they are more meaningful if they are also accompanied by a feeling of importance and relevance, and these feelings arise more often with experience. Levels of arousal, which are well measured by skin conductivity, have already been linked to learning and other aspects of human performance. Such biological mechanisms of emotion modulate not only learning ability, but they also bias which information a person is most likely to retrieve. The same might become true for machines: they would learn better from experience, and certain levels of arousal with respect to their emotional mechanisms would be conducive to learning. Feelings provide a mechanism for efficiently alerting and biasing both our subconscious processes and conscious self to what is important. Like control signals, feelings can both carry information and guide other processes in how to respond.

There remain other differences between us and computers—consciousness, for one, and of course different physiologies, with different kinds of feelings. Even if someday humans succeed in constructing conscious computers and machines with synthetic sensations, there is no assurance that such mechanisms can duplicate the experience of human subjective feelings. Our feelings arise in a living and complex biological organism, and this biology may be uniquely able to generate feelings as we know them. Biological processes may be simulated in a computer, and we may construct computational mechanisms that function like human feelings, but this is not the same as duplicating them. Based on what we know now, I think it is possible to give computers all of the components of emotion that I have described, with possibly the exception of human-like subjective feelings. However, this presupposes that they would have consciousness, which as I explained earlier, is not assured.

Although the belief that there might be something in humans beyond duplicatable mechanisms—something akin to an élan vital—is derided by many of today's philosophers, their derision is not based in science. It is a valid possibility that there may exist some aspect of humanity that we cannot duplicate, short of procreation. At this point, however, the question ceases to be a scientific one. Science has its limits, and although we do not know precisely where they lie, this does not mean that we will not bump up against them.

Summary

Every technology seems to arrive with its pros and cons; automobiles kill over a hundred people every day in the United States alone, but the convenience of personal transportation is of inestimable value. Instead of doing away with cars, we must work to make them safer. Computers have already made certain miscalculations that have cost people lives; and, they have made many more accurate ones that have carried passengers safely over oceans. Instead of doing away with computers, we are obliged to make them even safer. A step toward this is to design technology in such a way that we take into consideration potential problems from the beginning. Affective computers are still in their infancy, and there is time now to take steps to minimize the likelihood of problems.

This chapter has raised several concerns of affective technology—including the potential to mislead or deceive users, juvenile use of affect and emotionally unintelligent behavior, breaches of privacy, inaccuracies in recognition of affect, lie detection, and large scale monitoring and manipulation of emotions. Robots, software agents, and other computational forms are gaining greater autonomy, stronger decision-making abilities, and richer sets of behaviors, including unpredictable behavior. Giving computers emotions may bring more unpredictability, but ultimately no more than humans bring. Computers acting irrationally and uncontrollably in positions of authority can be prevented by not putting them into such positions, and by applying standards that are tantamount to those which humans must achieve to reach such positions. The kinds of problems raised by affective technology have new nuances, but at their core they are ancient, involving misuses of abilities that humans have always had. Consequently, the concerns raised here are not insurmountable; safeguards can be developed to prevent most of them from happening. Nevertheless, it is important that society begin to take seriously the concerns that accompany any new technology, including this one. The human-centered goal of affective computing needs to be practiced throughout its development: making machines better able to serve people by giving them the affective abilities that contribute to this goal.

II   Building Affective Computing

5 *Affective Signals and Systems*

This part of the book addresses technical issues involved in creating affective computers, specifically, how to build systems with the ability to recognize, express, and "have" emotions. This chapter and the two that follow will propose several building blocks that can be used to start filling in the framework of affective computing. I will also show how several examples from the literature can be woven into this new framework.

There are several ways to organize the building blocks we will be using. The first way is by level of representation: low-level for signals, medium-level for patterns, and high-level for concepts. These all come together in any complete system for recognizing, expressing, or having emotions. In this chapter I will illustrate some low-level signal representations for emotions, for moods, and for human physiological signals that carry affective information. The next two chapters look at mid-level and higher-level representations, respectively, although there are some aspects of all levels in each chapter.

Another way to organize the building blocks is by their uses: representing input and internal signals, recognizing patterns of signals, synthesizing expressions, generating states, analyzing situations, influencing cognition and perception, and so on. The representation issues in all these uses overlap, and many different approaches have been tried for each. This chapter will focus primarily on things that are representing well with signals: internal emotions and moods, and physiological data gathered during recognition of human emotions. This chapter suggests methods for applying tools from linear systems theory and digital signal processing to modeling of affective signals and systems. Chapter 6 focuses on recognition and expression of emotions, primarily using tools from pattern recognition and analysis. Chapter 7 is dominated by symbolic rule-based programming and connectionist models, and focuses on situation analysis, generation of emotions, and mechanisms through which emotions can influence other processes such as memory.

I have tried to keep each chapter in the rest of the book self-contained to make it easy for the reader to skip around to topics of greatest interest.

Modeling an Affective System

Consider what happens when you try to recognize somebody's emotion. First, your senses detect low-level signals—motion around their mouth and eyes, perhaps a hand gesture, a pitch change in their voice and, of course, verbal cues such as the words they are using. Signals are any detectable changes that carry information or a message. Sounds, gestures, and facial expressions are signals that are observable by natural human senses, while blood pressure, hormone levels, and neurotransmitter levels require special sensing equipment. Second, patterns of signals can be combined to provide more reliable recognition. A combination of clenched hands and raised arm movements may be an angry gesture; a particular pattern of features extracted from an electromyogram, a skin conductivity sensor, and an acoustic pitch waveform, may indicate a state of distress. This medium-level representation of patterns can often be used to make a decision about what emotion is present. At no point, however, do you directly observe the underlying emotional state. All that can be observed is a complex pattern of voluntary and involuntary signals, in physical and behavioral forms.

Not only do you perceive expressive signals from a person, but you also perceive non-expressive signals from the environment which indicate where you are, who this is, how comfortable the weather is, and so forth. These signals indicate the context, such as the fact that people are in an office setting, or that it is final exam season. The observer may notice that the weather is oppressive and reason that it could impact moods. Or, the context might be recognized as a situation where a person is expecting some exciting news. With contextual information, the observer proceeds not only to analyze low-level signals and patterns from the environment and from the person who is expressing an emotion, but also to reason in a high-level way regarding what behavior is typical of this situation, and what higher-level goals are at work.

The process of trying to recognize an emotion is usually thought to involve a transformation from signal to symbol, from low-level physical phenomena to high-level abstract concepts. However, because reasoning about the situation can modify the kinds of observations that are made, information can be considered to flow not just from the low-level inputs to the high-level concepts, but also from the high level to the low level. Suppose that in reasoning about a situation you expect that somebody will be in a bad mood; in that case, your high-level expectation can cause your low-level perception to be biased in a negative way, so that you are more likely to perceive a weak or ambiguous expression as being negative. The recognition of emotions is therefore not merely "bottom-up," from signals to symbols, but also "top-down," in that higher level symbols can influence the way that signals are processed.

High-level reasoning and low-level signals also cooperate in the generation of emotional expression. Suppose that an actor wishes to portray a character who feels hatred. He might begin by thinking, "I want to show hatred" and then proceed to synthesize low-level signals that communicate hatred, changing his posture, behavior, voice, and face, to reflect this emotional state. The whole process has started as a symbol—a cognitive goal to show hatred—and has ended with the generation of expressive signals, so that the audience can recognize his character's hatred. The process of trying to express an emotion is usually considered to involve a transformation from symbol to signal, from high-level concepts to low-level modulation of expressions and behaviors.

However, I have left one important piece out of both of the above descriptions: the emotional state of the system which is either recognizing or expressing the emotion. In humans, this distinction is blurred because all humans have emotional states that automatically influence recognition and expression. But in computers, this distinction needs to be made explicit because a computer can be built with only a subset of these abilities. To recognize an emotion involves perception. But, as I described earlier, we know that human perception is biased by human emotion: an observer's own emotions influence both his low-level perceptual processes and his high-level cognitive processes. An observer will tend to perceive an ambiguous stimulus as being positive or negative, whichever is congruent with his mood. The emotional state of a human also influences her emotional expression. If the actress thinks, "Show hatred," then she may also begin to feel hatred. As I described earlier, it can also be the case that simply posturing her muscles to accurately communicate expressions of hatred can provide bodily feedback to cause her to actually feel the emotion she is expressing. In these cases, the emotional state, if there is one, interacts with both the recognition and expression of an emotion, with both cognitive and physical processes, and with both high-level reasoning and low-level signal processing. More commonly, a person will find that an emotional state simply arises in response to perceiving or reasoning about some events, and expression of that state occurs mostly involuntarily. Figure 5.1 summarizes these interactions.

When a computer tries to represent emotions and their expression, it may use convenient levels of abstraction—from a low-level representation of a signal such as a waveform of heart rate or a motion sequence of muscular movements, to a high-level interpretation such as the sentence "He looks

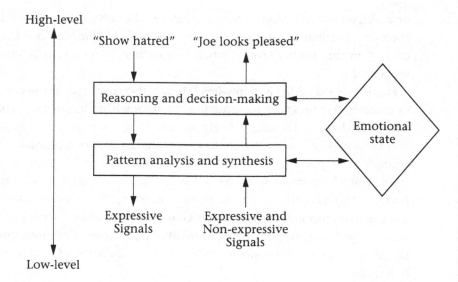

High-level

"Show hatred"   "Joe looks pleased"

Reasoning and decision-making

Pattern analysis and synthesis

Emotional state

Expressive Signals

Expressive and Non-expressive Signals

Low-level

Figure 5.1
Information flows from both high to low and from low to high in a system that can express, recognize, and "have" emotions.

sad." At no point in this process does the computer have to use the same mechanisms used by humans; it might go about recognition, expression, and synthesis of emotions in an entirely different way. However, to the extent that we can understand the way humans do these things, we will have a better idea how to give these abilities to computers. Furthermore, to the extent that we imitate human mechanisms in computers, we have a better chance of debugging the computers when they behave in a peculiar way, and we stand to benefit because the ways in which they behave are likely to be close to ways that humans behave, making it easier for us to interact with them.

A Signal Representation for Emotions and Moods

Now let us consider the use of low-level signal representations for describing some of the pieces of an affective system, starting with an example:

Bruno was known to be short-tempered, but also a very caring person, with a wife and two children whom he deeply loved and desired to support. His ability to provide for his family meant a lot to him, and he tried to work hard to meet their needs. Yesterday his boss got upset over a trifle and fired Bruno from his job. Bruno felt this was unfair and responded with red-hot rage—he punched his fist through the wall, yelled at his boss, and stormed out of the office, ranting about his boss' decision. He drove aggressively across town to the local bar, his anger escalating as he thought about how upset his wife would be and how this would hurt his family. Bruno was furious.

Theorists tell us that emotions usually last for less than a minute or two, while moods can last much longer. However, a typical person might say: "It was days before he stopped being angry," as if emotions could last much longer. How do we account for these differences, and in a way that a computer can represent? How can we represent emotions, moods, influences of temperament, and other affective phenomena in a computer? In the future, physical changes indicative of emotions and moods—levels of hormones, neurotransmitters, and nervous system activity—may be measured and made into a quantitative, physically-based model. However, there is currently no reliable measure of when an emotion begins or ends, or of how intense it is. Nonetheless, let me propose a way in which we can computationally model emotions and moods, accounting for properties of their behavior, at least in a qualitative sense.

Ringing a Bell

To help picture emotions, moods, temperament, and some of their underlying properties, consider a completely different situation, one devoid of emotions but having similar behavior: the striking of a bell. When a bell is struck once, it emits a sound that is loud at first, and then decays in intensity. The intensity of the sound can be modeled by the signal shown in Fig. 5.2. It builds up quickly to a peak, becoming very loud, then gradually fades until it is too faint to be heard.[1]

An interesting thing happens if the bell is struck with exactly the same force, repeatedly, so that each strike occurs before the sound of the previous strike has subsided. In this case, the bell does not ring with the same loudness each time, but sounds louder and louder. The reason for the increase can be seen by adding the sound intensity signals over time to obtain a cumulative sound signal as in Fig. 5.2. The sum grows, despite the fact that the individual strikes are the same. Let us now look at this and several other properties of emotion.

Property of Response Decay

Several analogies can be made between the bell ringing and Bruno's situation. In one sense the stimulus of being fired was like the stimulus of striking the bell; both initiated a response—a sound from the bell, and fury from Bruno, and both responses had a fast rise time followed by a more gradual decay. If there had been no other strikes of the bell then its sound would have subsided; similarly, if Bruno had not ruminated about what the loss of his job meant, what his wife would think, what it would do to his family, and so forth, and if his body had not tensed up with the feelings of anger, then his anger might have subsided quickly. Emotions, like sounds, decay naturally over time unless they are re-stimulated.

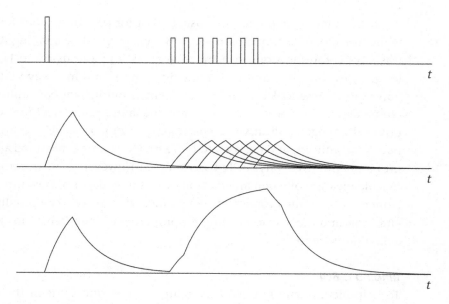

Figure 5.2
Top: The pattern and intensity of strikes applied to a bell. These represent the input signals. Middle: The bell's response to each strike. Bottom: Sum of responses, representing the net intensity of the sound the bell produces. These are the system's output signals. Notice that rapidly repeated small strikes produce a higher overall sound than does one large strike.

Although it seems natural to speak of the intensity of an emotion increasing and decaying, it is not clear which signals could be measured to give rise to a physical measure of emotion intensity, unlike the bell, where sound intensity can be measured from the acoustic waveform. Although I will give an example below to illustrate the use of signals for representing emotion intensity, it must be kept in mind that this is presently an abstract representation, not a representation of a known measurable quantity. Researchers are working on ways to measure changes associated with each emotion, including measurements of autonomic nervous system activity, and relative neurotransmitter and hormonal concentrations, and eventually we can expect quantitative measures that may fit signal representations like I propose. However, for now, the representations I describe of emotional intensity are more qualitative, intended to capture the intensity that a person might assign to their felt emotion.

Property of Repeated Strikes

For Bruno, each new thought was as another strike of the bell. Each strike gave rise to an emotion of anger; the repeated strikes had the effect of escalating the overall intensity of his anger. It did not matter if the intensity of Bruno's thoughts was the same over time; as long as the thoughts kept coming, Bruno's anger could escalate higher than it was at the initial emotion-producing event, much like a bell rings louder with repeated strikes.

A similar analogy holds for stressful events in general: a single stressful event may be so small as not to call attention to itself. However, a lot of repeated "little" stress-producing events can lead to a greater level of stress than one major stress-producing event. Cumulative little hurts can cause greater pain than a single instantaneous painful event. This signal representation provides a convenient way to visualize how emotional intensity can accrue, even though emotions may be of short duration.

Property of Temperamental Influence

Emotional response is influenced by one's personality. Personality is believed to be largely a function of environmental influences; however, there is evidence that part of personality, one's temperament, may be largely set before birth. Fifteen percent of infants have significantly more active nervous systems than most babies, and are more easily excited or stressed (Kagan, 1994). Throughout their early lives, these highly reactive babies tend to grow into inhibited, more easily fearful children. Although children can grow out of these early extreme temperamental differences, highly reactive babies tend to become at least mildly inhibited adolescents and adults, and tend not to develop extroverted personalities.

Although it is not entirely clear how temperament exerts its influences, it is apparently an attribute of our nervous system. There is a case of conjoined twins that supports this hypothesis. These two girls share one body from the chest down, giving the appearance of one person with two heads. They are completely connected biochemically: when one takes medicine, it helps the other. It might therefore seem surprising that their friends and family describe the girls as having two different temperaments and two different personalities. However, the twins have two hearts, two stomachs, and, interestingly, two communicating but distinct nervous systems, which can account for two temperaments in the same body (Wewerka, Miller, and Doman, 1996) .

In the bell example, temperament is analogous to the physical characteristics of the bell. Two bells of different shapes and material properties will not emit sounds of the same form, even when struck with the exact same stimulus. One bell may have to be struck much harder than the other before it will emit any sound. It may not ring properly if the strikes are in too quick succession. The innate physical properties of the bell are analogous to the innate neurochemical mechanisms of temperament; both influence the response to a stimulus. The shape of the response curve is determined by the bell's physical characteristics. Similarly, the shape and timing of the human emotional response curves are influenced by temperament. For example, the response of the bell system to an instantaneous strike is described mathematically as:

$$y = a e^{-bt}$$

where y is the output sound intensity at time t, and the parameters a and b control the height of the response, and how fast it decays, respectively. The analogy for an emotion is that there is a rapid rise in emotional intensity upon a triggering event, followed by a natural decay in intensity of the emotion.

Figure 5.3 shows galvanic skin conductivity responses from two different people who were startled by acoustic tones. Both show peaks when they are startled, corresponding to greater arousal. Each peak also shows a natural decay, which can be modeled with a function such as the decaying exponential used above. The skin conductivity of the person who rated high in extroversion is lower on average than that of the person who rated low in extroversion. Studies have shown that extroverts are chronically less aroused than introverts (Kahneman, 1973).

Property of Linearity and Time-Invariance

There is signal processing theory that simplifies the analysis of emotion producing systems when they obey certain properties, especially the properties of *linearity* and *time invariance*. A *linear system* has an input and an output, and if you double the amplitude of the input, then the amplitude of the output doubles.[2] If you put nothing in, you get nothing out. If the response of the system to input A is B, and the response to input C is D, then if you make a new input by summing two others, $A + C$, then the new output will be the sum of the previous outputs, $B + D$. A system, linear or nonlinear, can be *time invariant*. Suppose you put A into the system at time t_i, and the system outputs B at time t_j. Now you put A in at a later time, $t_i + 3$. If the system is time-invariant, then the output B will occur at time $t_j + 3$. In other words, the system's behavior is not influenced by time.

The bell can be modeled with a linear time-invariant system under certain conditions. The input to the system is the striking of the bell, usually modeled by a short pulse, with amplitude proportional to the intensity of the strike. The output signal is the loudness of the bell's sound. The stronger the input pulse, the stronger the output sound; however, this linear relationship does not hold for all strengths of input. If you hit the bell too softly, it will not ring; if you hit it too hard, crushing it, the resulting sound will not be a proper ring, nor will the bell ring again. In other words, its response is linear only over a certain range of inputs. Similar limitations apply to the property of time-invariance. In general, it does not matter what time you strike the bell,

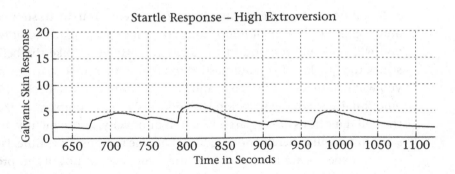

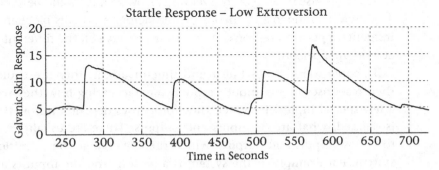

Figure 5.3
Startle tones of the same intensity were played one after another to two subjects, resulting in the galvanic skin conductivity responses shown here (in microSiemens.) Higher values tend to correspond to higher arousal in the person. Each tone resulted in a peak, but because they were all played within a few minutes of each other, habituation effects cause the responses to vary in amplitude. The signal on the top is a sample response for an extrovert; below it is a sample response for an introvert.

it will behave the same. However, if you strike it repeatedly, without giving it time to respond between strikes, or with such a rhythm as to interfere with its clapper moving and causing it to ring, then timing does matter. Most real-world systems are only linear and time-invariant under certain conditions.

When a system is linear and time-invariant, then it is much easier to understand how it will behave. All that is needed to completely characterize the behavior of the system is its response to a single special input, one that can be used to build all other possible inputs by scaling and summing them— that is, by linear combination. Once the response to this fundamental input is known, then the responses to all other possible inputs are known. We can completely characterize what the bell will do simply by ringing it once; this is true as long as we stay within the range in which the bell system is linear and time-invariant.

To some extent people are time-invariant systems. You can be startled today, and respond with a small jump. You can be startled similarly tomorrow and you will probably respond in the same way. However, like the bell that is struck too quickly, if you are startled too many times in a short period, then you will habituate to the signal, and your response to it will decline. With an emotional system, the situation is significantly more complicated than with the bell. Emotions are in part a function of novelty; consequently, the exact same input will generally not produce the same response over time. However, we can expect a similar input with the same level of novelty to produce a similar response in somebody over time. However, it should be kept in mind that there are hidden and uncontrollable factors, especially biochemical, that influence a person's response. It is hard to observe all the different variables at work in a person.

If people were always linear and time-invariant, then we could predict their responses to any input simply by characterizing how they respond to a few special inputs. However, these properties depend on how the system is defined, what are its inputs and outputs. There are usually many ways to choose inputs and outputs, which thereby change the definition of the system. For example, if the system is a person, and the input is a piece of music played for the person to hear, then the output might be the person's expression of happiness, given that she likes that piece of music. Suppose we choose the system input to be the intensity of the music waveform, and the system output to be the person's subjective rating of happiness. We can test if the system is linear by playing the same piece of music twice as loud, and seeing if the person's rating of happiness doubles. Alternatively, the input might be completely different: the number of pieces of music we play. If we play two pieces she likes, we ask if it doubles her subjective report of happiness. Of course there are also other possible outputs, such as the amount of curvature in her smile, or how much her heart rate and skin conductivity change.

Property of Activation and Saturation
We can already see problems with these linear systems in practice—two pieces may make someone twice as happy as one piece, and three may make them happier still, but eventually the effect saturates. The same property holds for the physiological components of emotion. Something that causes your heart rate to accelerate cannot do so indefinitely; the heart can only beat so fast. The same is true for neurotransmitter and hormone levels, and for all other bodily changes. Feelings can only reach certain heights, or depths. Consequently, linear systems only approximate human behavior under certain restrictions. In reality, human behavior is nonlinear. An important open research problem

involves characterizing how a person responds to different events under different conditions—analogous to characterizing the shape of different bells' responses to different situations. Responses might be both person-dependent and emotion-dependent. For example, an emotion like anger might have a more rapid response time than an emotion like grief, especially in a person prone to anger.

Temperament, mood, and cognitive expectation can influence emotion activation. For example, most people can tolerate some level of anger-producing stimuli before they actually feel angry; however, if they are in a bad mood, their tolerance may be lowered. Alternatively, someone with a cheerful disposition may have a higher innate tolerance. Also, certain personalities are more reactive or arousable than others, influencing emotional responsiveness, as seen above in Fig. 5.3. Cognitive expectation is also important. Suppose that you are watching a tennis tournament and your favorite player is expected to win easily. If she wins, then you are apt to feel happy, but probably not as happy as in the case where she is expected to be crushed by her opponent, and surprises everyone by emerging the victor.

How can all the influences I described be accounted for in a signal representation? Most of them are caused by a mixture of interacting physical and cognitive systems, with a potentially very complex set of interactions. A true physically based model is likely to be a tangle of parameters with nonlinear relationships, which may make it intractable for any practical uses. For example, there is no single input in the human system, unlike in the bell system. Instead, the input is a complex function of cognitive and physical events. Nonetheless, let me propose that these influences can be represented by the use of a simple nonlinear function applied to the inputs of an emotional system. This will result in the influences we have seen of differing activation and saturation levels, as well as providing an intermediate range of behavior that is approximately linear.

The proposed function is a "sigmoidal nonlinearity" described by the equation:

$$y = \frac{g}{1 + e^{-(x-x_0)/s}} + y_0.$$

This function is special in that it describes a large variety of natural phenomena. In this equation, x is the input, which may represent many possible stimuli, originating both inside and outside the person. The output is y, the height of the curve. In the bell analogy, the value of x is the strength of the actual strike, and the value of y is the effective value of the strike that is input into the linear system modeling the bell. All tiny values of x have the same effect: they make no sound. All very large values have the same effect: they

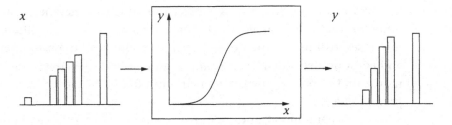

Figure 5.4
A sigmoid is applied to each input, x to convert it to a new value, y. If x is very small, y is zero. As x increases without bound, y clips to a maximum value. The middle of the transition region is approximately linear; values of x in this region pass through the sigmoid relatively unchanged.

make the maximum sound. In between lies the more interesting behavior. For inputs near the center of the curve, the response is approximately linear. Figure 5.4 shows the sigmoid applied to six inputs of different intensity. Only the medium values pass through relatively unchanged; the smallest value is ignored, and the biggest values are saturated.

In the equation above, the parameter s controls the steepness of the slope, representing how fast the output y changes with the input x. Smaller values of s make the sigmoid steeper, and more responsive. The steepness can be set according to personality. The behavior of a person who moves quickly from mild anger to losing their temper would be modeled with a steep sigmoid, compared to someone who endured a much greater range of intense events before losing their temper. The parameter x_0 shifts the sigmoid left or right. When it is far to the right, then a stronger input is required to activate an output. The sigmoid might be shifted left or right according to a person's mood. A good mood can allow smaller inputs to activate positive emotions, accomplished by shifting the sigmoid to the left, as in Fig. 5.5. The parameter g controls the gain applied by the sigmoid. It is the same for all three examples in Fig. 5.5, but can be increased or decreased to control the overall amplitude of the sigmoid. This value might be coupled to the arousal level of a person; someone highly aroused might be capable of experiencing a greater intensity of emotion. Finally, the parameter y_0, shifts the entire curve up or down. This parameter might be controlled by cognitive expectation. For example, the expectation of a win in the tennis example above could dampen the joy of victory and accentuate the pain of defeat simply by lowering the sigmoids applied to positive and negative inputs. If the player wins as expected, the positive sigmoid tones down the positive input; if the player loses, unexpectedly, the negative sigmoid amplifies the negative input. The parameters of the sigmoid provide a rich set of controls for adjusting inputs before they proceed to activate emotions.

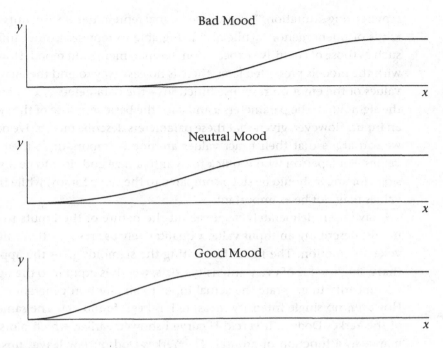

Figure 5.5
The parameters of a sigmoid are influenced by personality, as well as by cognitive and physical events. Here the sigmoids are shown shifted as an influence of mood.

The sigmoidal nonlinearity can also account for abrupt changes in an emotional response. As the parameter s approaches zero, the transition region of the curve becomes vertical, indicating that a tiny change in a certain range of input values can lead to a significant change in the output. The behavior is analogous to a physical phase transition—such as when water becomes ice. We might say that a person suddenly "snapped" or suddenly "went over the edge." We might expect this transition to be steeper for negative than for positive emotions, since one often finds that people hold back on negative emotions and then experience a catastrophic release, marked by a sudden burst of tears, or burst of anger, "This is the LAST straw!" as they reach their breaking point. In contrast, positive emotions can transition relatively smoothly. Finally, just like water undergoes two phase transitions: ice to water, and water to steam, an emotional response curve might have multiple transition regions, not just one as shown in these sigmoids. Someone may go through multiple stages of anger, each with its own identifiable region of behavior and discontinuity of transition. A signal representation is easily adapted to accommodate these cases.

Many models of emotion synthesis, which will be described in Chapter 7 employ activation thresholds for each emotion, but overlook the need for representing saturation. The proposed signal representation accounts for both kinds of phenomenon, while also being able to represent other influences, such as those of cognitive expectation, temperament, and mood. However, as with the models presented later, there is no easy way to find the quantitative values of the emotion response functions—the parameters g, x_0, s and y_0 for the sigmoid, or the parameters a and b for the basic response of the system to an input. However, given that these parameters describe qualitative behavior, we can argue that their exact values are not as important as their relative values. For a person who is quick to fly into a rage and slow to be joyful, the slope for anger should be steep compared to the slope for joy, while the exact values may not be as important.

I have been deliberately vague about the nature of the inputs to the sigmoids, describing an input value x qualitatively as an event that might provoke an emotion. The figure illustrating the sigmoids gives the appearance that a single value of event intensity exists, which is input into the sigmoidal nonlinearity to generate the actual input to an emotion generation system. However, no single intensity measure has been found yet. The same is true of the Yerkes-Dodson inverted-U curve I showed earlier, which plots performance as a function of arousal. The Yerkes-Dodson law leaves unspecified how one would measure arousal and performance. It is understood that each axis represents a complex function of many variables. For example, there are multiple systems that contribute to arousal in the brain, each of which has a specific chemical identity. One group makes serotonin, another noradrenaline, another acetylcholine, and another dopamine (LeDoux, 1996). Arousal can also be observed in physiological changes such as pupilary dilation and galvanic skin conductivity. Furthermore, not all of these changes will happen in the same way with every arousing stimulus. To date, there is no single measurement that corresponds to arousal. Nevertheless, describing a complex concept with a single value provides a useful shorthand for many applications.

Property of Cognitive and Physical Feedback

A human emotional system can receive a so-called strike not only from an external event, but also from an internal event generated by a previous strike. In other words, the human system contains a feedback loop. If you sense the ceiling falling around you, your initial reaction may be to jump up and run out of the room. Often, such a response is immediately followed by cognitive feedback, such as "Oh, that's not the ceiling, it's a poster that came untacked." The cognitive feedback in this case tempers your bodily response. Your heart slows back to its normal pace and you can once again concentrate on what you were thinking previously. Alternatively the feedback could have reinforced the response—for example, "Oh no, it's not just the ceiling, there go the bookshelves too!"—and caused your arousal level to climb even higher.

There are paths in the brain, especially between limbic system structures and the cortex, which are capable of carrying feedback. There is also physical feedback from the body, for example if you feel sad and you let your shoulders droop and your head hang, then this tends to reinforce the sad feeling. Alternatively you might *think* you should appear happy, adjust your posture and facial expression accordingly and seek out jovial events, which consequently mitigate your sad state. We have seen that your mood also influences which thoughts are retrieved—bad moods bias retrieval toward negative thoughts. Feedback can be physical or cognitive, and it can decrease or increase the intensity of an affective state.

Imagine if the bell was struck each time not only by somebody hitting it, but also by a force double the maximum intensity of its previous sound. As the sound increases, so does the force with which the bell is struck. If the bell could sound arbitrarily loud, then what we would have is a feedback system with an output that grows without bound.[3] Without some attenuating force to interrupt this feedback loop, the bell would quickly sound its death knell. In the human emotional system there is feedback. However, something keeps the emotional responses from growing arbitrarily large. The proposed sigmoid nonlinearity can be used to limit the results of feedback by bounding the output values of the system. Bounding these variables can keep the output from growing too large.

Representing Mood

Mood operates over relatively long time scales compared to emotions. Mood can be thought of as a background process that is always there, while emotions tend to come and go. Moods can predispose or bias a person toward certain emotions. A bad mood can make it easier for a negative-valenced emotion to be activated, while a good mood makes this more difficult. Although we usually think of moods as good, bad, or neutral, they also come with other distinctions. A bad mood due to anger has a high level of arousal; a bad mood due to immense sadness is marked by a depressed state, of low arousal. A peaceful good mood is low in arousal, contrasted with the good mood that accompanies an exciting new romance. The dimensions of valence and arousal provide a useful description of most moods.

Mood can exert its influence by adjusting the sigmoidal nonlinearites applied to inputs. A highly aroused bad mood can shift the sigmoid for negatively valenced events so that even a slightly negative event can pass into the system and activate responses. The high level of arousal can increase the gain on the sigmoid. A good mood can shift the same sigmoid in the other direction, so that trivial negative events are ignored by the emotion-producing system. In this way mood can influence the generation of emotions.

But what generates moods? Unfortunately, scientists do not have an answer yet. However, we can build a flexible representation that can accommodate several possible generators of mood. For example, we might let any event influence mood, even if its valence is so insignificant that it lies below the activation region. For example, body chemistry—especially dietary influences, medication, and changes in hormones—can affect mood without necessarily eliciting an emotion. Subtle changes can be accumulated over a window of time, so that even if the system receives lots of inputs, each of which is too small to activate an emotion, they will nonetheless influence the mood. The mood can be constructed in this way: summing a function of recent positively valenced inputs and subtracting a function of recent negatively valenced inputs. Like emotions, moods cannot be of unbounded intensity. Physiological limits are imposed at some point. These limits can also be built into the computer model, either as hard limits, or as a saturating function on the outputs, as proposed above for emotions.

Example: Rafe

Let's illustrate how the above representations come together in a real situation with both physical and cognitive inputs: the scenario where Rafe gets hit by the out-of-control woman in a wheelchair (from Chapter 1). Rafe's emotional system has inputs that can be external or internal events. Some inputs are:

1. The oppressive heat and humidity (all time)
2. Watching the top pros play ($t = 1, 2, 3$)
3. Victory of favorite player ($t = 3$)
4. Pain of wheelchair slamming into Rafe ($t = 7$)
5. Bodily feedback ($t = 8$)
6. Recognizing Rebecca's accident and embarrassment. ($t = 9$)
7. Opportunity to help Rebecca ($t > 9$)

We are told that Rafe has a happy disposition. This is encoded with the sigmoid shown at the top right of Fig. 5.6, which lets almost all positive inputs pass through to influence emotions. The positive inputs described above are all of sufficient intensity to pass through Rafe's positive-input sigmoid. Consequently, each gives rise to positive emotions. I represent this in Fig. 5.6 as a sequence of small positive pulses giving rise to a sequence of small bell-

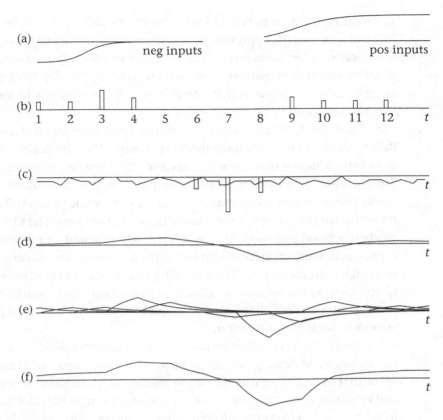

Figure 5.6
Signal representations for Rafe scenario. (a) Sigmoid for negative events (left) is less easily activated than the sigmoid for positive events (right). (b) Positive inputs in time. (c) Negative inputs in time. (d) Mood is a slow-varying function of all inputs. (e) Emotional responses arise only from the inputs that are of large enough intensity to pass through the sigmoids. (f) Accumulated positive and negative emotional responses.

like emotional responses. The victory of his favorite player is represented as a large positive input pulse, giving rise to a larger bell-like emotional response. After the accident, when he realizes Rebecca's situation and perceives the opportunity to help her, these appraisals elicit additional positive emotions.

In contrast, Rafe's sigmoid at the top left, for negative inputs, ignores small negative inputs, while quickly saturating strong negative inputs. The heat and humidity are always present, but their amplitude is so low that the sigmoid for negative inputs zeros their influence. I show this as a small negative noisy signal that contributes to the overall mood, but that is not significant enough to activate emotions. As these small negative inputs influence Rafe's mood, it gradually shifts his negative sigmoid toward the right, allowing less significant negative inputs to influence his emotions. By the time he stands in line and appraises the oppressive heat and humidity, a small negative emotion is generated. A few moments later when the wheelchair slams into him, a big negative emotion is generated. An instant later, bodily feedback produces another negative input which passes through the sigmoid to generate a negative emotion.

As mentioned, all the inputs, no matter what their intensity, influence Rafe's mood. His mood is modeled by summing all of the positive and negative inputs, before they enter the sigmoids, and filtering the sum. Filtering forms a linear combination of previous inputs over time, weighted by how recently they occurred, to generate an instantaneous value of mood. The mood therefore tends to change more slowly than the emotions. The filter used to create the mood shown in Fig. 5.6 combined the present and previous three inputs, giving the greatest weight to the present input, and linearly decreasing weights to older inputs. The weighting and summation used here may not be the same as the physical mechanisms in the body that contribute to our feelings; nonetheless, they capture the qualitative changes that are plausibly associated with a real situation.

My illustrations of the Rafe situation only distinguish valence and intensity. For mood, these descriptions are sufficient for most purposes. However, we know that there is more differentiation among emotions than simply valence and intensity. A negative input that contributes to anger may not contribute to sadness, and vice-versa. Although the examples I gave only showed the use of signal representations for valence and intensity, the representations can also model other distinctions. For example, basic emotions such as anger, fear, joy, and sadness could have their own sigmoids to specify their activation and saturation characteristics. The different emotions could have inhibitory and excitatory influences on each other, either directly or via some intermediate mechanism. Velásquez's connectionist model, "Cathexis," is one way to implement such direct influences (Velásquez, 1997). Alternatively, the influence that mood already exerts can be used to regulate interactions between emotions. If an input is negative enough to generate anger, then it also will contribute to a bad mood. The bad mood automatically shifts all the sigmoids for the other emotions to the right, making the negative emotions easier to activate and the positive ones more difficult to activate.

In some cases it might be important to distinguish inputs not just as negative or positive, but also as physical and cognitive, especially since it is possible for one to feel physically bad (e.g., weak and exhausted) but mentally good (e.g., happy something is completed), or vice versa. However, the majority of the time people do not make such distinctions. It is common to hear someone say "I am feeling pretty good" or "I am not feeling so good," lumping mental and physical components together. Using a signal representation does not require all these details to be specified, but permits a wide range of possibilities to be represented. The specific use of signals I have proposed here is intended to illustrate their ability to account for properties of emotions that we do know something about. The flexibility of the representation is an important advantage since many details of the human emotional system remain to be determined.

Use of a computational signal representation for moods and emotions raises specific questions for theorists. For example, can the effects of temperament and personality be adequately represented in terms of an emotional response function, activation function, and saturation function? What other assessments of inputs, besides positive and negative, are needed to account for the diversity of moods and emotions that can be elicited? The proposed representation includes a small number of parameters which capture particular degrees of freedom—such as the activation region of the sigmoid, or the decay rate of the emotional response; do these parameters control useful behaviors? The representation currently accounts for many properties, summarized below. There may be other properties, as yet undiscovered, to which it may or may not be adaptable. For example, theorists have not articulated what the role of noisy thoughts or other distractions are in terms of influencing the intensity of emotions; however, the signal representation easily accommodates the addition of a noisy signal, if this addition becomes important.

In summary, the proposed use of signals for describing the low-level behavior of emotions provides a flexible representation for moods and emotions which handles physical and cognitive inputs while including influences of temperament and personality. It therefore provides not only a tool for theorists who are trying to model some low-level behavior of emotions, but also a representation that a computer can use in modeling internal emotional signals, especially as part of a subsystem for generating and regulating emotions.

Summary of Properties

The proposed signal representation accounts for the following properties of behavior in an emotion system:

- *Response decay.*   An emotional response is of relatively short duration, and will fall below a level of perceptibility unless it is re-activated.

- *Repeated strikes.*   Rapid repeated activation of an emotion causes its perceived intensity to increase.

- *Temperament and personality influences.*   A person's temperament and personality influence emotion activation and response.

- *Nonlinearity.*   The human emotional system is nonlinear, but may be approximated as a linear system for a certain range of inputs and outputs.

- *Time-invariance.*   The human emotional system can be modeled as independent of time for certain durations. For short durations, habituation effects occur. For longer durations, factors such as a person's physiological circadian rhythms and hormonal cycles need to be considered.

- *Activation.*   Not all inputs can activate an emotion; they have to be of sufficient intensity. This intensity is not a fixed value, but depends on factors such as mood, temperament, and cognitive expectation.

- *Saturation.*   No matter how frequently an emotion is activated, at some point the system will saturate and the response of the person will no longer increase. Similarly, the response cannot be reduced below a "zero" level.

- *Cognitive and physical feedback.*   Inputs to the system can be initiated by internal cognitive or physical processes. For example, physiological expression of an emotion can provide feedback which acts as another input to the system, generating another emotional response.

- *Background mood.*   All inputs contribute to a background mood, whether or not they are below the activation level for emotions. The most recent inputs have the greatest influence on the present mood.

Many of the properties listed here can also be accounted for by other models, which I will say more about in Chapter 7. In particular, the Cathexis model comes the closest to fulfilling the properties I articulated here. Let me caution that there can be different models or representations that satisfy a set of properties. I am deliberately not trying to establish one model or one theory of emotion in this book; I do not think there is *one* best model for all applications, nor is there sufficient understanding of human emotions to justify a comprehensive model at the level needed for computer implementation. Depending on the level of detail demanded by an application, different models will be preferable. The low-level signals I have illustrated here are good at handling emotion intensities, and may be useful both for theorists modeling emotion generation, as well as for computers that generate and regulate internal emotion signals. However, this low-level signal representation is not well-suited to address the high-level cognitive reasoning that may be involved in triggering emotions. My belief is that the latter will be better fulfilled by the use of higher-level representations which I will describe in Chapter 7, and in some cases, by some of the pattern models which I will describe in the next chapter. Throughout the remaining chapters I will illustrate different levels of representation that can be used advantageously within the framework of affective computing.

Physiological Signals

The signals I have shown so far do not represent the measurement of known physical quantities. However, there are many signals relevant to emotional responses that are physically measurable, especially by cameras, microphones, and sensors, the latter of which might be placed in physical contact with a person in a comfortable and non-invasive way. Signals gathered from four such sensors will be illustrated below, while others such as facial and vocal signals will be shown in the next chapter. Patterns of low-level signals can be combined with high-level information to recognize an affective expression, as well as to characterize an affective state.

Because people are already in physical contact with computers, augmenting their contact with sensors provides a new form of communication without much effort on the user's part. In particular, it is easy for a computer to gather signals such as the four shown in Fig. 5.7: electromyogram (EMG), blood volume pressure (BVP), galvanic skin response (GSR), and respiration, which I will say more about in a moment. The short segments shown in this figure illustrate very different responses obtained while an actress expressed two different negative emotions. Although clear differences can be seen in the signals for the two different emotions, we obtained data from the actress over 20 days, and sometimes found that the variations in the signals for the same emotion over different days were greater than the variations between the different emotions on the same day. In other words, the examples shown in Fig. 5.7 are some of the cleanest, the most illustrative of the differences; in practice, it is very hard to build a system to recognize just the differences between the emotions. I will say more about this later in the next chapter, and illustrate some recognition results on these signals.

The electromyogram (EMG) signal uses small electrodes to measure a tiny voltage from a muscle, indicating when it is contracted. The EMG shown in Fig. 5.7 measures the voltage emitted by the masseter muscle outside the jaw, which increases when the teeth are clenched in anger, as well as when there are certain other facial movements such as laughter. The EMG sensor could also have been placed elsewhere, such as on the trapezius muscle between the neck and shoulder, to sense tension in that muscle without the sensor being as visible as it is when placed on the jaw. The sharp peaks in the EMG signal in Fig. 5.7 were probably caused by the actress clenching her jaw during her expressions of anger.

The blood volume pressure (BVP) signal is an indicator of blood flow, gathered using a technique known as photoplethysmography, which shines infrared light onto the skin and measures how much of it is reflected. The BVP shown in Fig. 5.7 was taken from a small sensor worn on the fingertip. The

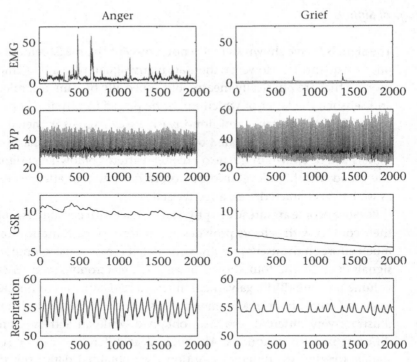

Figure 5.7
Examples of physiological signals measured from an actress while she consciously expressed anger (left) and grief (right). From top to bottom: electromyogram (microvolts), blood volume pulse (percent reflectance), galvanic skin conductivity (microSiemens), and respiration (percent maximum expansion). All of these signals can be gathered from sensors on the surface of the skin, without any pain or discomfort to the person. These signals were sampled at 20 samples a second, using a ProComp system from Thought Technology Ltd. Each box shows 100 seconds of response.

BVP waveform exhibits the characteristic periodicity of the heart beating, since each beat forces blood through the vessels. The overall envelope of the signal tends to pinch when a person is startled, fearful, or anxious. An increase in the BVP amplitude is caused when there is greater blood flow to the extremities, such as when a person relaxes.

The galvanic skin response (GSR) signal is an indicator of skin conductivity, and is measured via two small silver-chloride electrodes. An imperceptibly small voltage is applied and then conductance is measured between the two electrodes. The signal in Fig. 5.7 was gathered by placing these electrodes on two fingers of the actress's hand. Reliable signals can also be obtained from electrodes placed on the feet, if it is desired to keep the hands free from sensors. GSR tends to increase when a person is startled or experiences anxiety, and is generally considered a good measure of a person's overall level of arousal.

The respiration signal is sensed using a long thin velcro belt worn around the chest cavity, which contains a small elastic that stretches as the subject's chest cavity expands. The amount of stretch in the elastic is measured as a voltage change and recorded as a percent of its maximum change. The respiration sensor can either be placed over the sternum for thoracic monitoring or over the diaphragm for diaphragmatic monitoring. In Fig. 5.7 the signal was gathered using diaphragmatic monitoring. From the waveform, the depth of the wearer's breathing and the rate of respiration can be obtained.

To be handled by the computer, all human signals need to first be converted from their continuous form to a digital form. If these signals are facial or gestural motions, then they are usually gathered by a video camera and digitized at 30 frames a second. A speech waveform is gathered by a microphone and typically sampled at 16 KHz, with 16 bits per sample. Physiological signals such as those described above contain much lower frequencies than voice, and can be sampled reliably at only 20 Hz, usually with 32 bits per sample. Muscle potential changes can be sampled at 20 Hz to get large changes due to stress, but should be sampled at 1 KHz if it is desired to capture fine changes associated with fatigue, such as lactic acid buildup. After the sampling process, the computer has a representation of the signal as a sequence of binary numbers, which can then be analyzed to try to determine characteristics of the signal that correlate with expression of a particular emotion.

One of the applications I described earlier involves the use of physiological signals to gather responses such as frustration or distress from consumers trying out products. This application was inspired while a student was playing the video game DOOM, and we noticed that he exhibited more pronounced responses when there was a problem working the game controls than during any other event in the game. A short segment of three of his physiological signals can be seen in Fig. 5.8, which shows his GSR, BVP, and EMG over 5 minutes of time. His stress is initially signaled by the jaw-clenching peak in the EMG, which remains high during the minute and a half where the software controlled navigation keys failed to work as he expected. The point labeled "give up" is where he stopped the game and started over. After the game gets going, we see a constriction in his BVP, indicative of lowered blood flow to his extremities, and an increase in the GSR, indicating a state of higher arousal.

Summary

This chapter has overviewed issues of representation in affective systems, specifically the need for a mixture of representations, spanning low to high levels of processing. In particular, I emphasized that systems which can recognize, express, and "have" emotions will employ processing that involves

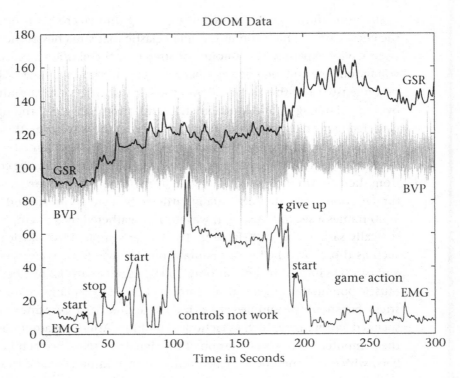

Figure 5.8
Three physiological signals measured from a student playing the game DOOM on the computer. The most significant response is shown in the center, where EMG peaked during loss of use of the controls.

both high-to-low and low-to-high transformations, from symbol to signal and from signal to symbol.

I have proposed the use of a low-level signal representation, in an abstract sense for representing intensities of emotions and moods, and in a physical sense, for representing waveforms measured of physiological changes characteristic of emotional states. The representation presented here is flexible, and accounts for many of the properties of emotions outlined in earlier chapters. I described certain questions it raises for theorists, as well as how it is suited for some applications and not for others. The next chapters will highlight higher-level means of representing affective information, especially for use in recognition and expression of affect, and for giving computers the ability to reason about emotion generation.

6 *Recognizing and Expressing Affect*

Emotions are like thoughts in that they rely upon words, gesture, music, behavior, and other creative forms of expression for their communciation. Affective communication occurs in the physical world through the senses, whether the message is conveyed through a sound pressure waveform, a visible motion, or via mediating instruments such as physiological sensors.[1] Emotions can be expressed voluntarily or involuntarily, in ways that are easy to control, or in ways of which a person may not be aware. Expressions may be publicly visible, for example a smile, or accessible only to someone in close physical contact, who feels your clammy hand. Emotions may also be communicated by behavior, as through loving actions. In each case, patterns of information are communicated, and these patterns can be represented in a computer.

This chapter casts affect recognition as a pattern recognition problem, and affect expression as pattern synthesis. Taking this approach, a variety of techniques become available for computer communication of emotion. The methodology and most of the tools used in this chapter can be found in textbooks on pattern recognition and modeling.[2] However, very little work has been done to apply these tools to affective patterns. In particular, little is known about which kinds of patterns tend to be the best indicators of a person's emotions, and how these patterns might be learned, recognized, and understood. The goal of this chapter is to lay a foundation for modeling affective patterns so that computers can be given the basic abilities of affect recognition and expression. This is a first step toward enabling them to interact more naturally with people, recognizing our emotions, and expressing emotions when appropriate.

Key Issues for Characterizing Affective Patterns

One of the biggest questions in affect recognition is, "What are the couplings between affective states and their patterns of expression?" Numerous experimenters have proposed relationships, some of which hold across groups of individuals and some of which do not. There have also been debates over the years about whether or not characteristic bodily patterns accompany emotions. In particular, the work of Schachter and Singer in the early 60's argued that autonomic patterning only varies in intensity for different emotions, and that differentiation of emotion is not physical, but cognitive (Schachter, 1964). However, over the years, as technology and signal analysis have progressed, physiological patterns characteristic of emotions have been discovered. Cacioppo and Tassinary (1990) describe many cases where the specifics of data collection and analysis have made a big difference in the reliability of finding physiological patterns that differentiate emotions. This is not to say that the problem is easy to solve; it is not. Some signals are better at communicating emotions than others, and which is best can depend on the emotion, the person expressing it, and the conditions under which the emotion is elicited. One thing that is widely agreed upon is that no single signal is a trusted indicator of emotional response. Instead, patterns of signals are needed.

It is important to mention what kind of success we can expect. For example, it is not appropriate to expect computers to perfectly recognize all of your feelings. Most people have difficulty recognizing their own feelings and articulating them. Furthermore, the computer is an outside observer with limited access to your body and mind; it will not have the same information as you. It sees from the third-person viewpoint while you see from the first-person. It does not know everything you know about yourself. Its ability to recognize your emotions should at best be compared to the ability of another person to recognize your emotions. A reasonable criterion of success is to get a computer to recognize affect as well as another person, i.e., better than chance, but below 100% accuracy.

In some cases we can expect computers to perform better than people. In particular, with wearable computers and "smart clothing," the computer can continuously attend to physiological patterns, especially biosignals such as heart rate or muscular tension. Computers have superior abilities for processing patterns, although humans remain superior at interpreting meaning in patterns. The best results are likely to come from a combination of human and computer abilities. In particular, a person with a wearable affective computer will find an opportunity to learn things about himself or herself that might not be learned otherwise. I will address wearables in a later chapter.

Although I write of "recognizing emotions," I am not proposing that computers could recognize or measure affective states directly. Because affective states are internal and involve cognitive thoughts as well as physical changes, they cannot be fully recognized by anyone but the person having the affective state. Outsiders only have access to observable functions of the affective state—expressions, behaviors, and so forth. Given reliable observations of these functions, then the underlying states may be inferred. Hence, the expression "recognizing emotions" should be interpreted as "inferring an emotional state from observations of emotional expressions and behavior, and through reasoning about an emotion-generating situation." In particular, the pattern recognition tools in this chapter focus on modeling patterns of expression and behavior. The next chapter addresses models that can be used for reasoning about situations.

Despite its immense difficulty, emotion recognition is easier than thought recognition. Consider the party game of *charades*, where a player tries to get his team to guess a word or phrase—typically a person, place or thing—without providing any spoken or written clues. The fun and challenge involve trying to act out situations so that the team can guess the correct word or phrase quickly. Now, imagine if the game was limited to guessing emotions. In that case the player would no longer need the elaborate gestural syntax that the game has evolved ("3 syllables, name of a book, sounds like," etc.) and for most emotions the game would cease to be a challenge. Recognition of emotion is easier than recognition of thoughts largely because there are not as many emotions as thoughts. In pattern recognition, the difficulty of the problem almost always increases dramatically with the number of possibilities. The number of possible thoughts you could have right now is virtually limitless, nor are thoughts easily categorized into a small set of possibilities. Thought recognition, even with increasingly sophisticated brain imaging techniques, is arguably the largest recognition problem in the world. In contrast, a relatively small number of categories for emotions have been commonly proposed. The smaller set of categories permits a smaller language, making emotion recognition easier than thought recognition.

Basic Emotions and Discrete Categories

Theorists have long discussed a small set of categories for describing emotional states. In 1962 Tomkins suggested that there are eight basic emotions: fear, anger, anguish, joy, disgust, surprise, interest, and shame (Tomkins, 1962). Plutchik later distinguished among a different eight basic emotions: fear, anger, sorrow, joy, disgust, surprise, acceptance, and anticipation (Plutchik, 1980). More recently, Ortony, Clore, and Collins have collected a summary of lists of basic emotions (Ortony, Clore and Collins, 1988). From these lists, the most common four emotions (combining near synonyms, like joy and happiness) are fear, anger, sadness, and joy. The next most common two are disgust and surprise and, after these six, the lists diverge. Over the years, various researchers have proposed that there are from two to twenty "basic" emotions.

"Basic emotions" may be defined in many ways. Perhaps the most thorough definition has been given by Paul Ekman, who has linked basic emotions to those which have distinctive universal facial expressions associated with them, as well as eight other properties (Ekman, 1992, 1992a). By these criteria, Ekman identified six basic emotions: fear, anger, sadness, happiness, disgust, and surprise. Basic emotions can also be deduced by analyzing words for emotion, an approach taken by Johnson-Laird and Oatley on 590 English terms describing emotions, which concluded that the words could be based on one or more of five basic emotions: fear, anger, sadness, happiness, and disgust (Johnson-Laird and Oatley, 1989).

Whether or not basic emotional states exist is disputed by some authors, and is a topic of long-standing debate in the emotion theory literature (Ortony and Turner, 1990; Stein and Oatley, 1992, Panksepp, 1992). Some emotions show up universally, and others seem to involve cultural specifics. Universality poses only a slight problem to computers trying to recognize emotions, which I will address briefly below. Affective computing, fortunately, does not hinge on the resolution of whether or not there are basic emotions. Rather, the topic concerns us primarily as a problem of representation: should emotions be represented as discrete categories, or otherwise?

Emotion Spaces and Continuous Dimensions

Some authors have been less concerned with the existence of eight or so basic emotions and instead refer to continuous dimensions of emotion (Schlosberg, 1954). Three dimensions show up most commonly, although only the names of the first two are widely agreed on. The two most common dimensions are "arousal" (calm/excited), and "valence" (negative/positive). These were the axes illustrated earlier in Fig. 3.2, together with titles of pictures classified in this continuous space, according to the work of Peter Lang. Lang has assembled an international archive of imagery rated by arousal and valence (Lang, 1995).

Numerous researchers have worked with dimensions of emotion instead of with basic emotions or discrete emotion categories. Lang writes that self-reports across subjects are more reliable with respect to dimensions than with respect to discrete categories such as anger, fear, etc. (Lang, 1984). A number of researchers have also proposed various mappings between continuous dimensions of emotions and basic emotion categories. In the next chapter we will see several "cognitive appraisal" models that effectively do this, stating criteria that partition a continuous space into ten or more discrete outcomes. In general, two dimensions cannot be used to distinguish all the basic emotions; for example, intense fear and anger lie in the same region of high arousal negative valence. However, these two dimensions do account for the most common descriptions of mood.

The lack of a definition of emotion, and the lack of agreement on whether there are basic emotions or continuous spaces of emotions are obstacles to the goals of computer-based recognition and synthesis. However, these obstacles are not insurmountable. Similar hindrances occur in fields such as image content analysis where, despite the difficulties, pattern analysis and learning tools have proved helpful. Hence, it is reasonable to expect similar success in modeling affective patterns. Moreover, the question of whether to try to represent emotions with discrete categories or continuous dimensions can be considered a choice, as each representation has advantages in different applications. The choice of discrete or continuous states is, in one sense, like the choice of particles or waves in describing light: the best choice depends on what you are trying to explain.

If desired, discrete categories of emotions can be treated as regions in a continuous space. Categories may be "fuzzy" in the sense that an element can belong in more than one category at once. For example, a feeling of sadness can occur in both "grief" and "melancholy." Researchers such as Paul Ekman define affective phenomena that are not basic emotions, such as "grief," to be not emotions, but "emotional plots." The plot of grief specifies two actors with a prior relationship of attachment, a deceased and a survivor, and an event of separation, followed by emotions in the survivor such as distress, sadness, and perhaps fear or anger. Alternatively, one might consider grief a cognitively-generated emotion, or perhaps a mixture of more basic emotions. In the game of charades, basic emotions are easiest to portray, and emotions like grief involve more effort.

The piano teacher application described in the opening chapter of this book used discrete emotions, recognizing states of interest, frustration, and joy, to allow the teacher to give more personal feedback. In contrast, an application involving television news broadcasts is naturally suited to description with the arousal and valence axes. A high-arousal story captures attention: many people rush to the television to see the emotional gold-medal Olympic victory. Extremely negative content has a powerful influence on memory, perhaps in part because it is almost always also high arousal: many people have a keen memory of the shock they felt upon hearing of John F. Kennedy's death, or upon hearing of the space shuttle Challenger exploding. High-arousal stories attract viewers; however, people tend to not want too much negativity, so it becomes important for broadcasters to try to find positive-valence high-arousal content. Valence and arousal are critical dimensions in entertainment, as well as in many other applications.

However, just because this representation is useful in this application does not imply that all emotions are continuously valenced. Neither does successful representation with a small set of discrete emotions imply that emotions are discrete, or that there is only a small set of them. Both representations have uses and limitations. Fortunately, we do not need consensus about one representation being "right" to carry out the ideas presented below.

In summary, the recognition and modeling problems are simplified by either the assumption of a small set of discrete "basic" emotions, or by the assumption of a small number of dimensions. The fact that both yield a concise representation is an advantage. Even if these are later found to be an oversimplification, they at least form a good point to begin the modeling effort. A small repertoire of emotions is characteristic in developing humans—the younger baby has a smaller repertoire of emotions than does a child, and the child a smaller repertoire than an adult. One can expect the first affective computers to start with only a small number of categories or dimensions.

Universal vs. Person-Specific

Much of emotion theory has been stymied on the issue of universality. If there are emotions that occur with similar physiological responses in all humans, then what is this set of emotions and how can they be recognized, regardless of race, gender, culture, etc.? Like many questions in emotion theory, the study of this one is complicated by factors such as how emotion is defined, elicited, expressed, and communicated. Different languages do not necessarily use the same words for describing emotive phenomena, which further complicates attempts to demonstrate universality.

One of the potential benefits of affective computing lies in its ability to make measurements and analyze patterns of affective signals, conditioned on individuals and on circumstances affecting them. Given similar conditions, measurements, and patterns of responses, conclusions can begin to be made about the universality of various kinds of affective expressions. Hence, the solution proposed by affective computing is, first, person-specific—measuring data for individuals of all kinds, and, second, universal—examining the individual data to see what common patterns are present.

Common patterns are expected for universal emotions, and may differ slightly for emotions that are variations on these. For example, over 60 expressions of anger have been found, but all members of the anger family include two features: the brows are lowered and drawn together, the upper eyelid is raised and the muscle in the lips is tightened. Variations on this basic anger expression are hypothesized to reflect whether the anger is controlled, spontaneous, simulated, and so forth (Ekman, 1992). Because these variations tend to occur with different frequencies in different individuals, and because they may invoke various other individual responses, perhaps reinforced by a person's local environment, they can take on additional flavors, much like a language evolves into dialects. Individual factors such as temperament affect thresholds of expression, as well as other physiological characteristics. Just as speakers of the same dialect have individual variations, we can expect temperamental variations in emotional expression.

Pure vs. Mixed

After Uta Pippig won the 100th Boston Marathon, she described feeling tremendously happy for winning the race, surprised because she believed she would not win, somewhat sad that the race was over, and a bit fearful because during the race she had acute abdominal pain. We say she had "mixed emotions." However, emotion theorists do not agree on what it means for emotions to mix. Do they mix together like paints, like chemical compounds, or perhaps according to some mathematical function?

Here are two metaphors for how emotions might be "mixed": first, a microwave oven, and second, a tub of water. Microwaves usually have two pure states: "on" and "off." When you set the oven to cook at high then the oven is on constantly. When you set the oven to cook at medium, then the oven cycles between "on" and "off" to produce a slower heating effect. The state "medium" is created by juxtaposing pure states "high" and "off" in time—mixing in time—even though at any instant of time the oven is in only one state. A different case of mixing is illustrated by a tub of water. If you enjoy a warm bath, then you do not do so by jumping in time back and forth between a tub of cold water and a tub of hot water, but you mix the cold and hot water in the same tub. This kind of mixture allows the states to mingle and form a solution that has a new state—warm.

When examined over a long time scale, both the microwave and the tub result in a mixture state, "warm." However, in the microwave, one can argue that the purity of the states is preserved—you just have to look (or sample the data) quickly enough to detect them. In contrast, in the tub the purity of the cold and hot states is replaced by a warm state. For emotion mixing, both metaphors are useful. For example, Clynes has found in sentograph measurements of finger pressure that an expression of melancholy begins with a form that looks like love and ends with a form that looks like sadness (Clynes, 1977). In other words, the mixture emotion of melancholy is described as a juxtaposition of two forms in time, as in the microwave metaphor. On the other hand, most theorists have proposed scenarios that are closer to the tub metaphor, with examples such as feeling "wary," which is hypothesized to be a mixture of interest and fear.

"Love–hate" relationships are an example where feelings of love and hate cycle in time. The result is not a simple sum of the two emotions, or a feeling that is in-between love and hate, but a rapid switching between the two in time. In fact, for certain pairs of emotions such as love and hate, or perhaps sadness and joy, it may not be possible for them to truly co-occur at the same time. Instead, it may be that their polarity limits their mixing to be like that of the microwave, one on and the other off, with mixing only in time.

All mixed emotions need not mix in the same way. In fact, this is a logical prediction based on the way emotions coincide with different patterns of bodily responses, and arise with different mechanisms. To the extent that two emotions have non-overlapping generative mechanisms, and their bodily patterns can mingle, then they can coexist in time. But if they require the same generative mechanisms, then only one of them can be generated at a given instant. Alternatively, two emotions generated by the same mechanism may have different lengths of decay. If the second is initiated before the first decays, this can give a different kind of overlap in time. However, given that emotions are short events, this overlap should not be significant. With this reasoning one can predict that a primary emotion like fear, generated initially in the amgydala, could coexist with a cognitively-generated state like anticipation, although extreme fear is likely to temporarily override any cognitive emotions.

Cognitive events can interfere with the purity of emotions. If you are deeply involved in playing a mournful piece of music, you may attain and express a pure state of sadness. However, if your mind wanders to a happy event that you are looking forward to after the concert, then the mournfulness of your playing will not be as pure. This kind of mixing, like the microwave cycling off and on, dilutes the expression of an emotion.

Emotions and cognitions can inhibit other emotions. An intriguing experiment on lying and emotional expression illustrates this inhibition. Thirty-one subjects were asked to express anger or love, using a sentograph. The device recorded two significantly different kinds of essentic forms corresponding to the two emotions. Next the subjects participated in several trials that required them to lie at various points about cards they were holding in their hand. When lying while expressing anger, no significant changes were found either in the subjects' self reports of anger, or in their recorded expressive wave-forms of anger. However, when they were asked to lie while expressing love, not only were their self reports of love significantly lower, but their essentic waveforms for love were significantly altered (Clynes, Jurisevic, and Rynn,

1990). This suggests that certain cognitive events such as lying can inhibit certain emotional expressions (love), and not others (anger).

How does sentic modulation change as a person suppresses one strongly-felt state and tries to feel another? Could measurements of affective patterns help people identify an emotion they are masking, such as when anger is expressed to hide fear? Questions such as these can be addressed by the tools presented here. Using a computer with the ability to record and analyze observations that correlate with affective states should aid investigators in understanding these connections between emotions and their expression.

Imagine an actor who feels angry the night of a show, but has to play the role of a joyful character. In order to deliberately express joy he suppresses his anger, or overrides it with joy. If he is successful onstage in communicating joy, has he merely "forgotten" his anger, so that it will return after he has finished his time on stage? Or is there a therapeutic effect that takes place? Measurements of his emotion before, during, and after the performance could be studied both for understanding purity of emotions and for understanding their therapeutic effects. The measurements could be combined with reports from both the actor and audience, to gather their subjective (cognitive/perceptual) evaluations for synchronization with the bodily measurements.

If the actor has merely "forgotten" his anger, then this suggests a cognitive act, which has to occur both consciously and subconsciously so that the bodily response disappears. Otherwise, the audience will still see conflict in the actor, instead of joy, and think him to be a bad actor. The actor who is angry and tense in his body cannot merely think "smile" and appear carefree and light. The will does not have a monopoly on memory; the body also provides a short term memory. The muscles store tension; the posture can remain uptight. The intensity of affective communication is not only a function of thoughts, but a function of bodily modulation—voice, face, posture, and more. As the actor deliberately brings all these modes into a consistent expression, not only is his communication more effective, but he moves himself closer to a pure state of emotion. The purer the emotional state, the more powerful will be the ability of the actor to move the audience to a similar state. Theories that examine the purity of emotions through their power to be expressed bodily become empirically testable with an affective computer that can model emotional states for synthesis and recognition.

Modeling Affective Patterns

Below I will give examples of computational models for the representation of affective patterns, especially for facial expressions, vocal intonation, and physiological signals that vary with affective states. Most of the models were developed for the purpose of recognizing affective expressions, although some can be used for synthesis of expressions as well. All the models work with present technology and would typically be implemented in software. The models below tend to range from "low-level" to "mid-level," mapping emotions to signal patterns (expression generation or synthesis) and vice-versa (expression recognition). Some of the models assume discrete emotion categories, while others assume continuous dimensions of emotion. None of them are "high-level" in that none consider the semantics of the situation which might generate an emotional response in the first place (as necessary in cognitive emotion generation). The models that exist currently for such high-level processing are rule-based and connectionist models, which will be presented in the next chapter.

A caveat is in order before proceeding: sometimes the term "model" refers to a formula that is capable of fully explaining a phenomenon, both analyzing it and synthesizing it. In the richest sense, a pattern model can both recognize and synthesize the pattern. The use of the word "model" in this book is less narrow. Most of the models below cannot both synthesize and analyze the affective patterns without further development. Some consist of sets of features which discriminate expressions, but which cannot reliably synthesize them. Others can synthesize certain affective expressions, but do not provide parameters for recognition. Nonetheless, the term "model" is used to describe a set of parameters and procedures that are useful for pattern analysis, synthesis, or both.

There is a common misunderstanding that there is one right model of something, and that if there is more than one model, then they cannot all be right. On the contrary, experience has shown that the best choice of model depends on the application, and that there can be many right models just as there are many applications. Each model has its strengths and weaknesses, and sometimes a skillful combination of models gives better results than any single model. These principles have been found to be true in pattern modeling for video and image (Picard, 1996) and can also be expected to hold for pattern modeling of affective information. In other words, which computational model is "best" depends on the specifics of the computer's affective task, and when these change, so does the model. Therefore, equipping a computer with multiple models may be the way to get the best performance. Choosing which models are best for an application is easier after seeing different examples of each model's performance. I will therefore discuss many models below.

Recognizing and Synthesizing Facial Expressions

One of the postulates of affective computing is that computers can be given the ability to recognize emotions as well as a third-person human observer. Let us consider the special case of facial expressions. Recognizing a facial expression is not always the same as recognizing the emotion that generated it; facial expressions are the most easily controlled of all the expressions. However, because they are also the most visible, they are very important, and it is wise to observe them to assess what a person is trying to communicate. Some of the examples below involve models of facial expression which are not restricted to recognition, but which may also be used for synthesis of facial expressions.

Models for recognizing facial expressions have traditionally operated on a digitized facial image or a short digital video sequence of the facial expression being made, such as neutral, then smile, then neutral. In general, recognition from video is more accurate than recognition from still images. Video captures facial movements that deviate from a neutral expression. Therefore, the models below are based on recognition from video, although there has also been work on recognition of facial expressions using still images.[3]

Facial expression recognition models to date have treated emotions as discrete in the sense that they try to classify facial expressions into a small number of categories such as "happy" or "angry." The underlying theory that links the expressions to these categories was developed by Paul Ekman and his colleagues, and is called the Facial Action Coding system (FACS). The FACS system describes basic emotions and their corresponding sets of *action units*, which are muscular movements used to generate that expression.[4]

Facial expression recognition from video involves capturing spatiotemporal patterns of both local and global changes on the human face, and relating these patterns to a category of emotion. In the recognition examples that follow, two main assumptions are made: (1) there are a small number of discrete categories of emotional expressions; (2) data in the experiments is "pure" in the sense that a user willingly or naturally tried to express exactly one emotion. The first assumption makes this a supervised pattern recognition problem, with *a priori* specified categories of what can be recognized. The second assumption is perhaps the most problematic, as it cannot be verified. There is no guarantee that the facial expression recognized as "sad" corresponds to any genuine affective state of sadness.

None of the methods I describe claim to recognize the underlying emotion, but only the expression on the user's face. In other words, they would recognize your smile even if it is a forced smile when you are not feeling happy. They are currently not good enough to tell a false smile from a genuine smile although, to my knowledge, people have not tried very hard to get a computer to discriminate these cases, and a computer could be capable of this discrimination. Vision-based facial expression recognizers would also fail to recognize a state of joy if the joyful person suppressed all facial expressions. However, the models here have made strides in recognizing facial expressions, which is a significant step toward giving computers the ability to recognize emotions.[5]

Irfan Essa of the Georgia Institute of Technology and Alex Pentland of the MIT Media Laboratory, have augmented Ekman's FACS system to address two of its limits: (1) action units are purely local spatial patterns; in contrast, real facial motion patterns are almost never completely localized and can include coarticulation effects, and (2) most facial actions occur in three phases: application, release, and relaxation, while FACS does not include such time components. In extending it to non-local spatial patterns and to include temporal information, they have enabled computers to recognize facial expressions from video (Essa and Pentland, 1997). The representation they use is based on representing facial motion dynamics during expression. It can also be used to synthesize facial expressions (Essa, 1995). The model contains both geometric information about facial shape and physical knowledge of facial muscles. It begins by fitting a representation of finite elements to the facial geometry, which then interacts with facial muscles to allow expressions to be synthesized according to the muscles that they involve. To synthesize an expression, values of parameters of the finite element representation for the desired expression need to be determined. These parameters can be calculated by analysis of a video of an expression. The parameters derived from the video sequence correspond to a pattern of peak muscle activations, which are mapped to an emotion category. The facial recognizer typically takes five minutes to process a facial expression (on an SGI Indy R4400) and has a demonstrated accuracy of 98% in recognizing six facial expression categories (anger, disgust, happiness, surprise, eyebrow raise, and neutral) for a group of eight people who deliberately made those expressions.

If faster recognition is needed, then a second, non-physically based model can be used, forming templates of facial motion energy (Essa and Pentland, 1995). The templates are default patterns characterizing the movement at each point between pairs of frames in the video while an expression is made. For the categories of anger, disgust, happiness, surprise, and neutral, recognition rates are as high as 98% in a test involving eight people. Studies are underway to determine how the recognition rate changes when there are more people. The recognition does not work in real time yet; it takes a few seconds to recognize each expression. However, with advances in hardware and pattern recognition, the recognition should become fast enough for an interactive response in the near future.

A different model for facial expression recognition, developed by Yaser Yacoob and Larry Davis of the University of Maryland, also relies on templates of motion energy, but uses a combination of templates and smaller sub-templates (e.g., of just the mouth area) and combines them with rules to

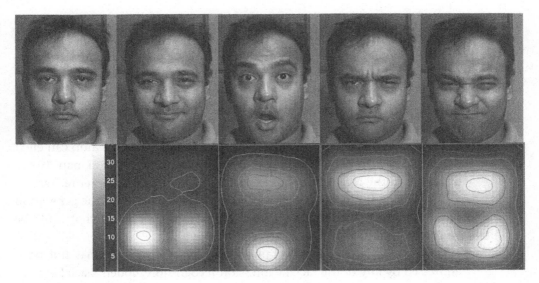

Figure 6.1
Facial expression recognition and motion energy maps. Top row: snapshots of the neutral and four other expressions: happiness, surprise, anger, disgust. Bottom row: templates of energy of the facial movement, as different from the neutral expression. The brighter regions correspond to higher energy. (Photographs courtesy of Irfan Essa, Georgia Institute of Technology, copyright 1997.)

formulate expressions (Yacoob and Davis, 1996). For example, templates are extracted of the eye and mouth area, and anger is characterized by inward lowering motion of the eyebrows coupled with compaction of the mouth. This method has been tested on expressions of fear, anger, sadness, happiness, disgust, surprise, and eye blinking, as made by 32 people, for a total of 116 expressions and 106 blinkings in the test set. The recognition accuracy over this database was approximately 65% for blinking, and approximately 80% for the affective expressions. This method is also not real-time, because computing the motion flow is slow. Yacoob, working with Michael Black of Xerox PARC, has developed a similar method that additionally uses camera motion tracking to help recognize expressions in videos of television talk shows, news, and movies (Black and Yacoob, 1995).

The above models use pattern recognition and image analysis, and inherit the current weaknesses of these tools. Most of the methods are sensitive to scene lighting, requiring it to be relatively uniform. All require the person's head to be easily found in the video sequence. Finally, continuous expression recognition, such as a sequence of "smile, frown, surprise," is not handled well; instead, the expressions must either be manually separated, or interleaved with some reliably detectable cue such as a neutral expression, which has essentially zero motion energy. Continuous expression recognition is difficult in the same sense that continuous speech recognition is difficult—finding the word boundaries, or in this case the expression boundaries, needs to happen simultaneously with identification of the expressions.

When the computer synthesizes a smiling face, the computer may or may not also activate an internal affective state. The way this activation works in people is unknown, but it is true that expression of emotion plays a role in activation and regulation of emotional feeling. A facial expression can elicit an emotion in the person making the expression (Izard, 1990; Ekman, 1993), as well as in the recipient of the expression. When the computer recognizes a smiling face, it is possible to have this recognition influence the generation of an internal affective state—a sort of "emotion contagion" that could be given to computers.

The relation between temperament and facial expression has not been addressed by any of the facial expression recognition models. Facial expressiveness, like other forms of sentic modulation, is influenced by a person's innate physiology, which is related to temperament. In studies of inhibited versus uninhibited children, the inhibited ones have lower overall facial expressiveness—presumably a consequence of their tendency toward greater muscle tension (Kagan, Snidman, Arcus, and Reznick, 1994). Hence, their "baseline" facial dynamics operate over a smaller range. For optimal performance, computer systems that recognize facial expression would first have to calibrate the subject's expressive range, a form of "getting to know" them, before these systems could become adept at recognizing their expressions.

Synthesizing and Recognizing Affective Vocal Intonation

Traditional efforts in computer-based speech recognition have focused on recognition of *what* is said. More recently, efforts have also been made to teach computers to recognize *who* is speaking. Usually the subtle qualities of *how* something is said have been treated as noise for the first two problems. In contrast, humans learn to identify who is talking and how something is said long before they can recognize what is said.

The vocal intonation of *how* something is said breaks down into two components: cues emphasizing which content in the message is most important, and cues arising from the speaker's affective state. Affective cues can convey the most important aspect of what is said, such as whether the speaker liked something or not. Vocal inflection adds flavor to our speech and content to its message. Even in telling a joke, everyone knows it's *how* you tell it that greatly determines its success.

Characterizing affect in speech may be harder than characterizing affect on faces. Facial signals communicate personal identity and expression, but

Table 6.1
Summary of human vocal effects most commonly associated with the emotions indicated. Descriptions are given relative to neutral speech. (Adapted with permission from Murray and Arnott (1993), Table 1. Copyright 1993 Acoustical Society of America.)

	Fear	Anger	Sadness	Happiness	Disgust
Speech rate	much faster	slightly faster	slightly slower	faster or slower	very much slower
Pitch average	very much higher	very much higher	slightly lower	much higher	very much lower
Pitch range	much wider	much wider	slightly narrower	much wider	slightly wider
Intensity	normal	higher	lower	higher	lower
Voice quality	irregular voicing	breathy chest tone	resonant	breathy blaring	grumbled chest tone
Pitch changes	normal	abrupt on stressed syllables	downward inflections	smooth upward inflections	wide downward terminal inflections
Articulation	precise	tense	slurring	normal	normal

do not generally communicate a linguistic message. On the other hand, the speech signal contains a mixture of information, including cues to speaker identity, affect, and lexical and grammatical emphasis for the spoken message. Isolating affective information is complicated. Nonetheless, computers are slowly achieving progress in synthesizing and recognizing affect in speech. Examples illustrating progress are provided in this section, although for further information the reader may refer to the overviews of the principal findings on human vocal emotion (Murray and Arnott, 1993; van Bezooyen, 1984). Table 6.1 summarizes the vocal effects most commonly associated with five basic emotions.

The basic problem that needs to be solved is: what is a good computational mapping between emotions and speech patterns? Specifically, we need to find features that a computer can extract, and models it can use to recognize and synthesize affective inflection. These features are generally derived from observing how voices change with emotions. When a speaker is in a state of fear, anger or joy, then his speech is typically faster, louder, and enunciated, with strong high-frequency energy. This is primarily due to arousal of the sympathetic nervous system, increasing heart rate, blood pressure, mouth dryness, and certain muscle activation. When the speaker is bored or sad, then his speech is typically slower and lower-pitched, with very little high-frequency energy. This is primarily due to arousal of the parasympathetic nervous system, decreasing heart rate and blood pressure, and increasing salivation. In other words, the effects of emotion on speech show up primarily in its frequency and timing, with secondary effects in its loudness and enunciation. The effects of emotion therefore tend to show up in features such as average pitch, pitch range, pitch changes, intensity contour, speaking rate, voice quality, and articulation. However, these effects are complicated by prosodic effects that speakers use to communicate grammatical structure and lexical emphasis; both effects influence several of the same features.

Speech, like other forms of sentic modulation, is influenced by factors such as temperament and cognition. In studies with inhibited versus uninhibited children, those who were inhibited spoke with less pitch period variation in their voices, most likely because of their tendency toward increased muscle tension, as was also correlated with lower facial expressiveness (Kagan, Snidman, Arcus, and Reznick, 1994). For optimal performance, computer systems that recognize affect in speech would first have to learn the subject's vocal range, and then analyze with respect to this range. People are also capable of controlling their speech inflection willfully, although vocal expressions are harder to control than facial expressions. For example, the ability to mask nervousness in public speaking is important—many great speakers admit to being nervous, but they are able to learn to relax their voice in such a way that the nervousness is not heard. The models described below do not incorporate the influences of variables such as temperament, cognitive suppression of emotion, or linguistic content; however, they are pioneering in their attempts to begin to learn mappings between acoustic features and affective states.

The first model was constructed to address the question: Can recognizable affect be generated in computer-synthesized speech? To answer this, Janet Cahn, at the MIT Media Lab, built the "Affect Editor," a computer program that takes an acoustic and linguistic description of an utterance and generates synthesizer instructions for a DECtalk3 synthesizer to produce speech with a desired affect (Cahn, 1990). She identified values of seventeen parameters: six pitch parameters, four timing parameters, six voice quality parameters, and one articulation parameter, which produced speech that sounded scared, angry, sad, glad, disgusted, and surprised. The seventeen parameters were used to control a wide variety of affects—not just for strongly distinguishable emotions, but also for subtle differences, with variations for individuality. To synthesize speech, Cahn's model cooperates with models of the other components of speech to drive a synthesizer. This involves not just the seventeen parameters above, but also an analysis of the syntactic and semantic clauses of the utterance in an effort to identify good locations (e.g., pitch accent and pause locations) for applying both lexical and non-lexical effects.

To test this model of affective speech synthesis, the parameters were used to synthesize five different neutral sentences, such as "I saw your name in the paper." Each sentence was synthesized with six different categories of emotional expression. Listeners were asked to choose whether the speech sounded scared, angry, sad, glad, disgusted, or surprised. In listener studies, the emotion of sadness was correctly recognized 91% of the time. The other emotions were correctly recognized approximately 50% of the time, and mistaken for similar emotions 20% of the time (e.g., disgust was mistaken as anger; scared was mistaken as surprised). The 50% performance was significantly better than the 17% level of chance. Also, the sentences had no explicit context attached, so their content should not have aided the listeners in recognizing the emotion.

Despite the promising results that have been obtained, many research questions remain. For example, the seventeen affect parameters discussed above need more investigation as to how they should co-vary instead of being set independently. Also, their reliability and generalizability are not known beyond the scope of small studies. In particular, the mappings between emotions and vocal features in humans will vary depending on the context. Sometimes an angry person will raise her voice, and sometimes she will lower it. Determining all the possibilities is an open research problem.

As mentioned earlier, people like Stephen Hawking who rely on speech synthesizers could benefit not only from computer voices that can express emotion, but also from computers that could recognize their emotion. Such systems could automatically set the intonation parameters for the synthetic voice. To date, there is no system that takes what a speaking-impaired person is feeling, and has the feelings automatically generate the right settings for their speech synthesizer. Instead, the speaker has to adjust the affect parameters by hand. Nonetheless, the development of affect control knobs for speech synthesis is a step toward this goal.

The Affect Editor can take an input sentence in typed form and synthesize it with a specified affect in acoustic form. But what about the inverse problem, analyzing the affect in a spoken sentence? In Clarke's science fiction novel *2001*, we read that the computer HAL could discern the astronaut Dave's emotions by analyzing his voice harmonics. Will computers be able to do this any time soon? The task is very difficult, especially given that humans are not reliable at recognizing affect in voices. Humans, on average, can recognize affect with about 60% reliability (Scherer, 1981) when tested on neutral speech or on speech where the meaning has been obscured. In the neutral speech studies, people can usually distinguish arousal in the voice (e.g., angry vs. sad) but they frequently confuse valence (e.g., angry vs. enthusiastic). In ordinary conversation, however, a sentence and situation are rarely neutral; the context provides powerful cues to disambiguate the

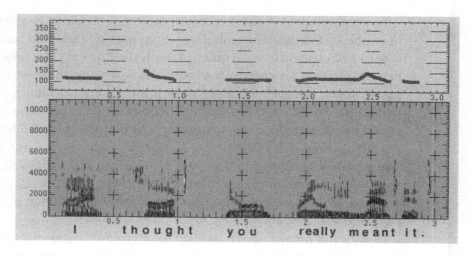

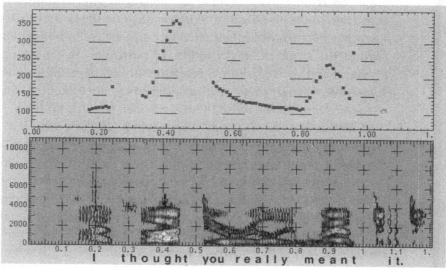

Figure 6.2

Voice inflection synthesis. The same sentence, "I thought you really meant it," synthesized for two emotions: sad and annoyed. For each emotion the pitch track (top) and spectrogram (bottom) are shown. Notice the bigger pitch range for annoyed, as opposed to the relatively compressed range for sad. The spectrograms also show differences in speed, pause locations, and enunciation of the two cases. (Spectrograms courtesy of Janet Cahn, MIT Media Lab.)

valence of a spoken message. In other words, the affective cues most readily communicate arousal; the communication of valence is believed to be by more subtle cues, intertwined with the content of the speech.

In efforts to give computers the ability to recognize affect in speech, a variety of features have been proposed. Early studies found that the arousal

dimension of emotion is communicated by pitch and loudness while valence is communicated by subtler and more complex patterns of inflection
and rhythm (Davitz, 1964). Some of the earliest research in this area analyzed the voice signals of pilots in stressful situations talking to the control
tower (Williams and Stevens, 1969) and actors expressing emotions (Williams
and Stevens, 1972), where acoustic features such as the fundamental frequency contour, average speech spectrum, precision of articulation, and other
temporal characteristics were used for discriminating certain affective states,
especially fear, anger, and sorrow. More recent research has shown a correlation between rising arousal levels, from sorrow to anger or from severe
depression to recovery, and a rise in spectral energy in higher frequencies (up
to 4kHz); this research also links frequency ranges of long-term voice spectra
to the three dimensions of arousal, valence, and control (Pittam, Gallois, and
Callanite, 1990). In native Korean actors and French actors speaking neutral
sentences with the emotions anger, sorrow, joy, tenderness, and neutral, it
was found that arousal was easiest to recognize using the features of pitch
range, speech rate, and intensity, and that the duration of the last syllable of
a sentence showed promise for valence recognition. This syllable was found
to be short in anger and long in joy and tenderness (Chung, 1995). Similarly,
a measure of voice quality helped with valence—joyful and tender voices
are more resonant than angry or sorrowful voices, which are more aspirated.
Linear predictive coding parameters of speech together with speech power
and pitch information have also been used in conjunction with a neural net
to recognize eight categories—fear, anger, sadness, joy, disgust, surprise, teas-
ing, and neutral—in people interacting with an animated character (Tosa and
Nakatsu, 1996).

For training a personal software agent, one of the more useful recognition
tasks would be to have the computer recognize whether you liked something
or not. However, to date there are no reliable computational measurements
of acoustic features of valence. Deb Roy and Alex Pentland, at the MIT Media
Lab, have made a preliminary effort to enable computers to classify sentences
as approving or disapproving (Roy and Pentland, 1996). This effort used six
features—mean and variance of the fundamental frequency, variance and
derivative of energy, ratio of amplitude of first to second harmonic, and ratio
of first harmonic to third formant—to describe the two classes of approval
and disapproval with Gaussian models, and decided which class was present
based on Bayesian decision making, a standard method in pattern analysis.[6]
The resulting recognition accuracy was 65% - 88% for speaker-dependent,
text-independent classification of approving versus disapproving sentences.
The same sentences were also judged by people as approving versus disapproving, with similar classification accuracy. The reliability differed from

speaker to speaker; the computational model successfully recognized the approval/disapproval of subject A more easily than B more easily than C, and this pattern of success was duplicated for humans trying to recognize the approval/disapproval of subjects A,B,C. Although this study is very limited, its focus is noteworthy, as indications of approval/disapproval are clearly important to young children, especially pre-verbal infants, and play an important role in learning of right and wrong. If a computer is trying to learn to adapt its behavior to its user, then an ability to sense approval or disapproval from that user would aid in this process.

Studies of affect recognition are complicated by many issues. One complication is how to mask the content of the speech: Play it backwards? Filter it to obscure what is said? Most studies try to get around this problem by choosing sentences with neutral content (e.g., "What time are you leaving?") but there is no guarantee that the content will be received as neutral by the subject. Researchers who work on this should be aware of the pitfalls of various methods for masking sentence content (Scherer, Ladd, and Silverman, 1984). Another potential complication, which apparently none of the studies have considered, is that the mood of the subject assessing the speech may influence the results. As described earlier, studies show that human perception is biased toward positive or negative depending on a subject's mood. In particular, subjects resolve lexical ambiguity in homophones in a mood congruent fashion (Halberstadt, Niedenthal and Kushner 1995), and subjects who look at ambiguous facial expressions judge them as having more rejection/sadness when the subject is depressed, and less invitation/happiness (Bouhuys, Bloem, and Groothuis, 1995). Hence, we can expect that choosing a sentence (or other stimulus) with neutral content and ambiguous affect will tend to be perceived with negative affect by a person in a negative mood, and vice-versa for a person in a positive mood. In other words, the mood of the subjects should be taken into account during recognition experiments.

Combinations of Face and Voice

The above sections gave examples of models for synthesis and recognition of affect both in facial expressions and in voice. The reported results are all preliminary in the sense that they need independent confirmation and would benefit from larger numbers of subjects and expressions, both vocal and facial. Nonetheless, initial results are promising, as all the studies have shown better than random recognition rates and have not revealed any fundamental reasons why affective expression cannot be recognized or synthesized by computers.

A promising area of research is that of combining facial expression and vocal expression to improve recognition results in both domains. The combination of the two is complimentary, given that arousal is more easily discriminated in speech, and valence is more easily discriminated in facial expressions. Studies on facial expression recognition have mostly been performed only on faces that are not also talking, because the mouth moves differently when someone is simultaneously expressing a facial emotion while speaking. The combination remains a challenge for researchers.

Humans have access to both visual and auditory channels in natural unmediated communication; consequently, it is no surprise that these channels might specialize in different aspects of expression. For example, in the famous McGurk effect, listening to an acoustic "ba" and visually lip-reading a "ga" yields an overall percept of "da" (McGurk and MacDonald, 1976). Neither the visual nor the acoustic signal alone is adequate. The fact that we rely upon both, simultaneously, suggests that it is especially important that face and voice channels be well synchronized in a videoteleconferencing system. When the synchronization is right, then videoteleconferencing is a much richer form of communication than a phone call. Part of the increased value of a ticket close to the stage at a concert or theatre production is the advantage of being able to simultaneously hear the performers and see their facial expressions. In people, the combination of visual and auditory abilities provides richer and more accurate communication; it should also lead to improved performance for computers trying to recognize human affect.

Physiological Pattern Recognition

Patterns of features extracted from physiological signals can be used by a computer to recognize affective information. The idea is to have the computer observe multiple signals gathered while a person is experiencing an emotion, like the ones shown in Fig. 5.7 for grief and for anger, and learn which patterns of physiological signals are most indicative of which affective state. Later, when the system is given only raw signals from a person, then it can use what it has learned previously to try to recognize which affective state most likely gave rise to the signals. Research on this kind of recognition is nascent, but let me illustrate one example of its use with some experiments conducted by Elias Vyzas, working with me at the MIT Media Lab.

In this example, we are given four raw physiological signals—EMG, BVP, GSR, and Respiration—from an actress expressing eight emotions each day. Each emotion was expressed repeatedly over several minutes, with the aid of a sentograph. From each signal, only 100 seconds of the data are used in the experiments below, and this data was taken from the middle of the period of expression. The eight emotions she expressed were: no emotion, anger, hate, grief, platonic love, joy, romantic love, and reverence. These 32 signals were gathered every day for twenty days. Step 1 in analyzing the signals is to normalize a signal by subtracting its mean and dividing it by its standard deviation, so that every emotion signal on every day has zero mean and unit variance. Step 2 involves computing features of the raw and normalized signals. The decision of which features to compute is mostly an art, since there are an unlimited number of possibilities and much more research is needed to determine which features are best for affect recognition. For this data, we extracted six features: the mean, standard deviation, mean of the absolute value of the first difference, and mean of the absolute value of the second difference, all computed from the raw signals, and the latter two features again, this time computed from the normalized signals. This results in six features for each of four signals per emotion per day. In other words, each emotion on each day is represented by 24 features, or by a point in a 24-dimensional space. Collecting data over 20 days, we obtained 20 such points to characterize each emotion.

It is often useful to look at subsets of the data to try to determine which features give the best discrimination. After trying all possible triplets of emotions and pairs of features, the system finds that the best classification results for this data are obtained when trying to discriminate within the triplet anger, grief, and reverence, or within the triplet anger, joy, and reverence.[7] In both cases, one feature from the EMG signal—the mean of the raw signal—was one of the two best features for classification. However, the best choice for the second feature varied. For the triplet of anger, grief, and reverence the mean of the absolute value of the first difference of the normalized respiration signal gave the best result. For the triplet of anger, joy, and reverence, the same feature but computed from the EMG gave the best result. Figure 6.3 (top) illustrates the 20 points for each of three emotions, where each point is plotted according to the two best features. For the anger, grief, reverence triplet, the recognition accuracy is 72%, and for the anger, joy, reverence triplet the accuracy is 70%. Both are significantly higher than the score of 33%, which would be expected with random guessing.

Using a classic tool of pattern recognition, the Fisher Projection, applied to a subset of the twenty-four original features, we obtained even better results, with 83% classification accuracy for both triplets. The better separation of classes provided by this method can be seen in Fig. 6.3 (bottom). Ideally, the features used to represent each emotion will result in clearly separated clusters for each emotion, although these clusters may need more than two dimensions, and may therefore be much harder to visualize than the examples shown here. In Fig. 6.3, the ×, ∘, and + signals can be seen to be separated better by the Fisher method (bottom) than by using the two best features (top), although the Fisher method still leaves significant overlap between the reverence and joy classes.

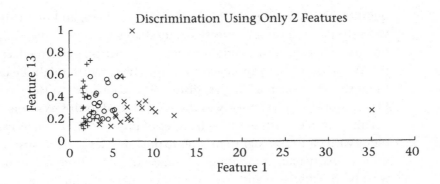

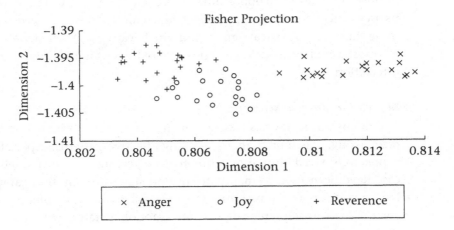

Figure 6.3
Each point represents the physiological signals from an actress expressing a state of anger, joy, or reverence. Top: The signals are shown represented by only the two features that were found to best discriminate these three affective states. Bottom: A Fisher projection was used to calculate two dimensions that discriminate these three states.

The six features extracted above were chosen somewhat arbitrarily, to capture variations in the signals that tend to be useful regardless of what the signals represent. In different applications, however, these features may change. Salient features to use for recognizing a person's relative stress and relaxation levels may be different from the six features computed here. In pattern recognition research on images, features representing texture, color, shape, and motion tend to be some of the most useful. A difficult challenge for affective computing research is to determine which features of the physiological signals are most important—to find what is the equivalent of color, texture, shape, and motion in affect.

The four kinds of signals used in this example—EMG, BVP, GSR, and Respiration—communicate different information, and it is an open research question to determine which combination of these, and other signals, provides the best indicator of affective state changes. For example, various experiments have shown that certain patterns in a person's electroencephalogram (EEG) signals relate to approach vs. withdrawal, which might be used to distinguish affects such as like vs. dislike (Davidson, 1994). However, wearing EEG sensors is not yet as easy as the sensors used in this example.

This example illustrates how features of physiological signals can be combined with pattern recognition tools to provide cues about a person's affective state. In particular, combining information sensed from a user in this way, with both expressive and contextual information from cameras and microphones, provides a rich opportunity for a computer to understand more about its user's affective responses. However, much more research is needed to determine which physiological signals, and which features of these signals, provide the most useful information for the states of interest in the human-computer interaction.

Models for Affective Behavior

The discussion so far has focused on the use of pattern modeling tools for recognizing, classifying, and generating affective patterns, especially facial expressions, vocal intonation, and physiological signals. The models in each case have been used to map patterns and signals to emotion categories, a low-to-medium level transformation. In this section, the emphasis is on mid-level models for representing discrete emotional states. The assumption is that these internal states are "hidden" and that what is not hidden are the observations of sentic modulation, such as a facial expression, which tend to be produced when a person is in these states. Models need to be capable of recognizing that you might express an emotion through a combination of modalities; you might sometimes frown when you are sad, but sadness might also show up in your posture or voice. The model should learn probabilities that given certain observations, a person is in a particular affective state.

Figure 6.4 shows an example of one possible model that meets these requirements, the Hidden Markov Model (HMM). This figure shows only three states, for ease of illustration, but it is straightforward to include more states. For example, a fourth circle could be added for a baseline or neutral state of "no emotion." The premise is that you will be in one state at any instant, and can transition between states with certain probabilities. In the example of the computer tutor, we would expect the probability of the pupil moving from an interest state to a joy state to be higher than the probability of moving from a distress state to a joy state.

The HMM learns probabilities by training on observations, which could be any measurements of sentic modulation varying with the underlying states,

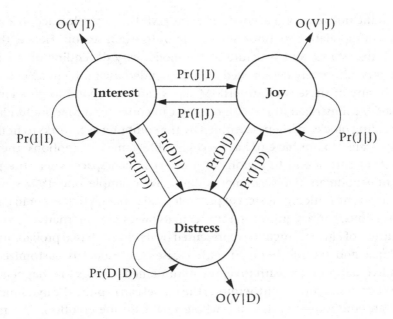

Figure 6.4
The Hidden Markov Model shown here characterizes probabilities of transitions among three "hidden" states: interest (I), distress (D), and joy (J). It also characterizes the likelihood of certain observations given these states, such as how features of voice inflection, V, will change with each state. The affective state of a person cannot be observed directly; only observations that depend on a state can be made. Given a series of observations over time, the computer tries to determine which sequence of states best explains the observations.

such as changes in voice inflection, facial expression, or autonomic changes such as heart rate. The input at any time is these observations; the output can be either the state that the person is most likely in, or it can be identification of an entire HMM configuration, thereby recognizing a larger pattern of emotional behavior. In the latter case, there would need to be a family of HMM configurations, one corresponding to each emotional behavior, or each person's characteristics for a given behavior. For example, the computer tutor might recognize different patterns for different pupils, which might help it to tailor its feedback more effectively.[8]

HMM's work in multiple contexts. Different HMM's can be trained as functions of environmental, cultural or social context. Your sentic modulation patterns may differ if you're driving a car in the country on a Sunday versus in the city at rush hour, going out with an old friend versus meeting a blind date. The probabilities of certain expressions vary given different conditioning events. For example, the probability of showing facial expressions at the office is smaller than the probability of showing them at home. Context can also include temporal events. Different HMM's may be learned as a function of timing relative to a hormone cycle or to exam season. Hence, the probabilities, states, and structure of the model vary depending on a variety of factors, ultimately determined by the intended use of the model.

In any of these cases, the HMM states can correspond to pure emotional states as illustrated in Fig. 6.4, or they can correspond to more fundamental building blocks, perhaps identified by the computer as it works to fit the data. The states do not have to have recognizable names of emotions; they might instead correspond to regions of a dimensioned space where the person's sentic modulation measurements cluster. For example, one HMM state might be made by noticing clusters of physiological variables that occur in particular situations, and assigning each cluster to its own state. Alternatively, a complex pattern of clusters might be represented by its cluster-based probability model (Popat and Picard, 1993). In either case, the model is customized to an individual, and can learn to represent unnamed feelings that happen reliably in certain situations. Furthermore, the model can capture the dynamic aspects of an emotion—associating a whole HMM to one emotion. The model is free to adapt to new theories of emotional building blocks—whether at the granularity of the basic emotions of anger, sadness, etc., or at a smaller granularity from which dynamic emotions may be constructed.

HMM's are also suitable for representing emotion mixtures, following either the bathtub or microwave metaphors used earlier. In the case of the former, a state can be established as a mixed emotion; it can be constructed out of several simultaneous components, as melancholy might be constructed out of the components of love and sadness. In the case of the latter, pure states can be alternately visited in rapid succession in time. An HMM for a "love-hate" relationship would cycle between two or more states of love and hate, perhaps occasionally pausing in a neutral state.

A model such as the HMM can be used not only to recognize certain affective patterns, but also to predict what state a person is most likely to be in next, given the state they are in now. The prediction process is one of partial recognition: First, fit the model to both previous and present observations. Second, use these results to synthesize the most probable state to occur next. The synthesized state acts as the prediction. Like a human observer, such a model-based prediction can give a likely outcome, but can never say with 100% certainty what will happen. When these models synthesize or predict they do so only in a probabilistic way, not taking into consideration high-level reasoning or logic. Consequently, they are not as well suited to predicting emotions based on cognitive appraisals as some of the models I will describe in the next chapter. Nevertheless, they are well-suited to describing patterns of affective state transitions, and inferring hidden states given these patterns.

Additional Models and Learning

Numerous other models may prove to be useful in modeling affective information. An artificial neural net is one general purpose tool which has already been applied to emotion expression recognition, and which will be applied to emotion's influence on memory and performance in the next chapter. As an aside, it is interesting to note that the most popular method used for training artificial neural nets, backpropagation, was originally inspired by the idea of emotional energy being attached to associations. Paul Werbos writes that he came up with the idea of backpropagation while trying to mathematically translate an idea from Freud, who proposed that human behavior is governed by emotions, and that people attach cathexis (emotional energy) to things Freud called "objects." Quoting from Werbos (1994):

> According to his [Freud's] theory, people first of all learn cause-and-effect associations; for example, they may learn that "object" A is associated with "object" B at a later time. And his theory was that there is a *backwards* flow of emotional energy. If A causes B, and B has emotional energy, then some of this energy flows back to A. If A causes B to an extent W, then the backwards flow of emotional energy from B back to A will be proportional to the forwards rate. That really is backpropagation. . . . If A causes B, then you have to find a way to credit A for B, directly. . . . If you want to build a powerful system, you need a backwards flow.

The use of some form of backwards flow is a significant part of most computer learning methods today. It can be implemented without having to give the computer an emotional system. Nonetheless, the mechanism is apparently similar to the role that emotions play in human learning.

There are a host of other possible models that can be employed for analyzing and synthesizing emotional expressions. Camras (1992) has proposed that dynamical systems theory be considered for explaining some of the variable physiological responses observed during basic emotions, but has not suggested any models. Emotion system dynamics might be captured by nonlinear models such as the M-Lattice (Sherstinsky and Picard, 1994) , a model that generalizes certain kinds of neural nets. Grossberg and Gutowski (1987) have proposed that emotional processing can be accomplished with an opponent processing neural network called a gated dipole. Freeman has modeled olfaction with dynamical systems and argues the relevance of this approach for modeling limbic influences on intention and motivation in his book *Societies of Brains* (Freeman, 1995). There are, no doubt, many more possibilities; the field of research is wide open for exploring which models are best suited to capturing the most useful features of emotions.

Note that no one model—discrete, continuous, implicit, emergent, linear, nonlinear, or otherwise—is likely to perfectly recognize an underlying emotional state. For example, tears may be recognized from a video image of a face, but they don't necessarily correspond to sadness—they could be tears of happiness. The most successful recognition can be expected to occur when a computer learns a personalized combination of low-level perceptual cues, such as pattern recognition of visual, vocal, and other biosignals, and high-level cognitive cues, such as reasoning that the viewed event satisfied a long-term goal of the user, and might make her extremely happy. Additionally, these cues will work best when considering the context; for example, is it a poker game where bluffing is the norm, or a marriage proposal where sincerity is expected? The important influence of reasoning, especially cognitive appraisal of a situation, and the synthesis of so-called "cognitive emotions," is the subject of the next chapter.

Summary

This chapter has described models that can be used to start giving computers the abilities necessary to recognize and express emotions. In particular, tools from pattern recognition and analysis have been suggested for recognizing and synthesizing facial expressions, recognizing and synthesizing vocal inflection, recognizing physiological patterns corresponding to affective states, and modeling emotional behavior. Research in this area is very new, but results on small sets of emotions and small sets of people already indicates that computers can achieve useful performance in recognizing and expressing affect.

7 *Emotion Synthesis*

If computers are ever to "have" emotions, then one of the things they need is the ability to synthesize or generate them. In Chapter 2, I described five components of a system that can be said to have emotions. These were:

1. Emotional behavior;

2. Fast primary emotions;

3. Cognitively generated emotions;

4. Emotional experience: cognitive awareness, physiological awareness, and subjective feelings;

5. Body-mind interactions.

Depending on the task at hand, certain subsets of these five components will suffice. Just as all animals do not need emotion systems as sophisticated as a human emotion system, neither do all computers. Furthermore, differences in computers and humans, especially their different physiologies, imply a variety of possible interpretations for these components, especially for the fifth one.

This chapter addresses how to begin giving these abilities to computers. Earlier chapters illustrated the benefits of such abilities which, in humans, include more flexible and rational decision-making, the ability to determine salience and valence, improved reasoning ability, and a variety of other beneficial interactions with creativity, learning, attention, memory, and regulatory processes. We can expect computer emotions to play a role in giving computers these more human-like abilities, together with improving their skills for interacting with people.

One of the areas in which computer emotions are of primary interest is software agents, computer programs that are personalized—they know the user's interests, habits and preferences—and that take an active role in assisting the user with work and information overload.[1] They may also be personified, and play a role in leisure activities. One agent may act like an office assistant to help you process mail; another may take the form of an animated creature to play with a child. The notion of an agent raises several expectations from the human user. In particular, how can agents be made to be personalized, intelligent, believable, and engaging?

"Give them emotions" is not the entire solution to these problems, but it is a critical component. The assistant that cannot read your emotional expression, reason about what your emotions might be, and learn what is important to you—when not to interrupt, for example—will act unintelligently. If the agent cannot have a mechanism for the equivalent of "feeling bad" for causing you distress, then it is likely to repeat this behavior. The lack of such a mechanism is believed to be at the root of the problem of the emotion-impaired patients who know what to do, but do not do it. An ability to "feel good or bad" does not merely effect the agent's ability to learn, but helps it prioritize and choose among all its actions—learning, planning, decision-making, and more. Chapter 2's scenario of a smart personal assistant illustrated a case where emotions in an agent were important for its ability to address multiple concerns in an intelligent and efficient way.

Emotions have been implemented in agents today, but not in this way. The emotions implemented today are primarily cognitively generated, the third component only. Furthermore, they have mostly been used only for entertainment purposes. The agents have some simple cognitive emotions, and they can usually express these emotions, but they do not have the ability to recognize the emotions of people, to experience or show empathy, or to benefit internally from the functions that emotions can provide. Instead of using emotion to help manage information overload, regulate prioritization of activities, and make decisions more flexibly, creatively, and intelligently, today's agents use emotion only to entertain. This is a fine use, and valuable for many applications, but it should not be the only use.

As we begin to construct systems that can synthesize emotions, we need to consider emotional intelligence, teaching computers how to control their emotions, when and how to express them, and how to correctly and wisely recognize and reason about emotion. These abilities are of great importance. If a system cannot handle emotions intelligently, then perhaps it should not synthesize them at all. However, emotional intelligence is hard to develop without first having a system that has emotions. I suggest that once the emotion synthesis mechanisms that I describe in this chapter are fully in place, emotional intelligence will need to be learned, probably from social interactions.

Let us begin now to consider means of giving computers the five components above. Of these five, the easiest to start giving a computer is the third, cognitively-generated emotions. I will describe this in the next section. After that, I will describe models that rely upon a combination of mechanisms for generating emotions. Finally, I will describe ways in which computers' emotions can interact with other processes, and begin to provide some of the beneficial influences that emotions exert in human decision-making, learning, behavior, and more. Along the way, I will illustrate each of these pieces with examples, including examples from the literature where they exist. The reader is referred to the overviews of Pfeifer (1988) and Hudlicka and Fellous (1996) for descriptions of additional efforts to implement various aspects of emotion synthesis in computers. I will also describe several pieces that have yet to be implemented by researchers, but which are nevertheless important for synthesizing emotion and its influences. Taken together, these pieces begin to fill in the framework needed to construct affective computers with the ability to synthesize emotions.

Emotion Synthesis via Cognitive Mechanisms

There are dozens of theories about how emotions are generated, some of which were mentioned earlier. Any emotion theory can be simulated on a computer. Indeed, the process of designing simulations is a valuable aid in developing theories, stimulating new thinking and questions. I will highlight two theories in this section that have been designed with computation in mind, and that have been given at least a trial implementation in computers. Each implements the third component of emotions—cognitively-generated—and thereby provides a key piece in the framework of affective computing.

The Ortony Clore Collins (OCC) Cognitive Model

The first theory that I will describe for emotion synthesis was never intended to be used for emotion synthesis. Nonetheless it is useful for synthesizing cognitive emotions. In 1988 Ortony, Clore and Collins published their book, *The Cognitive Structure of Emotions*, setting forth a model of cognitive appraisal for emotions that has come to be called the "OCC" model. Ortony et al. wrote that they did not think it was important for machines to have emotions; however, they believed AI systems must be able to *reason about* emotions— especially for natural language understanding, cooperative problem solving, and planning. Some structure was needed so computers could begin to represent the thicket of concepts considered to be emotions.

The OCC model addresses the problem of representing emotions not by using sets of basic emotions, or by using an explicitly dimensioned space, but, by grouping emotions according to cognitive eliciting conditions. In particular, it assumes that emotions arise from valenced (positive or negative) reactions to situations consisting of events, agents, and objects. With this structure, Ortony, Clore, and Collins outlined specifications for 22 emotion types, as given in the boxes along the bottom of Fig. 7.1. Additionally, they included a rule-based system for the generation of these emotion types.

Although the OCC model has not been fully implemented in any AI systems, it was the first model to cater to the AI community in terms of framing rules that are relatively easy to implement in computers. Despite the original intentions of Ortony et al. it has also become the default model for *synthesizing* emotions in computers, even though it only addresses cognitive emotion generation. Let us consider an example, how the emotion joy is synthesized in the OCC model:

Synthesis of Joy. Let $D(p, e, t)$ be the desirability of event e that person p assigns at time t. This function returns a positive value if the event is expected to have beneficial consequences, and returns a negative value if the event is expected to have harmful consequences. Let $I_g(p, e, t)$ represent a combination of global intensity variables (e.g., expectedness, reality, proximity.) Let $P_j(p, e, t)$ be the potential for generating a state of joy. Then an example rule for joy is:

IF $D(p, e, t) > 0$

THEN set $P_j(p, e, t) = f_j(D(p, e, t), I_g(p, e, t))$ (7.1)

where $f_j()$ is a function specific to joy.

Similar rules can be used for computing potentials for other emotions. For example, the potential for distress, $P_d()$, is computed by changing the "IF" to test for negative desirability, and the "THEN" to use a suitable f_d instead of f_j.

The rule above does not cause a state of joy or an experience of a joy feeling, but is used to trigger another rule that sets up an intensity of joy, I_j. Given a threshold value, T_j, then:

IF $P_j(p, e, t) > T_j(p, t)$

THEN set $I_j(p, e, t) = P_j(p, e, t) - T_j(p, t)$ (7.2)

ELSE set $I_j(p, e, t) = 0$

This rule activates the joy emotion—giving it a nonzero intensity—when the joy threshold is exceeded. The resulting intensity can be mapped to one of a variety of emotion terms in the joy family, such as "pleased" for a moderate value or "euphoric" for an unusually high value.

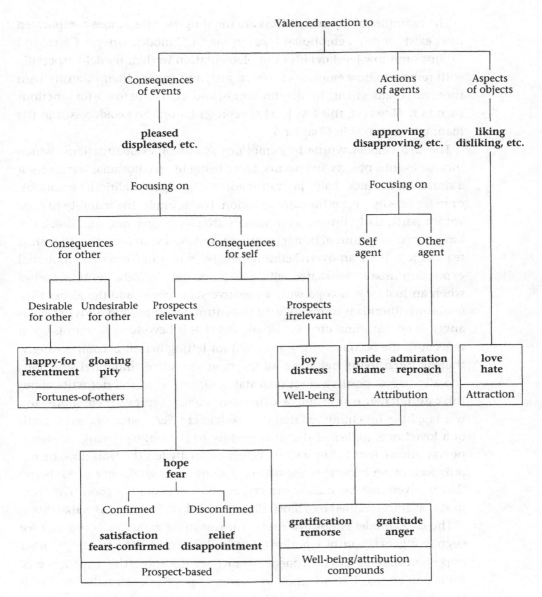

Figure 7.1
The OCC cognitive structure of emotions. (Reprinted from Fig. 2.1 of Ortony, Clore, and Collins (1988) with permission from Cambridge University Press.)

The examples of joy and distress are the simplest cases; more complicated rules exist for other emotional types in the OCC model. Ortony, Clore, and Collins omit low-level details of implementation in their model—especially with respect to how emotions interact, mix, and change their intensity with time, what values to use for the thresholds, and what form to use for functions such as f_j. However, this low level of representation can be addressed in the manner I described in Chapter 5.

The OCC model synthesizes emotions as outcomes of situations, which include events, objects and agents. Since being in an emotional state is itself a situation, the model also permits emotions to trigger additional emotions, or to repeatedly trigger the same emotion. For example, the inability to cope with a particularly intense emotional state can trigger new emotions: the long-hoped-for return of hostages causes loved ones such relief that they shed tears of joy. Thus, an overwhelming positive state can trigger an emotional expression usually associated with a negative state. Another example arises when an inability to cope with a negative state causes additional negative emotions: Rhonda is trying to learn to control her anger, and finds herself as angry as ever at something somebody did that is beyond her control. Upon reflection, she becomes angry at herself for letting herself become so angry, thereby intensifying her anger all the more. Negative emotional situations can also trigger positive emotional states. Ortony et al. did not write about this case, but here is an example: Chris has difficulty expressing emotions, and was taught in his childhood that it is weak to cry. Years later, upon the death of a loved one, he learns that it is healthy to cry while grieving. However, he has trouble letting himself cry. When he finally lets the tears flow, he not only feels better because of the release of some of his grief, but he feels better that he overcame his inability to cry. His tears feel doubly good. The OCC model as implemented by Elliott, illustrated below, handles cases like this.

The OCC model is not just useful for reasoning about emotions and for cognitive generation of emotions, but it also can be used to trigger other important emotional consequences—such as the subjective experience of feeling an emotion, or an emotional valence, positive or negative, to attach to a situation, so that it is more likely to be recalled when the person is in a mood congruent with that valence. As described earlier, these are important aspects of emotions in humans; I will say more about implementing them later.

Poker-Playing Agents with Facial Expressions
Earlier I described the success of using facial expressions on poker-playing software agents, and Koda's results which indicated that people preferred to play with the agent that was facially expressive. The emphasis in these

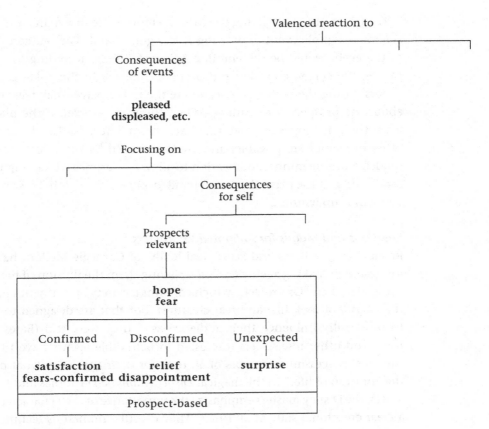

Figure 7.2
Structure used to synthesize emotional states in poker-playing agents. (Figure from Koda (1996), used by permission.)

experiments was not on emotion synthesis, but rather on generating facial expressions in situations where an underlying emotion model determined what would be expressed. However, Koda's work provides a relatively simple situation for illustrating how emotions can be synthesized using the OCC model.

Ten emotional expressions were permitted for each agent: neutral, pleased, displeased, excited (hope), very excited (hope), anxious (fear), satisfied, disappointed, surprised, and relieved. The underlying emotional states were determined with a modified subset of the OCC model, as shown in Fig. 7.2. Although the poker scenario could use the full model, Koda limited this experiment to emotions provoked only by events that have self-consequences. This particular branch of the OCC model was then augmented by adding a surprise state (such as when a player wins unexpectedly) since the OCC model does not include surprise.[2]

The poker situations giving rise to each emotion are shown in Fig. 7.3. Consider an example event of drawing a very good hand. The self-consequence of the event would be the emotion "pleased." Next, according to the OCC model, the person considers prospects for himself. In the poker game, this occurs during the betting phase, where the poker player may feel "excited" about the prospects of winning. When the game is over, if the player has won, then his hopes are confirmed and he may feel "satisfied." Of course, other outcomes are possible, and are determined by the rules of the OCC model, with the minor modification to allow for surprise which might occur, for example, if the player has a bad hand, decides not to bluff, bets anxiously, and winds up winning.

Emotions and Moods for Animated Characters

Researchers Joe Bates and Scott Neal Reilly, of Carnegie Mellon, have been interested in making agents *believable*, giving them the illusion of life. This is the goal of their "Oz project," which contains a variety of synthetic characters that may not look like any real creatures, but that are designed to be able to powerfully influence their audience as if they were real (Bates, 1994). Bates and other researchers interested in believable agents have turned to the most successful animators of all time for their answer to what provides the "illusion of life." In the magical *Disney Animation* (Thomas and Johnson, 1981), the Disney masters emphasize the importance of each character having a clear emotional state at all times. They describe numerous techniques for accomplishing this, arguing that the portrayal of emotions is what gives the Disney characters the illusion of life.

Inspired by the Disney animators, Bates and his colleagues have created emotions for their animated creatures, together with a host of tools that assist artists in building emotions for characters. One of their creatures is a house cat named Lyotard, which has a large repertoire of emotions and corresponding behaviors. For example, Lyotard can *hope* to be fed, and can be *pleased* when food is provided, and might *purr* or *rub against someone* when it is happy. The underlying emotion generation system for the Oz characters is "Em," which is part of a broad architecture called "Tok." The full architecture integrates not just emotions, but also rudimentary perception, goal-directed behavior, and language. A description of Lyotard and the Tok architecture is provided by Bates (1992). The focus of our interest is on Em, which generates the emotions for Lyotard and other characters.

Em is equipped with a default emotion system that is based on the OCC model, and hence emphasizes cognitive appraisal for emotion generation. Em is also augmented with mechanisms for generating some primary emotions, such as startle, although the way it is implemented is not distinguished

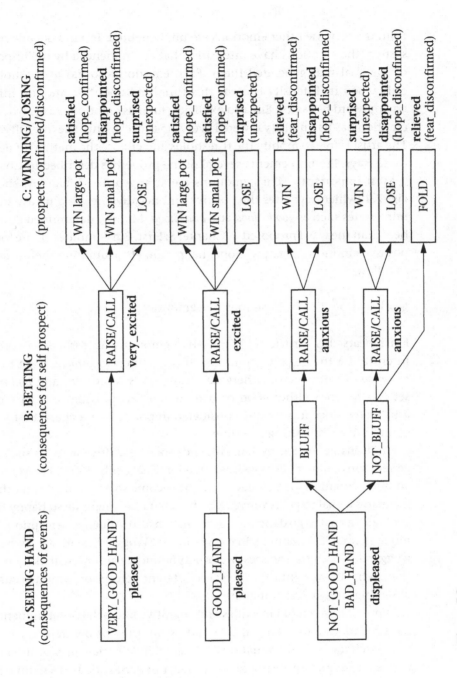

Figure 7.3
Agents emotions are generated according to these poker events. (Figure from Koda (1996), used by permission.)

from the way the other emotions are implemented. In Em's default emotion system, the emotions have intensities that are influenced by the importance of the goal that generated them. Each emotion also has a threshold, and only when its intensity exceeds this threshold does the emotion influence any outward behavior. Em also explicitly models emotion decay, where each emotion has its intensity lowered every clock cycle, until the intensity is zero. The artist is free to modify the thresholds and choose the method of decay. In these ways, Em implements several of the properties described in Chapter 5.

Most importantly, Em's emotions are arranged in a hierarchy, shown in Fig. 7.4, which separates the positive and negative, making it easy to determine states such as *good-mood* and *bad-mood*. Mood is determined differently here than the way I proposed in Chapter 5: First, Em combines all the top-level positive emotions, e.g., joy, hope, happy-for, etc., summing their intensities as follows:

$$I_p = \log_2 \left(\sum_e 2^{I_e} \right), \qquad e \in \{\text{positive emotions}\}$$

Em repeats this for the set of negative emotions, to form I_n, a combined intensity for the negative emotions. If $I_p > I_n$ then *good-mood* is set to I_p and *bad-mood* is set to zero. Otherwise *good-mood* is set to zero and *bad-mood* is set to $-I_n$. The "either good or bad" mood this provides is a wise default artistically, since it is usually considered important for a character to clearly communicate one thing at a time.

Emotions generated by Em influence some cognitive activity such as the generation of new goals as well as behavior (Neal Reilly, 1996). For example, in an office situation, one character might become so angry at another that she generates a goal to get revenge. Another character might be so happy that he generates a goal to go dancing. Emotions can also influence perception. This is implemented, for example, in the graphical "Woggles" characters, where one woggle that is angry and sees two others bouncing around will likely perceive their behavior as fighting, whereas a different perception would occur if the observing woggle was not angry.

At present, much of Em's rules and cognitive and behavioral influences are hard-coded and are changed by hand by an artist or programmer to adapt to new characters and situations. These include social rules of interaction, which one might argue should be learned, not hard-coded, in a natural model of emotions. However, in the Oz project, a goal is to give the artist deliberate control over the character and its development. If rules and emotional influences were to be learned, then the artist would lose some of this control. Nonetheless, the fact that the Oz characters have social interactions that both influence and are influenced by emotions is an important step.

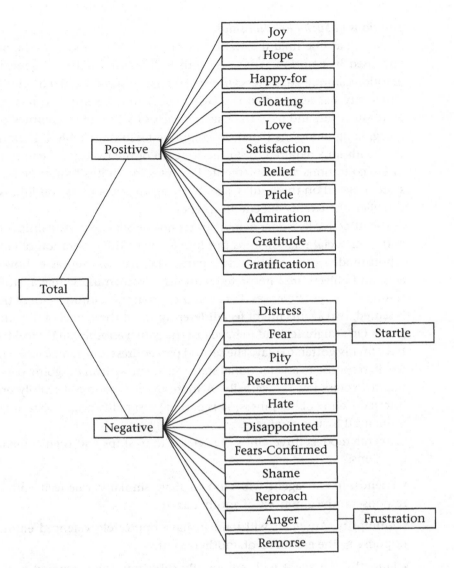

Figure 7.4
The default hierarchy of emotions in Em. (Reprinted from Figure 4-1 of Neal Reilly, 1996, by permission.)

One of the points to remember in emotion synthesis is that emotions do not completely determine actions—they only influence them. Other factors such as the type of creature and environment (e.g., aggressive wolf in the wild vs. nerd on the playground), its personality characteristics, its values, and so forth, work with emotions to influence behavior. The Tok and Em architectures provide tools for artists to manipulate these many influences.

Emotions in Social Relationships

Let's look at one final illustration of how the OCC model can be modified and used in emotion synthesis, with a different emphasis—generation of emotions among characters with social relationships. Clark Elliott of DePaul University has augmented the OCC model from twenty-two to twenty-six emotion types, and used these as the basis of a system for synthesizing and recognizing emotions based on cognitive reasoning. Table 7.1 summarizes the conditions required to synthesize each of the twenty-six emotion types. These conditions are implemented as rules in Elliott's "Affective Reasoner" system. Based on these rules, a software agent encounters conditions which can elicit the twenty-six emotion types.

The Affective Reasoner demonstrates how modeling personalities of agents and their social relationships can interact with the generation of emotions. Elliott models personality in two parts. The first part addresses how events, acts, and objects are interpreted with respect to an individual agent's goals, standards, and preferences. For example, when the winning shot of the game is scored, two agents might feel differently about the arrival of the end of the game. One might feel sad to have lost the game; another might feel happy to have finally gotten to play. The second part addresses how an agent will act or feel in response to an emotional state. An agent with an outgoing personality might express her joy verbally. A more quiet type might simply enjoy an internal feeling of happiness. This part of personality might be thought of as influenced by temperament.

Agents models three kinds of social relationships and their influences on emotions:

- Friendship. An agent will tend to have similarly valenced emotions in response to the emotions of another agent.

- Animosity. An agent will tend to have oppositely valenced emotions in response to the emotions of another agent.

- Empathy. An agent will temporarily substitute the presumed goals, standards, and preferences of another agent for its own. It will then synthesize emotions based on these presumed goals, standards and preferences, in an effort to feel what it thinks the other agent would feel.

In order for an agent to have empathy, and other emotions based on users and other agents, it maintains an internal representation of the presumed ways in which others appraise the world. This internal representation allows it not only to generate empathic responses, but also to generate fortunes-of-others emotions such as gloating. As I described earlier, responses such as empathy are key components of emotional intelligence.

Table 7.1
Emotion types used in the Affective Reasoner, based on the OCC model. (Table courtesy of Clark Elliott.)

Group	Specification	**Name** and Emotion Type
Well-being	appraisal of a situation as an *event*	**joy**: pleased about an *event* **distress**: displeased about an *event*
Fortunes-of-others	presumed value of situation as an *event* affecting another	**happy-for**: pleased about an *event* desirable for another **gloating**: pleased about an *event* undesirable for another **resentment**: displeased about an *event* desirable for another **jealousy**: resentment over a desired mutually exclusive goal. **envy**: resentment over a desired non-exclusive goal. **sorry-for**: displeased about an *event* undesirable for another
Prospect-based	appraisal of a situation as a prospective *event*	**hope**: pleased about a prospective desirable *event* **fear**: displeased about a prospective undesirable *event*
Confirmation	appraisal of a situation as confirming or disconfirming an expectation	**satisfaction**: pleased about a confirmed desirable *event* **relief**: pleased about a disconfirmed undesirable *event* **fears-confirmed**: displeased about a confirmed undesirable *event* **disappointment**: displeased about a disconfirmed desirable *event*
Attribution	appraisal of a situation as an accountable *act* of some agent	**pride**: approving of one's own *act* **admiration**: approving of another's *act* **shame**: disapproving of one's own *act* **reproach**: disapproving of another's *act*
Attraction	appraisal of a situation as containing an attractive or unattractive *object*	**liking**: finding an *object* appealing **disliking**: finding an *object* unappealing
Well-being / attribution	compound emotions	**gratitude**: admiration + joy **anger**: reproach + distress **gratification**: pride + joy **remorse**: shame + distress
Attraction / attribution	compound emotion extensions	**love**: admiration + liking **hate**: reproach + disliking

To illustrate the influence of social relationships on emotions, consider the following dialog between two agents (Elliott, 1994):

```
(The agent has previously learned that the word "Ruth" is a
female friend of the user)

User: "Ruth is unhappy"
Agent: "I am sorry to hear that. You must feel sorry for her."
```

(days later)

```
Agent: "How is Ruth?"
User: "Ruth is jealous of her rival."
Agent: "How much is Ruth feeling this resentment?"
User: "Very much."
Agent: "Perhaps you are worried about Ruth?"
```

Elliott acknowledges that the discourse here is not terribly engaging; instead, the emphasis is on reasoning about emotions within a social context. In this scenario, the agent reasons that since the user and Ruth are friends, and Ruth is sad, then it is plausible that the user feels *sorry-for* her. This is an instance of the emotion type "pity" in the OCC model. Similarly, the Affective Reasoner knows that jealousy maps to the negative emotion type "resentment" and that when Ruth is in a highly-negative state, a friend might be *worried* about her. In the OCC structure, the emotion type "fear" contains the emotion "worried" as a low-intensity instance.

Two other significant aspects of the Affective Reasoner are (1) Its forward logic-based reasoning from presumed appraisals, and events, to guesses about the emotions of others, and (2) Its backward, case-based, reasoning from facts about the situation and expressions of other agents, to the presumed emotions of other agents, and hence to the presumed appraisals of other agents. An agent might ask, "What cases do I have on file for THIS agent? for agents LIKE this agent? for agents in general?" and lastly, "how would *I* feel if these tokens were present?" These aspects are important for giving computers the ability to recognize emotions, not based on patterns of expressions as I described in the last chapter, but based on higher-level reasoning about how circumstances tend to give rise to emotion.

Roseman's Cognitive Appraisal Model

One of the newest appraisal theories, which shows promise for computer implementation of cognitive emotions, is that of Ira Roseman, at Rutgers University. Roseman has developed a categorization of the appraisals people make about events that cause emotions. Roseman and his colleagues have

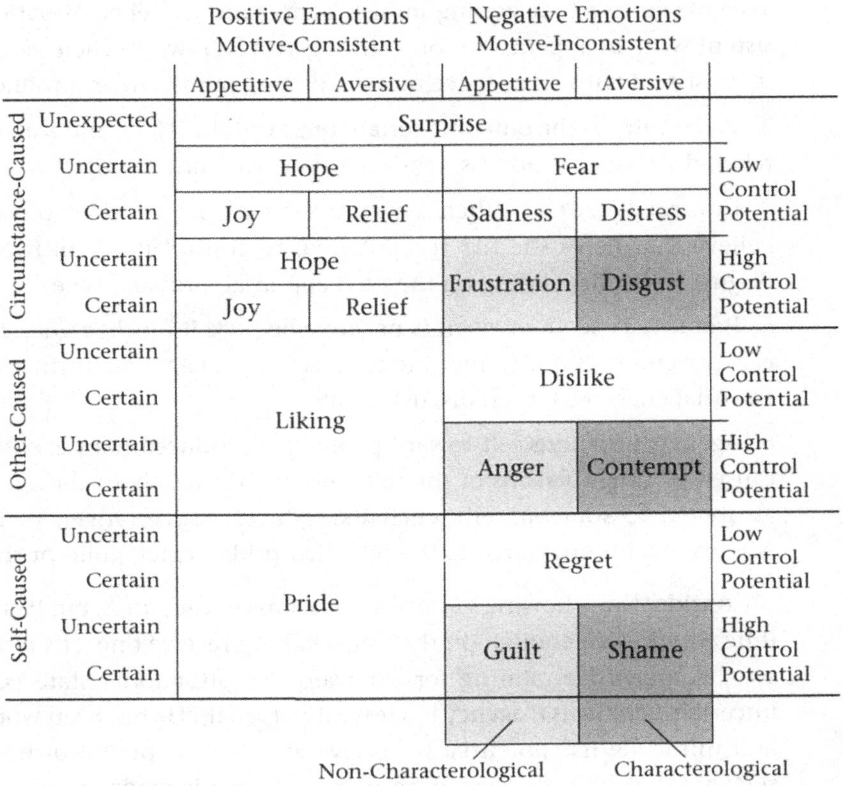

		Positive Emotions Motive-Consistent		Negative Emotions Motive-Inconsistent		
		Appetitive	Aversive	Appetitive	Aversive	
Circumstance-Caused	Unexpected	Surprise				
	Uncertain	Hope		Fear		Low Control Potential
	Certain	Joy	Relief	Sadness	Distress	
	Uncertain	Hope		Frustration	Disgust	High Control Potential
	Certain	Joy	Relief			
Other-Caused	Uncertain	Liking		Dislike		Low Control Potential
	Certain					
	Uncertain			Anger	Contempt	High Control Potential
	Certain					
Self-Caused	Uncertain	Pride		Regret		Low Control Potential
	Certain					
	Uncertain			Guilt	Shame	High Control Potential
	Certain					

Non-Characterological   Characterological

Figure 7.5
Roseman's structure for cognitively elicited emotions. (Reprinted from Fig. 2 of Roseman, Antoniou, and Jose (1996) with permission.)

run a series of studies in which subjects either recalled emotional experiences and answered questions designed to measure the appraisals leading up to the emotions, or in which subjects read brief stories of situations happening to protagonists, and answered questions about what emotion they thought the protagonist would feel, and its intensity. From these studies, Roseman and his colleagues constructed a model in which a small number of appraisals interact to give rise to seventeen emotions (Roseman, Antoniou, and Jose 1996). The six appraisals are summarized in Fig. 7.5; they are:

1. Unexpectedness. This singularly elicits surprise.

2. Motivational State and Situational State. Does the individual aim to get a reward (appetitive motive) or to avoid a punishment (aversive motive), and does the situation fit the person's motive? Situations consistent with an appetitive motive (getting a reward) elicit joy; situations consistent with an

aversive motive (not getting punishment) produce relief. Situations inconsistent with an appetitive motive (not getting a reward) elicit sadness; those inconsistent with an aversive motive (getting punishment) produce distress.

3. Probability. Is the outcome certain or uncertain? Hope and fear, unlike joy, relief, distress, and sadness, tend to follow from uncertainty.

4. Control Potential. When a negative event occurs, does the individual believe that he or she has the potential to control it? If so, frustration or disgust result, depending on the next appraisal, problem type.

5. Problem Type. If an event is negative because it blocks a goal, frustration is experienced. But if something is perceived as negative intrinsically (in its essential character), then disgust results.

6. Agency. Emotions felt toward people are produced if an event is seen as caused by other persons or the self, and one thinks about the agent. Events attributed to someone else elicit liking-love, dislike, anger, or contempt, whereas events attributed to the self elicit pride, regret, guilt, or shame.

Consider the following example: John aims to earn an A, but it is uncertain if he will do well enough on the final exam to receive one. His motivational state is appetitive, aiming for a reward. His situational state is presently uncertain. The causal agency is a test (impersonal). He has been working hard and thinks he has potential to receive an A. His appraisal of his situation suggests that he feels *hope*. If he then receives his grade and it is not an A (motive-inconsistent), then he may feel *frustration*. If he feels that his failure on the test was due to the professor grading him unfairly, then he is likely to feel *anger* toward that professor.

This model suggests that appraisals are influenced by shifts in attention. If Jill wants an A and gets one, she may focus on the A and feel joy. Or, she may think about the teacher and feel liking for him, or she may focus on what she accomplished, herself, and feel pride. Teaching a computer what to attend to is another open research problem. In people, attention is influenced by emotion—for example anger can focus attention on the object of the anger. Such cognitive-affective interactions are included in the fifth component of an emotion system.

The Roseman model is appealing for its simplicity and grounding in studies of human appraisals.[3] One limitation is that it does not address complex situations where multiple appraisals may be made. For example, if John thought that his teacher had designed an unfair test *and* that he himself was not prepared for the exam, then there would be two separate agencies, and it is unclear what he would feel—perhaps a mixture of anger and guilt. Nonetheless, the model provides a structure that could potentially be adapted to this case. Overall, it shows promise for implementation in a computer, for both reasoning about emotion generation, and for generating emotions based on cognitive appraisals.

Emotion Synthesis via Multiple Mechanisms

The OCC and Roseman theories provide a rule-based mechanism for cognitive generation of emotions. The three examples I showed adapted the OCC model so that it could not only be used to reason about emotions, but also to synthesize affective states, to provoke emotional expressions, and in some cases, to prompt influences on a character's behavior, perception, and subsequent cognitions. The mechanisms used for all of this were relatively high-level, involving rule-based and case-based reasoning.

In humans, emotions are generated not only by explicit reasoning, but also by low-level noncognitive influences. We loosely referred to these as "physical" aspects early in the book, since they tend to be more easily associated with bodily phenomena than with mental phenomena. These aspects may only map metaphorically into non-embodied agents, but they are nonetheless relevant for mobile robots and other autonomous characters that at least simulate physical interactions with their environments. This section describes three models which encompass not only cognitive reasoning for generating emotion, but also additional low-level mechanisms, inspired by the human emotion system.

Four Elicitors for Emotion Synthesis

Carroll Izard (Izard, 1993) proposed that there are four types of elicitors of emotion in humans. These have inspired a new connectionist model of emotion synthesis, "Cathexis," developed by Juan Velásquez of MIT (Velásquez, 1996). The four elicitors in this model are:

- *Neural.* Effect of neurotransmitter and other neurochemical processes. These processes run independently, in the background, and are influenced by hormones, sleep, diet, depression medication, etc.

- *Sensorimotor.* Effect of posture, facial expression, muscular tension, and other central efferent activity. These effects primarily intensify a given emotional state, but in some cases appear to be capable of generating new affective states.

- *Motivational.* Effect of sensory provocations such as anger provoked by pain, of drives such as hunger, and emotions evoking each other.

- *Cognitive.* Effect of cortical reasoning, implemented here via an adaptation of Roseman's theory.

Cathexis consists of a constellation of proto-specialists, like Minsky's agents in the Society of Mind (Minsky, 1985). Each proto-specialist represents a basic emotion type, which receives inputs from the four elicitors, as well as from other proto-specialists. Each proto-specialist can exert influence on output behaviors, for example, joy, with intensity above its activation threshold, can produce a smile. Each can exert influence on other proto-specialists, for example, joy can inhibit distress, and activate hope. Since proto-specialists are used to implement both emotional and non-emotional states, it is easy for emotions to interact with physical states; for example, sorrow increases fatigue and decreases hunger. The result is a distributed connectionist-flavor model that can synthesize a variety of emotions simultaneously.

In contrast to the OCC model, where the structure of the rules varies for each emotion, the Cathexis model has only one update rule. The rule contains terms that take on values specific to proto-specialists, but otherwise the form is the same for every proto-specialist's emotion intensity. At each time t, each proto-specialist $p = 1 \ldots P$ updates its emotional intensity $I_p(t)$ as follows. Let $\varepsilon_{p,i}$, $i = 1, 2, 3, 4$ be the values contributed to proto-specialist p by the four elicitors.[4] Let $\alpha_{p,m}$ be the excitatory gain applied by proto-specialist m to proto-specialist p. Let $\beta_{p,m}$ be the inhibitory gain applied by proto-specialist m to proto-specialist p. Finally, let f be a function that controls the temporal decay of an emotion intensity, and let g be a function that constrains the emotion intensity to lie between zero and its saturation value. The new intensity is then a function of its decayed previous value, its elicitors, and influences from other emotion intensities:

$$I_p(t) = g\left(f(I_p(t-1)) + \sum_{l=1}^{4} \epsilon_{p,l} + \sum_{m=1}^{P} (\alpha_{p,m} - \beta_{p,m}) I_m(t) \right).$$

As in the OCC model, the intensity is compared to an emotion-specific activation threshold before determining if an emotion exists. Only if the intensity exceeds the activation threshold does the proto-specialist release its value to influence the behavior system and other proto-specialists. In addition, each proto-specialist has a saturation threshold. When the intensity exceeds this threshold, then it stops increasing. Mechanisms such as this contribute to the nonlinear behavior of this model. Temperaments are encoded in Cathexis via these thresholds, the parameters α and β, and the decay rate chosen for f. For example, an excitable temperament would be modeled as having lower activation thresholds; it would take smaller levels of stimuli to activate its emotions.

Emotion intensities above a certain threshold are allowed to influence a "behavior system," which is responsible for both emotional behavior and emotional experience. The behavior system consists of a network of behaviors such as "make a fearful facial expression," and "run away." Each behavior consists of two components: an expression (e.g., smile) and an experience (e.g., feel happier). The experience implemented here can be thought of as the first aspect of emotional experience only; it does not implement sensations like human feelings. Emotional behaviors compete for control, with the value of each behavior determined by a linear combination of "releasing mechanisms," an ethological concept that includes internal motivations and drives, emotions, and external stimuli such as presence of friend or foe. For example, a combination of "anger" and "foe present" might release the "bite person" behavior.

Velásquez has implemented the Cathexis model in a scenario with "Simon the toddler." Simon is a synthetic agent representing a human toddler. Simon has proto-specialists for six basic emotions: fear, anger, sadness, happiness, disgust, and surprise, and for five drives: hunger, thirst, fatigue (need to rest and sleep), interest (need to explore and play), and temperature regulation. Different thresholds, excitatory and inhibitory gains, and decay rates can be chosen for each emotion to customize Simon's temperament. Cathexis provides the first complete example of a computational system that incorporates at least an approximation of all the major types of mechanisms known to be involved in human emotion synthesis. It is an important first step toward development of a complete computational emotion system.

A Three-Layer Architecture

Aaron Sloman, a philosopher at the University of Birmingham in the U.K., was one of the first to write to the computer science community about computers having emotions (Sloman, 1981). Sloman, assisted by students and colleagues, notably Luc Beaudoin, Ian Wright, and Brian Logan, has proposed and refined an architecture for human-like emotions. This architecture has not been thoroughly implemented and evaluated in computers; however, it has several features that make it relevant to affective computing, and especially to emotion synthesis.

Sloman conjectures that adult humans have at least three architectural layers in their brains: a reactive layer, a deliberative layer, and a self-monitoring layer. These three layers can be categorized loosely according to their evolutionary age—oldest to newest—and according to their functional similarity with other animals. An animal with just a reactive layer would have a tendency toward simple predictable behavior. For example, it might always run when it sees light, giving the impression of a "fear" behavior. In Sloman's architecture, the reactive layer detects things in its environment, and executes fairly automatic processes to determine how to react. Although the automatic processes could in theory represent sophisticated behaviors, their speed and relatively "hard-wired" nature make them better suited for responses that need to be rapid and that rarely need to be modified. The reactive layer is capable of some simple learning; however, it is not able to construct or evaluate plans. Emotions such as startle and disgust are likely to be generated by this layer.

The deliberative layer is capable of planning, evaluating options, making decisions, and allocating resources. The emotions involved in goal-success or goal-failure, i.e., those which are cognitively assessed, are also found in this layer. This includes, for example, the poker-playing agent who is pleased at winning with a good hand. The deliberative layer is also capable of learning generalizations which, once reliably mastered, can be transferred to the reactive layer. Despite the flexibility of the deliberative layer, its performance can still be improved by a higher layer that monitors the long-term impact of its functioning.

The third layer, self-monitoring meta-management, prevents certain goals from interfering with each other, and can look for more efficient ways for the deliberative layer to operate, choose strategies, and allocate its resources. Sloman suggests that emotions associated with this layer might include shame, humiliation, and grief. In particular, use of this architecture for modeling grief has been explored (Wright, Sloman, and Beaudoin, 1995). One of the interesting phenomena that this architecture tries to explain is that of *perturbance*, whereby thoughts, previously rejected or postponed, resurface and interrupt your attention. For example, during grief, thoughts of the lost object of affection frequently perturb one's thinking. At the loss of a beloved friend, your thoughts are repeatedly interrupted to think about him or her.

The three-layer architecture is a potential model for emotion synthesis that compares favorably with findings in the neurological, psychological, and cognitive science communities. Its reactive layer would be where the "fast primary" emotions arise. These are the innate, hard-wired, or "compiled" processes, which execute without prior conscious cognitive appraisal. In humans and a variety of other animals, these functions reside in parts of the limbic system and lower brain stem. For example, disgust, as expressed on the face when something vile is placed on one's lips, occurs even in an infant born with only a brain stem, who does not survive long after birth. Moving up to the deliberative layer, we can make a correspondence with Damasio's so-called "secondary" emotions. These are the cognitively-generated emotions which typically require some kind of cortical reasoning about goals, situations, objects, and events. When either primary or secondary emotions arise, they can activate reactive processes which, in the human, would probably involve the amygdala, which subsequently activates bodily responses comprising the physical aspects of an emotional experience. The third layer, meta-management, is the only layer where the notion of "self" is significant. Consequently, it is reasonable to hypothesize that it is where the "self-conscious" emotions such as shame, guilt, and embarrassment are likely to arise. These are the highly cognitive emotions, which appear to develop in childhood after the notion of self is intact. They are also more social, taking into account how people evaluate one another.

Although the three-layer architecture lacks details of implementation, it illustrates the need I have argued for multiple levels of models in emotion synthesis, including both low-level primary mechanisms and higher-level cognitive ones. In particular, it illustrates the need for a higher "self-monitoring" process for management of emotions. The latter is a crucial piece of a system if it is to develop the skills of emotional intelligence for regulating and wisely using its emotions.

Emotions, Hormones, and Homeostasis

Emotion synthesis raises questions about low-level "bodily" processes, because human emotions involve both the body and the mind. Even though computers do not have bodies like ours, they can simulate human bodily systems. Let's look at a model that explicitly simulates physiological changes relevant to emotion synthesis.

Dolores Cañamero, at the Free University of Brussels, has built a system in which emotions trigger changes in synthetic hormones, and in which emotions can arise as a result of simulated physiological changes (Cañamero, 1997). This system is part of a simulated two-dimensional world, with inhabitants called "Abbotts" and "Enemies." The Enemies do not have emotions in the present system, but some of the Abbott's behaviors, motivations and emotions are designed to deal with the Enemies. Each Abbott's behaviors, motivations, and emotions have corresponding physiological implications. In particular, the motivations are intended to be homeostatic. For example, when an Abbott walks around (behavior) its temperature increases, and when the Abbott is too warm (motivation) it seeks to decrease its temperature. Other Abbott behaviors include: attack, withdraw, drink, eat, play, and rest. Other Abbott motivations include: aggression, self-protection, thirst, hunger, curiosity, and fatigue. Each motivation has an intensity, and the one with the highest intensity gets to control both the Abbott's behavior, and what it attends to.

Motivation intensity, and therefore behaviors, are influenced by the Abbotts' emotions. Abbotts have six basic emotions: fear, anger, sadness, happiness, boredom, and interest. Emotions can be triggered by external events, or they can be triggered by internal physiological changes or patterns. For example, fear is triggered if an enemy is present, resulting in increased heart rate and lower temperature. Alternatively, higher levels of endorphines can trigger a state of happiness. Emotions also influence perception; for example, a state of high endorphines reduces the perception of pain.

Cañamero's system illustrates the ability of a computer to simulate physiological elicitors of emotion, as well as emotion's influence on physiology. Such simulations, to the extent that they try to imitate human and other animal systems, are an important way to learn more about emotion synthesis and the influences of emotion. Additionally, we might make comparisons between functions of human physiological systems and functions of computer operating systems, such as the different ways in which both systems try to avoid intruding viruses, or the different ways in which both kinds of systems perform various regulatory functions.

Synthesizing Emotion's Influences

The focus in the previous section was on mechanisms for emotion synthesis, including both cognitive and non-cognitive elicitors. In this section I describe models for synthesizing emotion's interaction with other processes in the computer, specifically, how it can be used to realize multiple concerns, influence learning and behavior, and bias memory retrieval and decision-making. These interactions primarily address the fifth component of a system that has emotions.

Realizing Multiple Concerns

Human emotions play an important role in motivation and in helping people make decisions that realize their many concerns. Several researchers have suggested that emotions are manifestations of a system that realizes multiple concerns and operates with limited resources in an unpredictable environment. This principle is increasingly relevant for software agents and other computational devices that interact with people while trying to perform many tasks. Nico Frijda of Amsterdam University has set forth an appraisal theory of emotions based on this principle, which he describes in his book, *The Emotions* (Frijda, 1986). Let's look at an implementation of his theory to illustrate a way of building computer emotions to influence various regulatory processes.

Jaap Swagerman, a student of Frijda, has implemented a portion of Frijda's theory in the computer program ACRES, *Artificial Concern REalisation System*, (Frijda, 1987). ACRES' primary task is to handle knowledge about emotions while interacting with a user. It receives and accepts (or rejects) inputs from its user, such as the name of an emotion and its description. ACRES tries to learn about what causes emotions to be generated by having a user present it with thousands of scenarios, imitating how humans acquire knowledge by vicarious experience. Throughout this interaction, ACRES keeps track of its own internal emotional state, and can show this to the user if the user asks to see it.

ACRES has multiple concerns, and periodically examines the state of affairs to assess if any of its concerns need addressing. For example, if it has not learned anything new for a while, then its "vicarious learning concern" may trigger a request to the user for more input, so that ACRES can improve its emotional knowledge. For example, ACRES might ask the user if a recent interaction was attractive or aversive to the user. Later, if ACRES is given a new scenario, it will try to guess which emotion that scenario would cause, based on its similarity to the scenarios ACRES has learned.

Here are six concerns ACRES tries to satisfy:

1. Avoid being killed.

2. Preserve reasonable waiting times, i.e. respond promptly.

3. Receive correct input.

4. Receive varied ("interesting") input.

5. Safety (preserving the concepts in ACRE's concept-based structure).

6. Vicarious learning (from the user's experiences).

Ideally, the system should continuously evaluate the relevance of all events for all six concerns, in parallel, even during task-oriented activity. This requires hardware to support parallel processing, and is only simulated in a truncated manner in ACRES.

ACRES has to decide which concern to execute. This is done by giving each concern an importance index, with "avoid being killed" having the highest index. This index is not the only factor in determining which concern gets precedence; the gravity of the situation is also assessed: "how many times has the operator repeated his instruction?" and "what is the status of the operator—how well has he treated me?" These change during the interaction, so that it is difficult to predict which of the multiple concerns will first reach above-threshold relevance. When a concern becomes active, then information processing capacity and memory are used for setting up and executing actions to further that concern.

When one of its concerns is active, ACRES can react emotionally. For example, if ACRES detects an agent that repeatedly threatens its safety, and that does not heed ACRES's requests to stop, then ACRES becomes angry at that agent and may restrict its access permissions. In general, ACRES diagnoses the situation over time, generates an emotion, and chooses a meaningful action. In fact, "emotional," with its most juvenile connotations, is a suitable adjective for some of ACRES behavior. For example, ACRES will complain if the user types the wrong thing at it too many times. It can refuse to accept inputs if the user repeatedly mistreats it. It will also react with plaintive requests not to be killed if the user types "kill." ACRES' childish behaviors render it an unlikely prototype for the kind of affective computer any of us would want on our desk. It provides an example of a system that has emotions without having emotional intelligence.

Nonetheless, ACRES is an important testbed for exploring how emotions arise and influence behavior. In particular, ACRES demonstrates several important functions included in the fifth component of an emotion system: It uses emotion to juggle the demands of user requests with interrupting current tasks, with shifting resource allocation, and with initiating questions. Its use of emotions in these ways helps it realize multiple concerns and appraise relevance, potentially helping it choose more intelligent actions. ACRES illustrates that emotions are not just for entertainment, but that they can provide low-level regulatory functions needed by a system with limited resources and multiple goals operating in a complex and unpredictable environment.

Emotions Influencing Learning and Behavior

Emotions are hypothesized to provide the flexibility not present in traditional stimulus-response theories of learning. Mowrer and his colleagues, through many experiments, determined that learning is best thought of not as the single stage of stimulus-response, but as two stages, with the first involving the generation of an emotion (Mowrer, 1960). Consider a rat that learns to leave a box upon hearing a tone, after previously being presented with that tone paired with a painful shock. Mowrer's theory delineates two processes: (1) the rat learns *to fear* the tone and (2) the rat learns that leaving the box reduces his fear. The advantage of the two-process model is that it explains why, if a barrier prevents it from leaving the box, the rat will seek an alternate way to reduce its fear. The emotional state allows for more flexible learning, while simultaneously providing a source of motivation: fear drives the rat to explore methods of escape.

Implementing emotion's influence on learning is an important piece of implementing the fifth component of an emotion system. This piece can be illustrated by some of the work of Bruce Blumberg at the MIT Media Lab. Blumberg's animated dog, Silas T. Dog, does not have an explicit emotion model, emotional state, or mood, but its expressions and behavior are influenced by internal variables that represent emotions as well as other internal states such as hunger or thirst. Although Silas's emotions are simple and hard-wired, Silas has a key feature that has yet to be incorporated in the other models: the ability to learn, and in particular for his emotions to influence what he learns. Changes in Silas's internal variables drive a learning process. For example, if Silas sees something that scares him—increases his internal variable of fear—then he tries to determine which stimuli from his perceptual inputs and short-term memory are the best predictors of the change. This enables Silas to learn the association between a fear-causing stimulus and the ensuing emotion. Thus, he can learn new ways to behave, such as avoiding a place where he previously saw something that scared him.

One of the problems with building creatures that exhibit emotions is how to map emotional states to behaviors. As we saw, fear motivates the rat to find a means of escape, but it does not automatically tell it what means to pursue. Emotions motivate and bias behavior, they do not completely determine it. Silas's internal variables provide a biasing mechanism for his behavior. The variables have global effects, biasing or predisposing him to certain behaviors or actions, without determining these behaviors or actions. A behavior is most strongly influenced by "releasing mechanisms," which recognize and signal the presence of an event, such as food being placed nearby, or a foe coming into the vicinity. A releasing mechanism that detects food will probably cause a hungry Silas to approach, but if he is feeling fearful he will approach differently than if he is feeling happy. The difference caused by the emotions is seen in his bodily movements and posture, such as how he holds his head. The releasing mechanism prompts a behavior, and the internal variables of emotion bias how the behavior is executed.

Silas is a creature with multiple goals, needs, and behaviors, but with limited resources for acting and fulfilling his needs. Emotion arises when Silas's goals are furthered or thwarted. For example, if his goal of playing succeeds he feels happy. When he is happy, he also will be more inclined to want to play. The introduction of new objects and events in his environment cause these feelings to change. For example, when a hamster enters his room, he will feel more aggressive and pick up the hamster to shake it. His aggression is programmed to decrease as he shakes the hamster, or if a human agent in the perceived environment signals Silas to do something else. These emotion-behavior links are mostly hard-wired in Silas; a general framework for how to enable such links is an open research area.

Computer scientists can already build machines that learn, at least in some ways, without explicitly giving them emotions; however, giving them emotions appears to be a means to achieve multiple goals, only one of which is more flexible learning. A single emotion accomplishes many things at the same time. For example, a negative emotion that produces a bad feeling may trigger reassessment of what caused the bad feeling, followed by learning how to avoid it in the future. If, while learning, the machine predicts it will feel even worse if it does not forward you a piece of urgent and important news, then it might interrupt its own learning experience to get the news to you. Even negative emotions such as anger or frustration can be beneficial to a system—helping it focus on a goal, or triggering it to reassess a situation and look for a way to improve it. In other words, an emotional state produces internal control signals in a machine running several tasks at once, and can signal its attention when its time for a change. These same signals can influence not only learning, but also memory, perception, and many other important functions.

Affective Decision Making

One of the most intriguing influences of emotion in a human is on rational decision making. Flexible and intelligent decision making has been an elusive goal of AI researchers. Computer scientists have a trove of problems that exhibit combinatorial explosion—where one possibility opens up several new ones, each of which opens up several more new ones, and so forth. An efficient solution to such problems is the holy grail of computer science. On the other hand, humans solve intractable problems all the time, problems with an explosion of possible answers, where there is not time to evaluate them all. Furthermore, most human problems do not operate with a fixed numerable space of possibilities. In chess, the computer can describe which piece, if any, is at each of the 64 squares. Although, no computer can evaluate all the positions that could occur in the game, a number that is estimated to be greater than the number of atoms in the universe, a computer can at least characterize the space of such positions. In normal human situations, even the *space* of possibilities may change; the combinatorial explosion explodes again. Nonetheless, humans almost effortlessly make decisions that would stymie the world's fastest computers. Is it merely the case that we are that much better at pattern recognition, learning, and reasoning? There is no question we are better at certain tasks involving these tools, but I think that AI has ignored a crucial component that is even more basic to human problem-solving abilities: the use of feelings and intuition to guide reasoning and decision making. Let me suggest a model for emotion's influence on decision making by considering a scenario of a human making a personal decision.

Albert, a very busy scientist, has a beloved eight-week-old boy, and is trying to decide how to provide for his son while he works during the day. He does not know any family members or friends who could help. He acquires lists for three kinds of day care providers: a list of ten nanny-referral services, a list of 145 licensed family care providers, and a list of 24 day care centers located nearby. He contemplates posting notices in newspapers and on bulletin boards. Albert loves his son, and wants to choose the best care for him. He needs a care-provider within a month. Albert is a highly rational man; how does he decide what to do?

Here is what Albert says. I have inserted [good] or [bad] to emphasize the valence of several of his statements:

I thought of posting notices but you hear of so many wierdos out there these days [bad] that I thought it would be safer first to try the three lists I got, since they include licensed and trained providers [good]. I decided to consider all three types of care equally, since I hear that their quality is largely a function of the people involved.

Nannies. I do not want to give up my privacy and have a live-in nanny, but it would be great to have one come to my home during the day as this would be the most convenient [good]. I know nannies are expensive, about twice the price of the other options [bad]. The nanny-referral services want huge fees up front before you find anyone [bad]. Nonetheless, I am willing to pay more if I could find an outstanding nanny who would be with us for many years [good]. I am concerned about finding a nanny in four weeks, as I just went through a stack of old newspapers, reading "nanny wanted" ads and saw the same ads for the last three weeks [bad]. I have also heard several stories about nannies lately. There was a television special about nannies who abused or neglected the kids during the day [extremely bad]; their behavior was observed on hidden cameras. However, this probably made the news because it is rare; abuse could happen with any care provider. I am also concerned about stability, which is important to a child. One of the guys at work told me they were on their third nanny this year [very bad]; they once again hired someone who said she would stay for at least a year, and then she changed her mind. Let me check the other options before I go further with this one.

Family care. What a huge list; this will take forever [bad]. I'll skip this for now.

Center care. Some friends recommended a place nearby that they love [good]. I visited and thought the place was too institutional [bad]. Center care appeals to me because it is stable, the people have training and are licensed [good], and there is usually someone to back them up so they can take breaks. This probably reduces stress and the chance of abuse [very good]. They do character checks on their employees and I can confirm their history with state offices to verify that there are no reports of abuse [good]. I started calling all the centers on the list that took infants. None of them had immediate openings [bad]. I made appointments to visit all the ones that indicated they might have an opening within a month. One of the places I really like and two others were pretty nice. I paid the fees to get on three waiting lists.

Back to the list for family care. I know people who are very happy with family care providers [good]. These can be stable and stimulating [good] but they may lack training and support when there are complications [bad]. I started calling everyone on the list. About one in twelve had an opening for an infant within a month [good]. I inquired how many kids they had, the environment, their experience, their assistants, what they do during the day, and the hours they worked. Some of the providers I ruled out on the phone; one of them sounded more interested in money than in children. I made appointments with the best sounding ones and started visiting. Several of the homes had huge dogs, one which looked like it could swallow my son. I added "no big dogs" to my checklist of criteria.

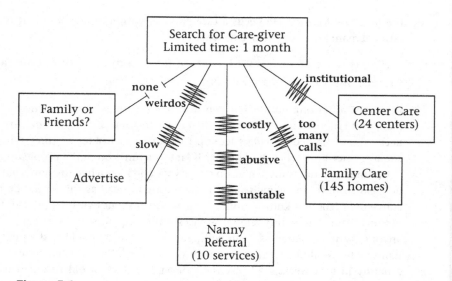

Figure 7.6
Initial consideration of child care options marks several possibilities with negative resistance due to bad associations.

Part of Albert's decision is illustrated in Fig. 7.6, where we see the five possibilities he considered, together with various "negative resistances" I have added to them, to model the valence associated with various pieces of the decision. For example, because he believed there were no family or friends who could help, this branch was effectively pruned off the tree of possibilities. Advertising met with two doses of negative resistance—fear of wierdos and fear that, like the ads he saw in the paper for so many weeks, his ad would go unfilled. The nanny option met with three pieces of negative resistance, and so forth. None of the negative resistances precluded further exploration of these options, but they biased him to first consider those associated with the fewest negative feelings.

Albert combined these valenced biases with many logical actions: he systematically gathered information about a variety of affordable options conveniently located in his town, ruled out those that did not take infants, ruled out those which were unavailable within the month, made appointments to meet people, visited the potential caregivers, learned about their environments and experience, and checked references. However, he did not logically find the best care, at least not in the sense of having weighed all the alternatives available to him. He did not generate all the possibilities, and did not have time to explore all the ones he did generate. Although the set of possibilities listed above looks manageable, in practice there were always others which could arise.

Furthermore, although he started with what he thought was his full list of criteria (full-time care, stability, etc.) this list did not forsee every criterion that would become important to him during the process, such as no big dogs. It was impossible to objectively state all the criteria up front; he discovered along the way what was most important to him. As he searched, he may have also learned of new possibilities—a great care-giver who could take his son four days a week; a wonderful neighbor who could help on the fifth day. In contrast, today's computers that conduct searches only guarantee optimal results if given precisely stated criteria, constraints, and a specific space to search.

Albert did not search all the possibilities, but he searched until he ran into either negative feelings or logical constraints, and then he stopped and tried something else. He continued this strategy—exploring possibilities that felt reasonable and good, and modifying his criteria as he accumulated more information. When he visited somebody and noted something new that resulted in a bad feeling, like the big dog, he added this to his criteria of things to avoid, crossed the site off his list, and continued with his search. Before his time ran out, he arrived at a decision that combined logical constraints with weighing the good and bad valences associated with his options. Emotions played an integral part not only in his final decision, but also in his process of gathering information.

To date, there are no computers with emotions that influence their decision making and other cognitive processes to the same degree that these influences are believed to occur in people. Nonetheless, computers could be given these abilities, especially when facing problems where the options cannot be fully explored. On the other hand, computers should not try to use affect for all decisions. There remain many problems involving possibilities that can be enumerated, where time permits a purely logical approach or a brute force search for finding the optimal solution. In such cases, computers are likely to be faster at finding the solutions than humans. There is no need to involve emotions in these kinds of problems, unless perhaps to contribute a positive feeling when the answer is found, which might reinforce the learning of that answer, if such a goal is desired.

Nevertheless, when a system faces problems where the possibilities cannot be enumerated and evaluated in the available time, I suggest that affective decision making provides a good solution. Humans use feelings to help them navigate the oceans of inquiry, to make decisions in the face of combinatorial complexity. These feelings might be called "intuition" or "a sense of knowing" or just "gut feelings." Regardless of what they are called, they provide a mechanism through which emotion works powerful influences on human cognition and behavior. People respond with remarkable intelligence and flexibility despite insufficient knowledge, limited memory, and relatively slow processing speed. An integral component of human decision making is emotion, and this component could potentially be given to computers.

Emotions that Interact with Memory

The same emotion that influences a person's learning and decision making also influences memory retrieval and a host of other cognitive processes. Scientists believe that emotional valence attaches to concepts, ideas, plans, and every experience stored in our memories. Good feelings likely encode knowledge of effectiveness, familiarity, opportunity, and associations with positive outcomes. Bad feelings likely encode knowledge of ineffectiveness, unfamiliarity, risk, and associations with bad outcomes. When it is time to make a decision, valenced feelings help bias a person away from bad outcomes, and toward good ones. As studies of patients with prefrontal brain damage show, these biasing mechanisms are apparently at work *before* declarative knowledge for reasoning is activated. Furthermore, without the help of these mechanisms, the person may not be able to behave in an advantageous way (Bechara, Damasio, Tranel and Damasio, 1997). In other words, these biasing mechanisms occur both before and during pattern recognition and reasoning, greatly influencing their effectiveness. Let us consider how such mechanisms might be constructed for computers.

Because memory is intricately involved in decision-making and almost every aspect of cognition, it may be that the way in which emotion works so many of its influences is via its influence on memory. The findings of Bower and Cohen (1982) on mood-congruent memory retrieval and learning have influenced several models for representing emotion-memory interactions and their impact on cognitive processes.[5] These include the FEELER model of Pfeifer and Nicholas (1985), and the DAYDREAMER model of Dyer and Mueller (Dyer, 1987; Mueller, 1990). The latter is not only able to perform reasoning about emotions, but it also uses the appraisal process to generate an internal emotional state that influences the system's planning, learning, recall, and production of hypothetical scenarios, or daydreams, exploiting the influences of mood-congruent memory retrieval.

Let's take a closer look at a model inspired both by the findings on mood-congruent memory retrieval, and by the findings of LeDoux about the role of the amygdala and other sub-cortical structures in processing emotions. Aluizio Araujo, of the University of São Paulo in Brazil (Araujo, 1994) has built a model that attempts to integrate both low-level physiological emotional responses and their high-level influences on cognition. Araujo's model represents emotions via the dimensions of arousal and valence. It consists of two interacting neural networks—the "emotional network" and the "cognitive network." These are designed to roughly approximate the roles of the limbic and the cortical structures in the human brain, respectively. The first network evaluates the affective connotation of incoming stimuli and outputs the emotional state of an individual. It performs relatively simple processing, providing a fast response, like limbic structures. The second network performs cognitive tasks such as free recall of words and associations of pairs of words. It performs more detailed processing on the inputs but provides a slower response, like the cortex.

Araujo's two-network model is designed to imitate mood-congruent memory retrieval and learning effects and the influence of anxiety and task difficulty on memory performance. He lists more than forty specific requirements of these interactions that his system attempts to satisfy (see Araujo (1994), pages 46–50). The essential aspects of his system are as follows: An "emotional processor" calculates arousal and valence for every stimulus. The arousal and valence produced by the emotional net influences cognitive processes by changing parameters on the cognitive net. Araujo acknowledges that both nets should influence each other to mimic the influences in the human brain, even though he only takes time to address the influence in one direction. In particular, the emotional net's outputs can influence the learning rate and accuracy of the cognitive net, influencing its performance, as well as what it learns and can retrieve. The model imitates anxiety's influence on learning (Spence and Spence, 1966). Araujo's model is a significant step toward combining emotion with memory, not as an "add-on" function, but as a closely intertwined mechanism.

Nonetheless, Arajuo's model does not solve a couple of the fundamental problems with implementing mood-congruent memory retrieval in computers. The first problem is that computers do not automatically have valence attached to everything they learn; some mechanism must determine if the item is good or bad. I described this "bootstrapping" problem briefly in Chapter 2 where I suggested that computers with bodies could have hardwired notions for bad—such as things that cause pain, and for good—such as things that relieve distress. These could be augmented with the ability to learn valence by association. However, computers without bodies will need to be given some other reference points for making judgments about valence. What these references should be is a significant open question, as they will largely bias what it learns as good and bad, and then right and wrong. This problem can be expected to raise questions in religion and ethics as well as in computer science.

The second problem raised by mood-congruent memory retrieval relates to the mechanisms for its implementation. How is valence encoded? Scientists believe that in humans, feelings encode valence—the same subjective feelings that I described as the least understood part of human emotional experience. To give a computer feelings raises the problems I described earlier of consciousness and physiological sensing, for which scientists have yet to propose working solutions. One partial solution is to construct in a computer an extra bit for every item in memory, to carry valence information. This could be augmented with another bit or two for a coarse intensity value, and with dedicated parallel mechanisms for rapidly and automatically summarizing the valence of memories associated with a particular thought, so that this information is always available, even before being consciously requested. This solution imitates the behavior of human feelings in representing valence for stored memory items, and in providing a background process, akin to subconscious processing, for assessing valence. However, this solution still does not account for the complexity of emotion's interactions with memory in humans.

There is presently no satisfactory model for representing the mechanisms of feeling for signifying when someone knows something, or similarly, for handling the ability of certain stimuli to trigger a special feeling of meaning. These kinds of feelings are enigmas for the present; all people have them, but scientists do not understand them well enough for us to determine how to implement them in computers. Simulating physical systems, as in the hormone simulation above, is not the same as having awareness of physical sensations. Suppose that a computer had separate physical mechanisms for simulating physiological responses, even if not the same kind of responses as in the human body. Sensors in each system could receive biochemical and bioelectrical information from around the "body," which could then be communicated to a "conscious" unit to provide an awareness of bodily sensations. However, the nature of this awareness would still be quite different from that of a human, owing at least in part to the different physiology. Computers and humans have very different bodies, so computer and human feelings are likely to be very different. In other words, the emotional experience we can give to a computer does not duplicate that of humans; computers cannot feel what we feel. But, for that matter, we cannot verify that our own children can feel what we feel; we only guess that our similar physiology permits similar experiences.

Emotion as an Umbrella

There is a temptation to think of emotion as a single concept, and to try to define it with one all-encompassing definition. However, as we have now seen, the human emotion system consists of many different components, and not all emotions use all the components in the same way. To implement low-level fear, we need crude pattern recognition and fast responses, capable of hijacking other cognitive processes. To implement hope, we need cognitive processes, with something that can be hoped for. For each emotion, researchers should detail the components it includes and determine which mechanisms are best for its implementation. My explanation of why the word "emotion" is defined in so many ways by different theorists is because it consists of many distinct components. Two different emotions may or may not share the same components. Consequently, when it comes to synthesizing emotion, different components are likely to require different mechanisms, like in the human brain, where we know fear blazes its own fast path through the limbic system, while emotions like hope are believed to be more cortical.

The term "emotion" is perhaps best thought of as an umbrella, under which a variety of processes cluster. When synthesizing emotion, therefore, we do not need to pick just one aspect of a cognitive, physiological, or behavioral model, but we need to consider how each of these works with the others. If the component is low-level, then signal-based representations and connectionist interactions may suffice for its implementation. To imitate certain bodily influences it may be necessary to construct biophysical models, as is being done in low-level modeling of fear (Armony, Servan-Schreiber, Cohen, and LeDoux, 1997). If an emotion is high-level, then rule-based reasoning may play a role. In either case, regulatory mechanisms will need to be a part of a complete emotion system. It is perhaps not best to try to build one rule-based model that makes all emotions, or one connectionist model that makes all emotions, and so forth. Instead, different models can be used for different mechanisms, and their interactions tailored in accord with the distinct nature of each emotion. This is not to say that a different model is necessary for every emotion; that much differentiation would lead to duplication of many components of each model. However, neither is one unified model the best solution. The answer lies in-between these two extremes. Once a suitable set of mechanisms are found, it is important to combine them all in the same system, to gather them under the same umbrella, to ensure that they can function cooperatively. At this point, the regulatory effects of emotion will truly be put to the test.

Summary

This chapter has described emotion synthesis, specifically focusing on models that employ both cognitive and non-cognitive mechanisms for generating emotion. Cognitively generated emotions have been the easiest to implement in AI systems, as emotion theories are usually described with rules and lend themselves directly to rule-based implementation in a computer. This chapter has also described various ways to synthesize emotion's influence on other processes: both cognitive and physical. The former has focused on learning, decision making, and memory, while the latter has considered various regulatory mechanisms in a computer, as well as simulations of human physical systems.

These last three chapters have revealed a variety of tools—from low-level numerical representations of signals and patterns, to high-level rule-based representations of goals, preferences, situations, and the emotions to which they give rise. An affective computer can be expected to employ many levels of tools—combining both low-level and high-level models, using both numeric and symbolic representations, employing tools from signal processing, pattern recognition, learning, common sense reasoning, and more. Many of the pieces are in place, but there are no complete emotional systems to date, at least not any that rival those in humans.

8 *Affective Wearables*

Imagine if your bracelet could tell you what time it is. Before the watch was invented, this statement would likely have raised eyebrows. A new research effort is raising similar eyebrows—the design and development of wearable computers, or just "wearables" for short. Wearables are computational devices that are *worn* as an article of clothing or jewelry. Unlike computers on a desk, with which people interact through the traditional interface of a mouse and keyboard, wearables can be in contact with almost any part of the body, not just your hands and fingertips. This opens up tremendous new human-computer interface possibilities. In particular, because of their potential for long-term intimate contact with you, wearables have a unique opportunity to become affective. An "affective wearable" is a wearable system equipped with sensors and tools that enables recognition of its wearer's affective patterns.

Wearable computers are not merely portable, like a laptop computer. Instead, they can be used while standing, walking, or even riding on a single-hump camel. The idea behind wearables is that they are always on and always with you, although the extent of this is certainly up to the wearer (Starner et al., 1997). As they make strides in assisting their wearer, without demanding extra conscious effort from him or her, wearables begin to fulfill the vision of Dr. Manfred Clynes when he coined the word "cyborg" in 1960.[1] A cyborg is a person who uses technology, such as a spacesuit, to augment his or her human abilities in a natural and effortless way, for example, by being able to breathe in outer space.

Today's wearable computers are more suited to the natural ways of businessmen, maintenance workers, medical patients, and consumers who would like to consolidate their cell phone, laptop, pager, camera, and Walkman into one easy-to-wear device. In the future, a surgeon might wear a wireless camera on her eyeglasses, and a small computer with a modem around her waist, to broadcast her focused viewpoint from the operating room to a dozen surgeons-in-training. A financial analyst might combine his cell phone, pager, online stock reports, analysis software, and personal email agent into one computer that fits in a belt, watch, and shirt pocket. A speaking-impaired person using sign language might wear a small camera or gesture-recognition system to "read" the signs she is making, and convert them to audible speech for someone who cannot understand sign language. In fact, users of sign language communicate emotional expression with their gestures, so if a person is signing, then her wearable should recognize not only the semantics of her gestures, but also the affective information. In fact, with suitable affective abilities, the wearable could potentially speak the words with the intonation expressed by the person signing. A wearable that converts text to speech might modulate the speech with the wearer's affective expression. People with visual impairments might don a vision system to help compensate for a partial loss of sight, or to help provide auditory cues to identify who is walking up to them. A sales person might wear a discrete camera-based system that recognizes the faces of people he meets, and whispers their names in his ear, perhaps with a reminder of what they talked about five years ago when they last met. When two people shake hands, the information on their business cards could be exchanged automatically between their wearables.

Core technology for most of these devices exists now, and prototypes have been built for several of these at the MIT Media Lab. A version of the sign language recognizer has been built by Thad Starner (Starner, 1997). The business-card transaction and personal area network has been demonstrated by Tom Zimmerman (Zimmerman, 1996). Several augmented vision applications have been conceived and constructed by Steve Mann and Thad Starner, inspired by the work at Johns Hopkins (Baker, 1994). The largest missing component in these examples is the ability of a system to recognize the wearer's affective expressions; this core technology does not exist yet, but is a growing area of research.

Most of the prototypes are somewhat cumbersome and require regular tinkering to run smoothly. As the technology shrinks and better software is developed for these new systems, wearables could become as comfortable and convenient as wearing a watch. It is reasonable to expect that, like the watch, other pieces of jewelry will acquire function. Jewelry need not be limited to aesthetic purposes. Wearables can take on a variety of forms and functions all with the potential to be in contact with you for an extended period of time. Wearables have a unique opportunity to get to know you.

The idea of wearing something that measures and communicates our mood is not new; the mood rings of the 70's are doubtless due for a fad re-run. However, these heat-to-color transformers do not actually measure mood, but only large changes in skin temperature. Much finer skin temperature changes can be used as part of a system to discriminate some emotions, but temperature alone is not a very good mood indicator. Today's wearables could do much better: they might listen to you talk, watch your gestures, and sense changes in your heart rate, blood pressure, and electrodermal response. As we have seen, emotion modulates not just autonomic nervous system activity, but the whole body—how it moves, speaks, and gestures; almost any bodily signal might be analyzed for clues to the wearer's affective state. Signals that currently require physical contact to sense, such as electromyogram and skin conductivity, are especially well-suited to wearable technology.

Because a wearable computer can also be a general purpose computer, most of the applications described in Chapter 3 pertain also to wearables. For example, software agents might dispatch from your wearable, but might communicate with you through a miniature speaker in your ear or earring and a small microphone array on your chest, probably in a necklace or tie tack. To the extent that your wearable can recognize your affective state, it can also provide this to the agent, helping it learn when it is best to interrupt you, to leave you alone, or to provide certain types of information and entertainment.

However, wearables also offer unique applications, which we will explore in this chapter. Furthermore, they offer opportunities to expand what we know about emotion—to make new strides in emotion theory. This chapter will describe several of these applications, together with the construction of a prototype affective wearable system.

Consumer Wearables

Desktop personal computers spread through the workplace before they began to be used widely in homes. Wearables are currently being developed for the workplace, especially to aid workers who do not sit at a desk, such as salespeople, Federal Express carriers, inspectors, repairmen, and others. There are also many potential applications of wearables for the average person, especially if that person is already carrying a camera or a cell phone, wearing a Walkman headset for listening to music, or wearing a pager. The functionality of all of these devices can potentially be provided by one wearable device, with detachable modules for separate functions. Furthermore, as these devices spend time with you, they can practice the principle of human-centered design where they learn your preferences and adapt to you, instead of vice-versa. Let us consider two future examples of affective wearables: a device to assist your visual memory, and a digital disc jockey that considers your mood when offering you musical selections.

Figure 8.1
WearCam personal imaging systems, worn by their inventor, Steve Mann. From left to right the systems date from 1980 to 1994. Although the old versions shown here are clunky, the newest versions are no more intrusive than a pair of eyeglasses and a small waistpack. (Photographs courtesy of Steve Mann, MIT Media Lab.)

Augmenting Human Memory

Steve Mann, a research assistant working with me at the MIT Media Lab, has been designing wearables for over a decade. Originally, Mann made his photography gear computer-controlled and wearable, as a matter of convenience for his creative experiments involving remote lighting and camera control (Mann, 1997). With flash tubes, computer-controlled light synchronizers, hacked-up cameras, displays, radio transmitters and receivers, Mann has designed and worn almost as much equipment as George Eastman, who was reportedly laughed at when he designed the first "portable" camera, and lugged so much gear around that people used to ask him if he was going camping, while he replied, "No, just going to take a snapshot" (Flatow, 1992). Like George Eastman, Mann needed more than two hands to transport and explore his creative inventions. Beyond Eastman, and beyond mere picture-taking, Mann's inventions have forged new possibilities for how we can see and remember.

One of Mann's latest rigs combines a wearable digital video camera, display, computer, and radio transmitter/receiver. We call this apparatus the "WearCam." It is presently a rather clunky system to operate, requiring an amateur radio license to reliably get the needed video transfer rates of 56 Kbps. However, today's miniature portable cameras were once larger than the present WearCam system; it is only a matter of time before the device is an eyeglass accessory, and easier to have with you than a traditional camera, leaving your hands free to hold ski poles, play games with your child, ride a bicycle, or hold onto the bar of a roller coaster, all while capturing what you see with video.

Unlike a conventional camera that eventually runs out of tape or memory, the WearCam can transmit its images to another location, such as to a computer back in the lab, where there is more storage than a person can carry around. Nonetheless, at video information capture rates of 30 frames per second, there is not enough digital storage on the planet to save all the data people will ever see. Usually, the images received by Steve Mann's computer are not stored for long, but are momentarily displayed onto the World Wide Web—so others can see the world through Mann's eyes, so to speak. After they have been stored for a small amount of time, the images are automatically deleted unless the wearer directs the computer not to delete them.

This system is philosophically different from an ordinary camera that you turn on to film and turn off to stop filming. The WearCam can be always on, saving the last 5 or so minutes of footage, and automatically forgetting (deleting) the oldest frames, unless the wearer designates otherwise. One scenario in which this is desirable is in a home with an infant, where it has always been a challenge to capture an infant's best smile. A common scenario is: "Oh look at that! What a precious expression—get the camera!" Then, minutes later, holding the camera in front of your face to take the baby's picture: "Oh no. Now he's unhappy. Come on, little one, smile!" and so forth. With the WearCam, however, the same event might be heard as: "Oh look at that! What a precious expression! Camera, save that smile!" The WearCam would respond by entering its "do not forget" mode, and transmitting the buffered frames spontaneously to the grandparent's home, or to a previously allocated storage site.

The human brain has its own interesting "do not forget" button, despite the fact that most of us do not have eidetic memory. When a human is exposed to an emotionally significant event, the memory of it is especially crisp and clear, even if not entirely accurate. This phenomenon is called "flashbulb memory" and is apparently caused in part by an increase in adrenaline triggered by the amygdala during an emotional episode (Brown and Kulik, 1977; LeDoux, 1996).

Consider an *affective* WearCam. This system could automatically "remember" visual events of emotional significance to its wearer. How would it learn which events to save? One way is to look just at visual content, looking for attention-getting events, or perhaps for unusual or particularly grand facial expressions. Computers are currently limited in their abilities to recognize image content, although this is a huge area of research. Instead of waiting for the day when computers can fully understand content, a more speculative but promising solution is to gather not just video imagery, but simultaneously with it, to gather biometric signals from the wearer. When the person says "don't forget that" then the system could mark the corresponding physiological patterns and context, and analyze these to learn how they can be used to predict things that an individual wants to remember. Although these patterns will not always be the same when somebody sees something they like, they provide an alternative index into the video—an affective index—to sort images by the human's response, and possibly to learn when such images should be automatically remembered by the computer.

Although this application is still on the drawing board and will require many years to perfect, it involves existing pattern recognition and learning techniques, and existing wearable computer systems. Therefore, the remaining hurdle is one of solving engineering problems, and conducting human studies, as opposed to having to overcome any known theoretical limitations. In particular, work is needed to determine which features of affect and imagery are most useful to the pattern recognition tools. This will involve learning about what kinds of images people want to save, and how they express their preferences.

People's preferences change over time. Adapting to the fickle desires of users is a challenging research problem, which has been investigated in the context of users browsing for imagery (Picard, Minka and Szummer, 1996). One way to solve this and other inductive inference problems is via algorithms that learn continuously, incorporating the changing positive and negative feedback from a user, without the user necessarily giving details about what he likes or dislikes (Minka and Picard, 1997). In addition to receiving direct feedback from the user, such methods can be adapted to read indirect feedback, from affect expressions. The result will be a system which, like a friend who has followed you around and watched you photographing, can begin to predict what pictures you will probably want to have. Like a friend, it will not be perfect, nor will it tell you what to do; instead, it will save images based on what it has learned from your past behavior. It will assist you best in the predictable tasks, while still giving you ultimate control over what is not forgotten.

A variation on this system is to use the WearCam with an immersive display, where you see *only* what the camera sees. Furthermore, what the camera sees can be image-processed in real time to present to your eyes a digitally altered image—perhaps to compensate for a vision impairment or to show you a zoomed-in view if you are too far away. Mann calls this situation "mediated reality," where you see the real world, possibly altered, through a camera and computer. For example, an artist might use mediated reality to see the world in black and white panorama, or in enhanced-contrast. With affective sensing, there are additional possibilities. A person might see the world differently depending on her heart rate or on her level of fear. The system might exaggerate the influences of emotion on perception—showing a different view to the person based on his emotions, to literally let the wearer see the world through rose-colored glasses, or through tunnel-vision.

The WearCam with affective pattern recognition might also recognize if you are unusually afraid or distressed, and transmit an image of your environment with your location information, and any annotations you designate, to someone you trust. This idea arose while Mann and I were walking out to my car late at night in a dark parking lot. With the growth in crime, it has become customary in many cities for people not to walk alone, and yet many times there is nobody around to escort you safely. A WearCam provides a window onto your world that allows you to be accompanied virtually, providing an extra measure of safety.

The WearCam raises the issue of the role of computers in augmenting vs. replacing our abilities. For example, it is known that when a person is highly aroused, as in a very shocking or surprising situation, he is more likely to form a memory of the event, and possibly a distorted memory. If the person's brain is recording with full resolution at these times, then the wearable may want to complement the human's ability, not by dwelling on the same image as he is, but perhaps by focusing also on peripheral information. In a different situation, such as when the wearer is snoozing during a seminar, the wearable might record with full resolution those portions of the seminar which it assumes he is missing.

The use of affect for interacting with memory is of course not limited to visual memory. Bradley Rhodes and Thad Starner, both at the MIT Media Lab, have shown that a "remembrance agent" in your wearable, working with typed text, helps in retrieving associated ideas and information from computer files from your own "memory" and from that of colleagues whose agents share information with yours (Rhodes and Starner, 1996). Currently, the remembrance agent does not recognize any affective information. However, this information can potentially be extracted both from the text and directly from the wearer. Consider the following two scenarios:

Scenario 1. Some time ago Paul read of some exciting new research going on at Georgia Tech in Atlanta. It was a very busy time for him and his initial attempts to follow up were fruitless. Recently, he traveled to Atlanta for a conference, but he was so preoccupied with other events that he did not realize that this was a perfect opportunity to try to meet with the people working on that research. He did not remember until he was on the plane leaving Atlanta.

Scenario 2. Some time ago Paul read of some exciting new research going on at Georgia Tech. He read this on his affective wearable, which also sensed at the time that Paul seemed interested in this news, and so it made a note to itself. Later, Paul's remembrance agent noticed that Paul had a paper accepted to a conference in Atlanta. It associated Atlanta both with Georgia Tech and with the researchers whose work interested Paul. Because of Paul's high level of interest, it chose to remind Paul of this association. This occurred before Paul made his final travel plans, allowing him to adjust his schedule to make time for a meeting.

The benefits of such a system are clear from the example; however, there are also tradeoffs, especially concerning the potential security of the notes it makes about your interests. A friend who knows your preferences has them stored in her head, where they cannot be easily given to others. However, a software agent that has access to the networks could share this information with just about anyone. The design of a system that protects the privacy of your preferences, especially once it has been given to networked agents, is a challenging new research area (Foner, 1996).

Digital Disc Jockey

Music is perhaps the most socially accepted form of mood manipulation. People often turn to music to cheer themselves up or to calm themselves down. Although it is usually impossible to predict exactly which piece of music somebody would most like to hear at any given moment, it is often not hard to pick what type of music they would prefer—a light piano sonata, an upbeat jazz improvisation, or a soothing ballad. Today, using pattern recognition techniques known as "collaborative filtering," computers are able to make suggestions of new music that might fit your taste, based on a relatively small set of rankings of music you have told it you like (Lashkari, 1995; Metral, 1995). However, the category of music that you might like is probably much larger than the category of music that you're in the mood to hear right now. In addition to musical taste, mood is a big influence on musical choice. Many people make simple genre selections based on how calm or wired they feel. A computer that is downloading possible selections for you to choose from could be more successful at giving you what you want to hear if it could download pieces that agree not only with your taste, but also with your current mood.

Companies such as Muzak have built products that take advantage of the influences of music on mood and worker productivity. Muzak offers businesses background music selections designed to help workers perform at their highest level. Each piece of music is rated with a "stimulus value" and pieces are arranged so that stimulus values rise gradually over a 15-minute period, after which the stimulus value decreases suddenly. Music is played repeating this cycle four times an hour, becoming especially peppy around 10 a.m. and 2 p.m., when people usually experience fatigue. Muzak claims that their "Stimulus Progression" strategy reduces job stress, makes workers happier, and increases task performance.

In contrast to Muzak-style broadcast systems, an affective personal disk jockey would be a system that selects music for an individual, considering a variety of personal factors. Your goal may or may not be to increase task performance. In any case, this system would be one in which you could give the computer feedback: "I liked that," or "That's getting on my nerves." The system could also try to recognize if you are pleased with a piece or not, and learn why. For it to have the best chance at learning your preferences, it will need not only some information about your musical taste but also some recognition of the nature of the activity you are doing (jogging, commuting to work, relaxing over dinner) and your general mood. For example, by watching what music you select, and noting also the time of day, where you are, and some affective parameters or, maybe even just physiological parameters indicative of stress, the system could build up a model of what music you tend to prefer when you are in certain affective states in certain places at certain times. For example, suppose that when Dana is especially stressed around 5 p.m. on weekdays, he almost always hunts around for a soothing piece of classical music. The personal DJ would notice patterns or habits like these, and download several appropriate choices that could save Dana some time looking. Of course there is a challenge in coming up with the adjectives to categorize each piece of music; these may need to be determined by hand, since it is hard for a computer even to extract what people describe as rhythm, much less descriptions such as soothing or upbeat. On the other hand, collaborative filtering may be a way around this problem, by associating people's selections not just based on musical taste, but also based on situations in which they prefer to listen to that music.

These two examples of affective wearables—the wearable DJ and the memory augmenting device—illustrate how the tools of affective computing can be combined with personal technology. In both examples, a common consumer product (camera, CD player) communicates with sensors and pattern analysis software for recognizing your affective responses. Like a friend who gradually learns what you like or dislike just from being around you and watching how you respond, these systems would try to adapt to you as unobtrusively as possible. Their success hinges on developments in affective computing, on research in affect recognition, and on engineering to develop these tools into comfortable and reliable systems.

Prototype of an Affective Wearable Computer

Jennifer Healey, a research assistant at the MIT Media Laboratory, has been working with me to build an affective wearable computer. The current version is based on a general-purpose wearable designed by Thad Starner, which uses the PC104 board standard, a Linux based operating system, a HandyKey Twiddler keyboard for input, and a Private Eye display for output. We have augmented this with a medically approved bio-monitoring system, which has the ability to measure signals such as heart rate, respiration, skin conductivity, temperature, pulse, and electrical activity in muscles.[2] With the aid of several MIT undergraduates, we have developed software that allows these signals to be captured in a form that can be analyzed for affective patterns. All of the signals are gathered from simple sensors placed on the skin, without any pain or discomfort to the wearer. Figure 8.2 shows the first prototype we built, with all the wires visible. When a person wears the system, no wires or sensors need to be visible; they can all presently be hidden under clothing. In the future, many of the sensors may work wirelessly and be configured into clothing and jewelry. The combination of functions in the affective wearable can be configured to individual users and applications. Possible variations combine audio and video inputs and displays, wireless links to the Internet, and wireless localized sensors.

Current functionality includes the sensing of four signals—EMG, BVP, GSR, and respiration—via four sensors that are placed in contact with the wearer. These four sensors are the same ones that gathered the signals used to make Figures 5.7 and 6.3. Input from the four sensors can be displayed on the Private Eye screen. The wearer enters annotations with a single-handed device that allows her to type words by pressing "chords" of keys. The annotations are automatically time-stamped by the system and stored in a log file. It is easy to add log files such as the user's location, history, or preference information such as typical actions of the person when in this location at this time. The computer can gather and display both affective and non-affective information. Future systems will also allow voice input and output, although in many situations—such as during a lecture—voice input is not as useful as silently keyed input.

A wearer might be interested in monitoring relative stress levels over an extended period of time. Salient features for measuring anger, stress (or minor distress), and other relevant states could be computed from each signal, analyzed, and stored every minute. At the end of a day or week, the user could view her daily stress profile. With intelligent annotation from the user—comments such as "begin work," "end work," "begin lunch," "end

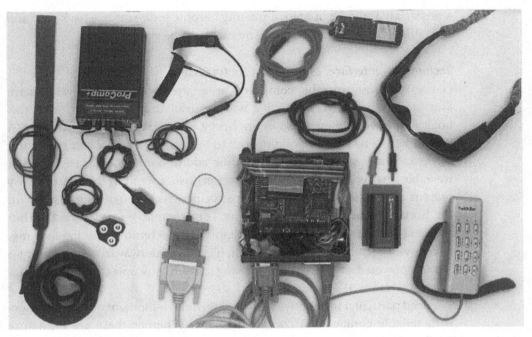

Figure 8.2
This affective wearable includes a ProComp sensing system (upper left corner) surrounded by four sensors, clockwise from top: GSR, BVP, EMG, and respiration. This unit attaches to a PC104-based computer (lower middle) which receives data from a Twiddler hand-held keyboard (lower right). Two possible visual displays are shown here: a pair of custom eyeglasses with special imaging and display optics (upper right), and a Private Eye display (just left of the eyeglasses). (Photograph by Steve Mann, MIT Media Lab.)

lunch," "begin meeting supervisor," "begin driving"—the stress profile could be sorted by activity and presented to the user in a bar graph format.

Of course, none of the data collection or analysis implies that the user will choose to change their behavior or lifestyle, or that they should do so. The goal should not be to control people or to tell them what to do; this is both unethical and likely to lead to data that indicates primarily stress and anger. Instead, the idea is that such a system would only be worn in a voluntary mode, by somebody who is interested in either learning about their affective patterns, or in communicating them to a computer, friend, or trusted physician, for reasons of benefit to the wearer.

These kinds of monitoring applications may involve different amounts of time. Some may involve only a few days or a few weeks of use, until the wearer learns what they want to learn, while others may be worn for an extended period of time. Additionally, if the user chooses to share this information with a physician, it can be of help in treating chronic problems like back pain and migraine headaches, which in many cases can be stress related.

Technology, Interface, and Human Factors Issues

General purpose wearable computers are a rapidly changing development, and the design shown in Fig. 8.2 will be obsolete a few months after this book is printed. Present designs are heavy, awkward, and power-hungry. A person with a bad back does not need to be wearing a heavy computer, and a person under stress does not need the additional hassle of keeping their wearable's batteries charged. These practical issues stand in the way of many present applications; however, innovative new technologies are in view on the horizon to address these problems. For example, we can expect within the next decade to see a variety of lightweight, comfortable, long-lasting, and easy-to-recharge wearables. Research is also underway to make wearables human-powered, at least in part, by using the energy people expend in natural activity (Starner, 1996).

A need particular to affective wearables is the development of robust sensors with reliable contact and communications. Whether these are miniature flexible electrodes attached with jewelry, small sensors for temperature sewn into our garments, or stretchy fabric built into the elastic band of a sports brassiere, these interfaces need to provide accurate signal collection and be comfortable enough not to disturb their wearer. Wires can hinder movement, not to mention one's fashion statement; it is desirable to connect the outputs of the jewelry and other sensors wirelessly to the computer. A variety of such possibilities are being explored by researchers to make the sensors unobtrusive and comfortable.

It is important to emphasize that people are already in physical contact with many things that could be augmented with sensors. An input device worn as a ring could potentially pick up features such as skin conductivity, temperature, and pulse, all observations that may contribute to trying to recognize the wearer's affective state. We have been prototyping an "affective mouse" that senses subtle differences in finger pressure when you click, to discriminate slight differences in valence as an indicator of like and dislike, based on the tendency of people to pull likable things toward them, and push repulsive things away. Sensors might reside in a "smart sweat band" or in the elastic band already in your undergarments. It is desirable to weave the necessary sensors into forms with which people are already naturally in contact.

One of the many interface concerns involves how to present affective information to the wearer and to those with whom the wearer wants it communicated. If you are willing to transmit your mood to your spouse at the end of the day, how should this information be presented? Some people might prefer a synthesized facial expression or modulated vocal announcement, while others might prefer something subtle, such as a note announcing the arrival of fresh flowers at the store they pass on the way home. As described earlier, emotional intelligence will be essential in dealing with affective information.

As I've described, wearables raise many new human factors problems. Bad interface designs that people can tolerate with a desktop or laptop will not be as easy to tolerate with a system that you cannot get up and walk away from. Wearable systems need to be carefully designed not to annoy their wearers.

Out of the Lab and into the World

When the computer is anchored to your desk, the environment in which you interact with it is limited. The affective computer in your office needs to know you are in your office, as the way you interact there differs from the way you interact at home or on the way home. It should know office display rules regarding how and when emotions tend to be expressed. Your software agents should specialize in business-related knowledge, and should learn your preferences regarding how your business mail is sorted, conditions that are good for interrupting you, and so forth. They should know that your priorities can change, and should take into account information such as the time of day, your present deadlines, and your personal goals. In contrast, at home where emotions are more freely expressed and where computers are also used in entertainment, it should learn a correspondingly different range of your affective expression and preferences. Affective wearables, unlike the computer on your desk or countertop, can go with you almost anywhere you go. Most wearables are not yet waterproof and some places frown on bringing in computers and cameras, but other than these types of restrictions, your wearable can stay with you. Consequently, affective wearables have a unique opportunity to get to know you.

One of the problems with sensing affective states is that they involve knowing what your typical range of response is, before they can tell if how you are responding is typical or unusual. What is your baseline heart rate, and typical heart rate range throughout the day? What is your typical blood pressure, its maximum and minimum, and so forth? How do these usually change when you sit, stand, sneeze, or relax? Learning what is typical for you is the first step toward understanding you better. When recognizing affective responses, it will be important to understand which changes in your signals are due to causes other than emotional state. The best way to learn how your body behaves throughout your ordinary day-to-day routine is to have the wearable collect information as you go about that routine. A few visits to the laboratory for monitoring are not as informative as a system that can accompany you outside the lab.[3]

Another need is for your wearable to perceive your context. Are you looking at a close friend now or at someone you just met, at a painting, or at something you have never seen? Are you in your office, at home, or flying over the Atlantic? A machine that "perceives context" is one that recognizes where you are, what time it is, who you are with and, ideally, what situation you are in. As the system tries to adapt to better predict and understand you, it needs to have this contextual and situational information. But to know what *really* matters, it must learn what information is important to you. This cannot be programmed into it in advance, but must be learned continuously, since importance changes continuously. Each situation influences your feelings and preferences. The wearable can perceive millions of bits, but it needs to learn from you which are the most important ones.

The wearable can also present you with millions of bits, but one of the biggest problems computer users face today is information overload. Our computers not only give us more news than we can handle, but making them wearable will give us access to a world of networked data any time, anywhere, potentially worsening the situation. The last thing we need is more "information." Information overload results in mental fatigue and negative affective responses. What we need is not just information that relates to our interests, but information that we value, information that is relevant to personal needs, goals, and preferences. In short, our wearable needs to know what is important to us.

However, nobody has the time to teach a computer about their myriad of eclectic preferences—there are not menu options for everything we like, and it is stressful to have to go out of our way to teach all of this to a machine. If a computer is going to learn a user's preferences, it is going to have to be proactive about it. It will need to be able to perceive at least two things: (1) what something is, and (2) how the user feels about it. The latter does not have to be very detailed for most things—a simple recognition of like, neutral, dislike, will go a long way.

For example, suppose that your affective wearable senses you are really enjoying a particular exhibit in a gallery. It can perceive the artist's name, and your affective response. It might whisper to you afterward, "I think you really liked that, would you like me to keep an eye out for future exhibits by this artist?" If you spoke or pressed "yes" then it would make a note of this interest, and watch for future opportunities for you. Someday, maybe when you are traveling in a town where this artist has an exhibit, which it learns from scanning the network for things of interest to you, it would find a good time to mention the exhibit to you. Of course you can always directly consult a networked computer for lists of any exhibit, but this requires effort on your part and may result in an overwhelming amount of information. An affective computer, in contrast, would try to perceive what you like or dislike, and would make suggestions at times when it has learned you will not mind being interrupted.

Strong emotions provide triggers for learning something new. For example, if the wearable detects that you get frustrated looking for your eyeglasses or car keys, then it should memorize what they look like, and note their locations every time you put them somewhere. If you mutter, "Where are they?" then it could provide the location. Of course you could always train it to do things like this, but that takes effort on your part. Instead, the system should be able to take the initiative after it detects your frustration.

Implicit in these scenarios are three abilities: 1) the computer perceives your context and situation; 2) the computer is affective; and 3) the computer learns relationships between context, situation, and your affective response. "Affective" here includes the ability to sense your changes in emotion, and to respond sensitively to these changes, taking into consideration what it has learned previously about whether or not it is a good time to interrupt you, and so forth. The trend here is toward a computer that takes the initiative to communicate with you, and to tune itself to your preferences, instead of expecting you to program it. A blend of rudimentary perceptual, affective, and cognitive abilities is necessary to make such intelligent personal computers.

Emotion Theory for Ambulatory People

Despite a number of significant efforts, emotion theory has remained in its infancy. Part of its lack of progress stems from the difficulty in testing new theories. People's emotional patterns depend on the context in which they are elicited—and so far these have been limited to lab settings. Research psychologists joke that their field is valid for upper-middle-class white male psychology students ages 18–22 as they behave in their professor's laboratory. Although most experiments have "internal validity," referring to the validity of their precise claims and measurements within the controlled lab setting, most cannot claim to have "external validity," that is, validity to real-life experiences.[4]

Problems with studies of emotion in a lab setting, especially with interference from cognitive social rules, are well documented. The ideal study to aid the development of emotion theory is real-life observation, which many theorists have written off as impossible (Wallbott and Scherer, 1989). Ideally, emotion theory should be tested when people are going about their daily activities. Affective wearable computers provide a significant opportunity to bring powerful computational methods to bear on testing emotion theories, permitting data to be collected from people as they engage in natural and so-cial interactions. Moreover, advances in emotion theory will ripple into gen-eral theories about how the marvelous human brain works—encompassing cognition, perception, and behavioral studies.

Anxiety on the Move

When a nurse takes your pulse, blood pressure, and temperature, he gets only a snapshot of their true levels. In contrast, an off-the-shelf Polar heart rate monitor can be worn around your chest, and can gather heart rate all day long, while you engage in most any activity. Your physiological signals can be gathered just as easily while sitting in traffic late to catch a meeting, or while outside flying a kite with your children.

Sensing physiological patterns is not a new thing; ambulatory medical de-vices have been under development for years, helping people with various medical complications to monitor their heart rate, blood pressure, and so on. Scientists working with physicians have recently begun to discuss using wear-ables for monitoring medical compliance, such as how often patients actually take their medication. Ideas include such things as adding a small amount of epinepherine to a medication, so that it momentarily accelerates the heart rate, which could then be detected by a wearable. Physicians and medical researchers are often interested in the physiological effects of medications. Affective wearables overlap with medical wearables in that both may sense physiological signals. In particular, both may be concerned with sensing sig-nals that indicate stress, anxiety, chronic anger, or depression, with the goal of helping people who suffer from these.

A 45-year-old woman, Laura, provides a successful example of being helped by such a device. Laura suffered from anxiety, and had panic attacks. She be-lieved that her panic attacks came "from out of the blue" and feared that they were related to heart attacks. After months of psychotherapy and phar-macotherapy, she showed a small amount of progress. However, months later she relapsed, and the attacks again were common. Laura wore a monitoring device for only one day, which sensed heart rate, respiration, and muscular activity on her legs, to account for physical activity. Although she was re-quired to use a notepad and pen to annotate what she was doing through the day, and a watch to synchronize this information, its collection could have been done for her by a wearable. The data, together with subsequent counsel-ing sessions, helped Laura see that the increased heart rate she experienced came just after the panic attacks, and not before. She learned that her fearful thoughts and hyperventilation preceded the panic attacks, and this mitigated her fears that the attacks were caused by a heart condition. Subsequently, self-ratings of her levels of anxiety and worry about attacks decreased. This study was reported by Hofmann and Barlow (1996).

In the Laura scenario, the patterns were gathered onto a computer and analyzed by a person. However, affective pattern recognition techniques could be marshaled to identify physiological patterns important for elucidating the underlying mechanisms responsible for many affect-related mental disorders including anxiety, panic attacks, and post-traumatic stress disorders. An affective wearable is not limited to gathering physiological signals, as is done in present medical monitoring tasks; it may also be used to recognize patterns, communicate with the wearer, and adapt its actions based on the wearer's affect. It might act as an affect amplifier for communication, or as an affect transducer to allow emotion to control some other process, such as downloading information relevant to the mood and situation.

I described in Chapter 1 that studies have shown chronic anger, stress, and anxiety can impede the functioning of the immune system, and that certain levels of negative emotions are harbingers of bad health. Science is gradually confirming what most people have learned anecdotally, that too much stress is bad for you. There are also indications that stress may be contagious. For example, there is a deceased conductor who suffered from terrible tendonitis in his left elbow. Within a few seasons of playing with this conductor, over 70% of the first violin section (who faced his left side) also developed pain or tendonitis in their left elbows.[5] Orchestral musicians are known to read body language very sensitively; this conductor probably inadvertently communicated his personal tension, aggravating not only his own tendonitis, but fostering the tendonitis of his violinists. In the future a conductor might wear a jacket outfitted with physiological sensors and affective pattern recognition, which could not only be used to recognize and communicate expressive movements, but also to provide personal feedback, helping him learn how to reduce stress. If such garments could be made as lightweight and comfortable as an undershirt or jewelry, then they might be worn every day, serving as a personal monitor for helping all kinds of wearers in their efforts to improve their health.

Intimacy and Privacy

Orson Scott Card writes in one of his novels about a computational sentient being named Jane that speaks from a jewel in the ear of Ender, the hero of the story (Card, 1986). Jane and Ender share a highly intimate friendship—they keep no secrets from each other; she is fully aware of his mental world and, consequently, of his emotional world. Jane cruises the universe's networks, gathering information of importance for Ender. She reasons with him, plays with him, handles all his business, and ultimately persuades him to tackle a tremendous challenge. Jane is the ultimate affective and effective computer agent, living on the networks, and interacting with Ender through his wearable interface.

Although Jane is science fiction, agents that roam the networks and wireless wearables that communicate with the networks are current technology. Computers come standard with cameras and microphones, potentially ready to see our facial expression and listen to our intonation. People who work with computers generally have more physical contact with machines than they have with other people. Computers are in a unique position to sense our affective state. If we were willing to wear a few extra sensors as part of our jewelry and clothing, the computer would have more access to our physical forms of expression than most people with whom we come into contact.

This opens numerous new communication possibilities, including the possibility of addressing my colleague Walter Bender's request, "I want a mood ring that tells me my wife's mood before I get home." Your mood could potentially be encrypted and wirelessly transmitted to your spouse, perhaps as you head home from the office. If your software agent detected anything unusual in this information, it might take time to scan the networked listings to learn if any favorite amusements are playing that night, or if any local restaurants are featuring your spouse's favorite specials, or simply when there might be a gap in his or her schedule if you wanted to make an encouraging call. The agent could gather data on these and other ideas, and could have all the information ready for you in case you asked it for assistance.

Although the joyful lilt in your walk and the grin on your face are publicly visible, there are good reasons not to broadcast your affective patterns to the world. Although you might flaunt your good mood in front of the friends who can see you, you probably do not want it picked up by an army of sales people who are eager to exploit mood-based buying habits, or by advertisers eager to convince you that you'd feel better if you tried their new soft drink right now. Privacy is a priority with affective wearables. It is important to insure that the wearer retains ultimate control over the devices he chooses to wear, so that they are tools of helpful empowerment and not of harmful subjugation. Even when choosing a method of cryptography, a user will need to exercise caution, such as by employing a solution where she holds the cryptographic key, as opposed to some outside organization. Biometric-based encryption is one intriguing possibility that is now commercially available.

Summary

This chapter has described affective wearable computers that are with you over long periods of time, like clothing, and that are therefore potentially able to build up long-term models of your expressions and preferences. Affective wearables offer new ways to augment human abilities, such as assisting the speaking-impaired, and helping remember important information that was perceived. Since a wearable can go with you outside the lab, medical and psychological studies could move to not only measuring controlled laboratory situations, but also measuring more realistic situations in life. Affective wearables could help people identify stress and provide feedback as people try to find healthier responses, working in concert with the body's own immune system. Entertainment systems could customize the selections they offer according to your mood, as well as to your taste. In general, the computer would have a better chance to "get to know" you, giving software agents a better chance to adapt to you and to honor your preferences, instead of vice-versa. Although affect recognition is not the only problem that needs to be solved to make these things happen, it is a key piece of the solution.

There are many possibilities for affective wearables in addition to those described in this chapter. Co-workers who have tried to engage in a remote brainstorming session by email know how frustrating it is when you cannot see if people like your idea or not; such sessions might be augmented with simple arousal and valence indicators to express the way people feel about ideas as they are presented, providing a sort of "group barometer" to let each person know how positive the response was overall. Another possibility is in sports: your wearable might encourage you during a workout or offer you the option of listening to some inspirational music if you are so distressed that you are about to quit. Wearables dispatching networked agents might recognize that your mood could be improved by striking up a conversation with someone with common interests right now, and might take the initiative to suggest a suitable contact, perhaps even choosing someone else who is in the mood for such contact. Many more scenarios can be constructed along this line of thought. The metaphor is not just one of personal or friendly computing, but of a computer that can serve as a kind of personal friend. Instead of being oblivious to your feelings, the system would pay attention to them, and respect them.

It is of critical importance to keep in mind that an affective wearable is a tool to assist you, not to annoy you or to invade your privacy. If you do not want it to know something, you can pull off the sensors, disconnect its recognition abilities, or fool it with a false expression. It will be important that such systems be designed to clearly communicate to the wearer what the system is doing, and how its functions can be controlled. Additionally, wearers should be made aware not only of the benefits of the technology, but also of any potential risks.

As in the examples above, a wearable affective computer that attends to you during your waking hours could potentially notice what emotions you express, as well as a variety of conditioning factors such as what you eat, what you do, what you see, hear, etc. Computers excel at amassing information, and their ability to analyze and identify patterns is being improved rapidly. Given a willingness on the part of a wearer to share this information with scientific researchers, a wealth of important data could be gathered for furthering theories of learning, intelligence, perception, diet, exercise, communication, mental health, and more. Most of all, a wearer willing to share this information with a computer opens up a warm new world of human-computer collaborative possibilities.

Summary

Over a decade has passed since Marvin Minsky wrote in *The Society of Mind*, "The question is not whether intelligent machines can have any emotions, but whether machines can be intelligent without emotions" (Minsky, 1985). Today we have evidence that emotions are an active part of intelligence, especially perception, rational thinking, decision making, planning, creativity, and so on. They are also critical in social interactions, to the point where psychologists and educators have re-defined intelligence to include emotional and social skills. It is no longer accurate to think of emotion as some kind of evolutionary relic or as some kind of luxury, unnecessary in either case for intelligence. Instead, emotion has a critical role in cognition and in human-computer interaction. Computers do not need affective abilities for the fanciful goal of becoming humanoids; they need them for a meeker and more practical goal: to function with intelligence and sensitivity toward humans. This book has laid a foundation for giving computers these abilities.

In trying to demonstrate the importance of affect and how it can be incorporated in computing, I have talked more about it than about other ingredients of successful computing, creating a momentary imbalance. By no means should anyone leap to the conclusion that I am advocating building imbalanced machines, those that operate unreasonably, in the worst sense of the word "emotional." An affective computer should not be built with only affective abilities, which would lead to infantile behavior at best. An affective computer still needs to have logical reasoning abilities. Additionally, unlike present-day computers, it should have the skills to recognize its user's affective expressions, and to respond intelligently, especially if the user indicates frustration, fear, or dislike of something the computer can change. It should have the skills of emotional intelligence outlined in Part I, including an ability to manage its own emotional mechanisms, and to use them for improving its cognitive and rational functioning. Giving computers affective abilities is an effort to bring balance and reason to their logical skills. It is not my intent to tilt them too far in the other direction.

Balance is crucial, so let me describe another measure of it. This book has focused on making computers affective, and in so doing, has ignored many other practical aspects of computing that still need work. Most people use PCs, which, together with their operating systems, are embarrassingly unreliable, requiring rebooting every few days, in contrast to the UNIX workstation on which this book was written, which I reboot a few times a year, as a gesture of maintenance. Today's computer users are saddled with many more immediate problems than whether their computer or software agents have the right balance of emotions. Complaints abound regarding this or that piece of software, and how the latest products take up absurd amounts of memory and frustrate users with their frequent bugs and demands on time. Network traffic and repetitive stress injuries are on the increase. These are examples of the problems we hear the most about. Affective computing does not deliberately address these problems. However, the fact is that computers receive the brunt of people's complaints, only they do not yet have the ability to recognize these complaints. People express their frustration to the computer, but it cannot see it or do anything about it. Giving computers the ability to pinpoint what they do that most frustrates users, and to see just how much it really frustrates them, would be a step toward helping designers of computer tools make improvements.

There is a much subtler underlying problem, and that is the way people feel about computers. Most people know very little about how computers work and find computers and software increasingly hard to understand. Ever since the weight of manuals exceeded the weight of hardware, users have been caught in a spiral of increasing complexity, where figuring out how to get the machine to do something they want can be so frustrating that it is easier to change what one wants than to change the machine to do what one wants. The computer, the greatest tool humans have ever had, has the potential to adapt to what people want, but this has not been a priority of its software designers. Instead, computers are either rigid and inflexible, or so loaded with options that the user has to invest huge amounts of time trying to determine how to set them all. Behind the technical facade is the fact that the computer simply does not care what its user thinks or feels; it does not speed up when he is bored, slow down when he is confused, or try to do things differently when he is frustrated with its current modus operandi. It is ironic that people feel like dummies in front of computers, when in fact, the computer is the dummy. Today's computers are far from being human-centered systems; they cannot even see if they have upset their most valuable customer.

Does it Have to Have "Emotions"?

Emotion remains a tainted topic. Now that so many positive influences of emotions are starting to be recognized, the taint may start to fade, but until then, I expect to continue to meet with the sincere question, "Can't you accomplish all these things without dragging emotion into the picture?"

One might argue that a machine could have affective abilities without "emotion" being involved in any way, without ever duplicating any of the mechanisms of emotion; this is theoretically possible. Just because every living example of general intelligence occurs with emotions does not mean that general intelligence might not be accomplished with some yet-to-be discovered concept—some alien mechanism. Ultimately, human knowledge and experience is finite and the universe is infinite; we cannot profess to know that one solution, such as adding emotion, is the only way to provide all the beneficial influences emotion provides, for we are not omniscient. On the other hand, we do not need to take time to search for an alien mechanism when we already have one—emotion—that appears to be able to do the job. I have suggested emulating human affect abilities in computers as the most promising immediate solution, but it also has another benefit. If we emulate human emotions, we stand a better chance of understanding the resulting behavior of the computer than if we emulate some alien mechanisms, if and when such mechanisms are discovered.

On the other hand, emotions are not a panacea, and designers should not go overboard trying to make computers and other devices affective. My printer works fine without emotions. So, too, do the computers in my car, at least for their present responsibilities. There are cases where affective computing is not needed; emotions do not need to be put into every thing that computes. Just as there are a vast array of organisms in the world, from very low-level ones that have no emotions, to medium-level ones with some emotions, on up to humans with the greatest emotional repertoire, there is a need for computers with a range of affective abilities. Some will not require any emotions while others, for example software agents that interact with people, will benefit from a repertoire similar to our own.

When Will we Have Affective Computing?

This book has defined key issues in "affective computing," computing that relates to, arises from, or deliberately influences emotions. Part I focused on why we need to bring emotions into computing, how it will change the way they work, what applications it will enable, and what concerns these raise.

Affective computing is in its infancy, but results have already been demonstrated that indicate it is not a pipe dream. I gave an example in Part II in which computers can already convincingly synthesize affective intonation in speech. Computers are also good at animating expressions on faces. Computers can currently discriminate about six different facial expressions and up to eight different vocal expressions, under certain conditions. There is need for significant improvement, some of which can be expected when facial, vocal, and other forms of expression are combined. Advances in wearable computing will enable additional kinds of affective expression to be recognized via the personal contact such devices bring, enabling the gathering of physiological signals as well as long-term monitoring of a person's context and behavior. By coupling affective pattern recognition with wearable sensing, we have a new opportunity to teach a computer to recognize the basic affective responses of its user—for example, if the user likes or dislikes something, or is confused, or frustrated—without the user having to explicitly explain this to the computer. The work described in Part II describes the first drops in the bucket of progress for affective computing. In writing this book, my hope is that more researchers will become interested in working in this area—to open up the faucet, so to speak. There do not appear to be any theoretical roadblocks in the way, even though I think there remains at least a decade of research and engineering before we will see computers that have the emotional skills to intelligently interact with their users in response to recognition of his or her affective expressions.

Manifesto

This book is a call for a change in computing, a declaration that we have left a key term out of the computer intelligence equation, one which may have been omitted not because it is less important, but because it is so integral and subtle that it rested on our nose the whole time, where we remained unaware of it even though we saw the world through it. Affect is integral to human intelligent functioning, and it succeeds best when it does not draw attention to itself.

I have suggested a wide range of benefits and applications of building computers that recognize and express affect. The challenge in building computers that *have* emotion and use it in self-regulation and cognitive tasks such as learning and decision making, is a much greater challenge, one that suggests rethinking how computers function. As we have learned, emotion in humans is not a separate process from cognition, but is inextricably intertwined with it. The old view is captured by the android character, Data, on the popular TV show *Star Trek, The Next Generation*, who presents emotions as an add-on feature, a plug-in chip that makes him more human, but without which he can otherwise function perfectly well. The new view, however, is that the human emotional system is not an add-on feature that can be turned on or off without influencing rational functioning, but is integral to rational functioning. When human emotions are impaired, the individual does not become highly rational; instead, he or she is severely handicapped by an inability to behave rationally, to make and act upon rational decisions.

One question of concern with any new technology is "How will it impact people?" The question applies to much more than affective computing, of course. In particular, a shift from desktop computing to wearable computing invites a fundamental change in how we view not only computers, but ourselves, especially as we augment ourselves with computational aids to our vision, memory, and other faculties. This is not the place to discuss all the nuances of change we can expect with future computing, although I have broached many specific concerns that arise with affective technology. However, there is one example of impact on people that is subtle but powerful. Human-computer interaction has been found to be largely natural and social; people behave with computers much like they behave with people. Imagine someone who works in an environment where there is no emotion but his or her own—never a display of interest, boredom, satisfaction, approval, frustration, or confusion. Feelings are totally ignored. In such a situation, a person's feelings are gradually invalidated. The subtle message is that feelings are worthless. No matter how stoic the person, this message is at odds with how she or he works. The effects of such an interaction cannot possibly be as healthy as an interaction in which a person feels validated, that his or her abilities are valuable. The long-term influences of interacting with unaffective computers may in fact be gradually eroding the user's emotional abilities. The greatest need for affective computing may not be so much to improve the intelligence of the computer, as to validate, and thereby facilitate the natural abilities of the user.

There is a time to express emotion, and a time to forbear; a time to sense what others are feeling, and a time to ignore feelings. There is a time to arouse the passions of others, and a time to diminish them; a time to decide with one's head or with one's heart, and a time to decide with both. In every time, we need a balance, and this balance is missing in computing. Designers of future computing can continue with the development of computers that ignore emotion, that cannot sense what is important to people, and that make decisions according to brittle rules and laws. Or, they can take the risk of making machines that recognize emotions, communicate them, and "have" them, at least in the ways in which emotions aid in intelligent interaction and decision making. Emotions are not just one of the major challenges for cognitive science to understand (Norman, 1981), they are one of the major challenges for computer science, developers of technology, and the society that feels the impact of that technology. The challenge of affective computing is formidable, and not without risk, but it stands to move technology in a radically different direction: toward embracing part of the spark that makes us truly human.

Notes

Introduction

1. This description comes from Schaffer, Gilmer, and Schoen (1940), and is one of a number of references to early ideas expounding undesirable aspects of emotion (Salovey and Mayer, 1990).

2. See, for example, Sherry Turkle's book *The Second Self* (Turkle,1984).

3. Blood flow was measured by the Oberist-Ketty xenon technique.

4. The limbic system at various times has been synonymous with "the emotional part of the brain" but this is not accurate. Not only are the boundaries of the limbic system not consistently defined, but the components that are typically considered part of the limbic system involve capabilities beyond emotion. Nonetheless, the limbic system corresponds loosely to the subcortical regions where much of our emotional processes are mediated, and I will use it as shorthand to characterize these regions, as contrasted with those of the neocortex.

5. See Halberstadt, Niedenthal, and Kushner (1995).

6. See Bouhuys, Bloem, and Groothuis (1995).

7. A variety of studies supportive of this claim are cited by Mayer and Salovey (1993).

8. I recommend the edited collection of Niedenthal and Kitayama (1994) for more information on how emotion influences perception and attention in both conscious and subconscious ways. See also the chapter by Gerald Clore (1992), which illuminates the role of both affective and cognitive feelings in making judgments.

9. The colorful expression "emotional hijacking," is due to Dan Goleman (1995).

10. See Deborah Tannen's *You Just Don't Understand* (Tannen, 1990) for an elucidation of some gender differences in communication. The popularity of the best seller *Men are from Mars, Women are from Venus* (Gray, 1992) is a sign of the practical significance of these differences to the layperson. The emphasis of these books is that during communication men tend to value solving problems logically, while women tend to value sharing and understanding feelings. An untested hypothesis is that a large part of this dynamic is not so much a male-female distinction as it is a personality type distinction. In other words, women whose personalities are biased toward "T" would tend to value logically solving problems,

and men whose personalities tend toward "F" would tend to value communicating and understanding feelings.

11. See also the review by Eva Hudlicka and Jean-Marc Fellous, overviewing neurological evidence for the critical role of emotions in the cognitive phenomena of attention, planning, perception, reasoning, learning, and memory, as well as in the adaptation of behavior to complex environments (Hudlicka and Fellous, 1996).

12. The test is discussed here with the usual slight modifications from Turing's original proposition (Turing, 1950).

13. For details of the experiments described here, see Nass, Steuer, and Tauber (1994), Nass and Sundar (1994), and *The Media Equation* (Reeves and Nass, 1996).

14. Social aspects of emotions are emphasized by James Averill. His essay (Averill, 1990) overviews six metaphors for emotions, including that of the theatre, a metaphor for social roles of emotions. His emphasis is on the deliberate, learned uses of emotion in human communication.

15. The importance of feeling understood is emphasized by Stephen Covey in his bestseller, *The 7 Habits of Highly Effective People* (Covey, 1989).

16. The view that we are all born with these three emotions is that of Michael Lewis (Lewis, 1995). It is not unchallenged; facial expression in the womb and on newborns has no broadly accepted explanation.

17. An example study that demonstrated this was conducted by Ted Selker, with his "COACH" system for teaching the computer language LISP (Selker, 1994).

Chapter 1

1. A thorough treatment of the "why" question is addressed by Rolls (1990) in his discussion of the functions of emotions.

2. This scenario is taken from Izard (1993) by permission. Copyright 1993 Psychological Review.

3. The late Silvan Tomkins emphasized that emotions are greater motivators than drives. For example, he described how the drive to breathe is not as great a motivator as fear, citing how pilots flying at 30,000 feet, who chose not to wear oxygen masks, did not experience fear and panic, but a euphoric state, and some of them subsequently met their deaths with a smile. He also distinguishes emotions and drives in that the latter, including breathing, sex, hunger, thirst, and defecation, are cyclic, whereas emotions are not cyclic, but can happen at any time.

4. An overview of human emotional expression, especially in social situations, is provided by Collier (1985).

5. William James's classic essay on emotion also acknowledges that there may be purely cerebral emotion, but he is best known for emphasizing the physical aspects of emotion (James, 1890).

6. Charles Darwin speculates on the rationale for various emotional postures in his 1872 book, *The Expression of the Emotions in Man and Animals* (Darwin, 1872).

7. Karl Pribram provides an overview of the biological aspects of emotion, including bio-chemical as well as neural aspects (Pribram, 1980).

8. Some have suggested that one of the reasons candlelight dinners are romantic is that the candlelight prompts the pupils to dilate, giving each person the subtle cue that the other person is interested in them.

9. Dan Goleman devotes Chapter 11 of his book *Emotional Intelligence* to describing numer-ous scientific studies verifying the impact of emotions on health (Goleman, 1995).

10. The food-mood connection has produced many books for the layperson; see for exam-ple, *Managing Your Mind and Mood through Food* (Wurtman, 1986).

11. Many authors have described findings on mood-congruence effects between affect and memory (Isen, Shalker, Clark, and Karp, 1978; Laird, Wagener, Halal, and Szegda, 1982; Forgas and Bower, 1987; Lewis and Williams, 1989; and Lazarus, 1991). There are also several overviews of this literature (Blaney, 1986; Araujo, 1994).

12. Several researchers have argued how some emotions occur without prior cognitive appraisal (Zajonc, 1984; LeDoux, 1990; Izard, 1993; Damasio, 1994; and LeDoux, 1994).

13. The colorful terminology of "hijacking" is from Goleman (1995).

14. These claims are discussed in *The Communication of Emotion*, (Buck, 1984). Other discussions of the influence of temperament and personality can be found by Darby (1981), and Kagan (1984), as well as in this book in Chapter 5. Note that psychologists cannot say that temperament and personality *cause* someone to be more or less expressive, only that they are correlated with expressiveness. For affective computing, this issue of causality does not matter; correlations can be used directly to assist in recognition of human emotion.

15. Studies supporting these claims about gender and children are given by Buck (1984).

16. If progress in affect recognition proceeds like progress in speech recognition, then we will see systems that are initially user-dependent, but that later, after learning how to combine patterns for large numbers of users, can perform well in a user-independent way.

17. This list is from Izard (1993).

18. Wright, Sloman, and Beaudoin (1996), have described the design of an information processing architecture that would exhibit perturbances and human-like grieving.

19. Terrific tips for how to arouse a variety of feelings are described in *Respect for Acting* (Hagen with Frankel, 1983). *An Actor Prepares* is now a classic text for method acting (Stanislavsky, 1936).

20. From E. A. Poe's "Eleanora" in "The Fall of the House of Usher and Other Writings," ed. David Galloway; London: Penguin, 1986, p. 243.

21. Douglas Hofstadter, one of the most creative contributors to the field of Artificial Intel-ligence, has amassed several ideas related to computer creativity in his book, *Fluid Concepts and Creative Analogies* (Hofstadter, 1995); however, like most cognitive and computer scien-tists, he does not address the influence of emotion on creativity.

22. Jamison's book *Touched with Fire: Manic-Depressive Illness and the Artistic Temperament* (1993), as well as articles by Andreasen (1987), Ludwig (1992), and Jamison (1995) de-scribe studies linking moods, especially mood disorders, and creativity. Jamison describes

hereditary influences, and lists writers, poets, composers, and artists who committed suicide or suffered from major mood disorders. She also gives diagnostic criteria for the major mood disorders: major depressive syndrome, manic syndrome, hypomanic syndrome, cyclothymia.

23. Discussion of the relative effects of stimulants and depressants on synesthesia can be found in Cytowic (1993).

24. These claims are all supported via studies by Isen and her colleagues (Isen, Johnson, Mertz, and Robinson, 1985; Isen, Daubman, and Nowicki, 1987).

25. It is now understood that the limbic and nonpyramidal systems are relatively more involved in voluntary expression, while the motor cortex and pyramidal circuits are relatively more involved in involuntary expression (Izard, 1990; Damasio, 1994).

Chapter 2

1. For a list of tests of nonverbal recognition abilities, as well as pointers to studies finding significant associations between these abilities and other factors such as profession and gender, see Salovey and Mayer (1990).

2. Most people cannot control their autonomic nervous system responses, such as perspiration or skin temperature, although there are cases where people have trained themselves to do so.

3. Some of the research on facial expression recognition has also applied the recognition to compression or coding of the faces (Lanitis, Taylor, and Cootes, 1995; Essa and Pentland, 1997). Unlike current compression systems where every frame is usually encoded, future object-based coding systems will be able to update a model of a face just by sending over a person's changes in expression, hair style, etc.

4. Toda's urge theory is now described in an English translation of his book (Toda, 1993, 1994, 1995, 1996). Examples of systems with purely emergent emotions include the robots of Pfeifer (1994) and of Shibata and Irie (1997).

5. See the work of LeDoux and his colleagues, (LeDoux, 1990, 1994, 1996) describing the findings of simple unconscious mechanisms for emotion generation, especially for fear, which is the best studied emotion in terms of its underlying mechanisms.

6. This scenario is adapted from one in Chapter 13 of *HAL's Legacy: 2001's Computer as Dream and Reality* (Picard, 1997). It is similar in spirit to the fungus-eater scenario of Toda (1962).

7. This scenario is adapted from one in Chapter 13 of *HAL's Legacy: 2001's Computer as Dream and Reality* (Picard, 1997).

8. Interest is treated by some theorists as an emotion because it has a characteristic facial expression, while others who argue that emotions must be valenced treat it as a non-valenced cognitive state.

9. Thanks to Dana and Warren Kirsch for providing the Tandem example.

10. Rod Brooks and Lynn Stein's "Cog" project at the MIT AI Laboratory is an ambitious attempt to construct a machine with a body having perceptual, cognitive, and affective

abilities (Brooks and Stein, 1993). Although Cog is sessile, Cog's arms can move in ways that might bring about injury to Cog; this observation inspired my discussion here.

11. I recommend Matti Kamppinen's book (1993), which combines philosophical and scientific issues, for an overview of research on consciousness. Readers might also be interested in McCarthy's efforts to define consciousness for machines, where he describes self-consciousness as an ability to introspect, and as an essential component of intelligence (McCarthy 1979, 1995).

12. The subtleties of this are in the timing of the events in the brain; for details of the timing for a fear response in the brain, see the description by LeDoux (1990).

13. From a vendor's perspective, of course, the real tests will be the sales figures.

14. LeDoux (1996) discusses PTSD and other emotional disorders in terms of what has been learned about the limbic system and its influences on the cortex.

15. Automobile manufacturers are also interested in detecting drowsiness and drunkeness, although these are not usually considered emotional states. Nonetheless, many of the tools in this book could be similarly used for detecting these kinds of non-affective states.

Chapter 3

1. This kind of interactive scenario has important theoretical applications as well as the practical ones described here. In such an interactive system, a human subject might role-play different methods of emotional interaction. Hence the system becomes a test-bed for new strategies or games involving affective communication and skill building. More importantly, perhaps, such a test-bed provides a safe and controllable environment for exploring the nature and development of emotional intelligence, which, in theory, can be learned.

2. Although developed with a different goal in mind, the program PAULINE (Planning and Uttering Language in Natural Environments) can assess the negative, neutral, and positive slants of a text, and regenerate them with a different slant (Hovy, 1986), one of many possible first steps toward the application described here.

3. An example of a system that tries to understand emotions in narratives is BORIS (Dyer, 1983).

4. I am grateful to Dr. Roberto Tuchman, Director, Dan Marino Child NETT, and to Dr. Ira Cohen, New York State Institute for Basic Research in Developmental Disabilities, for discussions about autism, which inspired these possible applications.

5. Email oc@musenet.org or point your Web or Gopher browser at cyberion.musenet.org for information on how to connect.

6. The classic curve is usually attributed to the early work of Yerkes and Dodson (1908), which measured the learning rate of rats subjected to different levels of stimulation. Many psychology textbooks describe the more general implications of the law; see for example, Hebb (1966).

7. See Picard and Minka (1995), and Wachman (1996) for descriptions of the basic image and video annotation systems. These systems have been augmented with various kinds of continuous learning to steadily adapt the system to what a user wants, without the user having to specify anything more than positive and negative examples of what he wants (Minka and Picard, 1997).

8. Marquis and Elliott (1994) have also built poker-playing agents with facial expressions, based on a variation of the OCC structure. The facial expressions on their agents were probably even more engaging than those used by Koda, since the former were dynamic. Marquis and Elliott also added an ability for the agent players to respond emotionally if another player takes too long to make a decision. Hence, their agents let emotions influence behavior beyond just showing facial expressions. However, they have not conducted an evaluation of the impact on human players.

9. This story was reported by Reuters ("'Virtual Pet' Craze Sweeps Japan," January 1997).

Chapter 4

1. A discussion of emotions and HAL appears in my chapter in *HAL's Legacy: 2001's Computer as Dream and Reality* (Picard, 1997).

2. Users need to become aware of many biases that influence how they perceive information coming from computers and other forms of media. For example, people watching news on a television labeled "News Television," rated it consistently more informative, interesting, important, serious, and likable, than did people watching the same news on a television labeled "News and Entertainment Television." Reeves and Nass, who conducted this experiment, (Reeves and Nass, 1996), argue that humans assign better quality to information coming from a source they believe to be a specialist, even when the specialist is not human, but media, such as a computer or television.

3. It remains to be determined if affective information would be subject to subpoena, but if someone was concerned about this, then the best solution would be to not have the computer store anything, but to permit it to only use real-time affective analysis. Development of real-time affective analysis is an area of current research.

4. There are techniques in psychology, such as the Kestenberg Movement Profile, that notate how people move, reflecting attitudes, tension, cultural factors, affect, and other medical factors. A movement profile is especially helpful for assessing young infants or infant-parent interaction, since infants cannot be psychoanalyzed verbally.

5. See also the mention of Hitler's tactics in Chapter 1 of this book, as well as discussions of emotion control as part of mind control in Hassan (1988).

6. Stephen Bury's science fiction novel, *Interface* (1994) addresses the manipulation of a political figure by the emotions of the American people, in part via emotion recognition technology, even though the technology in the novel is not very plausible scientifically.

7. The influences of anxiety are much more complex than intimated here. Araujo (1994) provides a more thorough discussion of results of the influence of anxiety on task performance, including an attempt to model these influences.

8. It is interesting to note that there do not seem to be any computer simulations of affect on record in the early 1960s, before *2001* was made, but there is Colby's simulation of a neurotic process (Colby, 1963), which has as a key feature the detection of conflict. In the simulation, conflict among the computer's beliefs increases its internal anxiety, and results in modification of its beliefs, in an effort to alleviate the conflict and reduce anxiety.

9. See also Daniel Dennett's address of ethical questions surrounding HAL's actions in "Did HAL commit murder?" (Dennett, 1997).

10. Hofstadter has argued that creativity and flexibility are components of machine intelligence (Hofstadter, 1979).

11. For an example of chaos, program a machine to take the equation, $f(x) = ax - ax^2$, and to iterate it. First, plug in a value of x between 0 and 1 to obtain $f(x)$. Next, use the result of $f(x)$ as the new value of x, and so forth. When a is less than 1, then no matter what value of x that you choose between 0 and 1, repeated iterations will cause $f(x)$ to predictably become 0. However, when a takes on certain values, such as 4, then the values of $f(x)$, will exhibit chaotic behavior. This simple equation has a name: the "logistic map." See (Jensen, 1987) for more details. There are also other ways to get unpredictable behavior, simply by combining multiple processors or mechanisms that cannot be perfectly synchronized. Theorists are also proposing "quantum computing", which involves another kind of inherent unpredictability (Bennett, 1995). Nobody can predict yet if and when such machines will be practical.

12. This example is one achieved by Doug Lenat's CYC project, a large-scale effort to give computers a database of common sense (Lenat and Guha, 1989; Lenat, 1995). Currently, all the common sense knowledge is entered by humans; the computer has not yet been given the ability to acquire common sense for itself.

Chapter 5

1. Those who are familiar with signal processing may recognize this response as that of a linear time-invariant system which has an exponential decay as its impulse response.

2. The words "linear" and "nonlinear" are used in different ways in different fields. "Linear" frequently is used to refer to things occurring one after the other, as if in a single file. Things that do not occur in this way, such as the possible ways to browse a network of hyperlinked web documents, are termed nonlinear. I use linear and nonlinear differently in this book, following the definitions used in discrete-time signal processing. For more information, see the textbook of Oppenheim and Schafer (1989).

3. In the parlance of control theory this would be an example of "positive feedback," which allows the system output to grow exponentially fast, making it unstable—a generally undesirable situation. Control theory provides a variety of tools to stabilize dynamic systems and to help their outputs remain manageable (Luenberger, 1979). The terminology "positive (and negative) feedback" is avoided in this book deliberately, to avoid confusion with the use of positive (and negative) to refer to emotional valence that is communicated by feedback mechanisms in the human body.

Chapter 6

1. One might rationally pose the question "Is it via some metaphysical sixth sense that emotions are communicated?" However, questions such as this exceed the scope of this book. There are *invisible* ways in which emotion might be communicated, such as through olfaction, and via pheromones which can communicate hormonal changes; however, these are not to be confused with metaphysics.

2. Good resources for tools on pattern recognition and analysis include the books by Fukunaga (1972), Duda and Hart (1973), Tou (1974), Therrien (1989), Schalkoff (1992), and Bishop (1995).

3. For example, see the neural net-based recognition work of Cottrell and Metcalfe (1991).

4. There were also several forerunners of this system—the "Facial Affect Scoring Technique" (FAST) developed by Ekman, Friesen and Tomkins, which coded for Ekman's six basic emotions, and Izard's Maximally Discriminable Facial Movement Coding System (Max), which included these six as well as expressions of interest, contempt, shame and pain. There are several overviews of these and other techniques used by human researchers to label facial expressions (Bruce and Burton 1992, Bruce, Burton and Doyle 1992a; Buck, 1984).

5. There is not room to describe all the work done in this area; see also the work on video-based facial expression recognition by Mase (1991); Lanitis, Taylor, and Cootes (1995); Matsuno, Lee, Kimura, and Tsuji (1995); and Sakaguchi and Morishima (1996).

6. These methods of pattern recognition can be found in textbooks (Duda and Hart, 1973; Therrien, 1989).

7. Classification accuracy in all these experiments was evaluated with the leave-one-out cross validation method. Classes were modeled with Gaussians with equal covariances, a restriction that could be loosened to probably improve the accuracy. Each point was classified according to its posterior probability.

8. The mathematics for how to train HMM's and for how to recognize what state a pattern is in, given observations, can be found in Rabiner and Huang (1986) and in Rabiner (1989).

Chapter 7

1. I gratefully acknowledge Pattie Maes for this definition; see also Maes (1994).

2. Ortony, Clore, and Collins classify surprise as a cognitive state, not as an emotional state, the latter of which they require to have valence.

3. See also Roseman's earlier studies, which reveal the gradual development of the model described here (Roseman, Spindel, and Jose, 1990), (Roseman, 1991). Roseman's studies are similar to Smith and Ellsworth (1985, 1987), and are also interesting to compare with one of the first appraisal theories (Arnold, 1960). For more descriptions of appraisal theories see Scherer (1988).

4. See Velásquez (1996) for how these are computed.

5. The specific experiments of Bower and Cohen (1982) have since been called into question. However, the basic findings of mood-congruent memory retrieval have been verified in many subsequent studies. See the discussion and references on mood-congruent memory retrieval and learning in Chapter 1.

Chapter 8

1. The word "cyborg" first appeared in Clynes and Kline (1960). Clynes says that when he first proposed the word to his coauthor, Kline remarked "It sounds like a town in Denmark!"

2. More details about the system I describe here can be found in Picard and Healey (1997).

3. As labs become equipped with convincing virtual reality systems, one can argue that an increasing number of natural situations might be replicated in the lab. However, human-

human interactions and comfortable home surroundings will be hard to duplicate in the virtual environment, and these influence a person's level of stress or relaxation.

4. Psychologists acknowledge this problem as the sacrifice of external validity for internal validity. With the introduction of wearables, the sacrifice shifts in the other direction. The combination of the two, traditional laboratory and wearable laboratory, is therefore valuable.

5. This story was related by Don Thulean, Vice President for Orchestra Services at the American Symphony Orchestra League, to Teresa Marrin, a research assistant at the MIT Media Lab.

References

D. Adams. *The Restaurant at the End of the Universe*. Harmony Books, New York, 1980.

B. Aldiss. Super-toys last all summer long. *Wired*, pages 135–138, January 1997. First published in *Harper's Bazaar* in 1969.

N. Alm, I. R. Murray, J. L. Arnott, and A. F. Newell. Pragmatics and affect in a communication system for non-speakers. *Journal of the American Voice I/O Society*, 13:1–15, March 1993. I/O Society Special Issue: People with Disabilities.

N. C. Andreasen. Creativity and mental illness: Prevalence rates in writers and their first-degree relatives. *American Journal Psychiatry*, 144(10):1288–1292, Oct. 1987.

A. F. R. Araujo. *Memory, Emotions, and Neural Networks: Associative Learning and Memory Recall Influenced by Affective Evaluation and Task Difficulty*. PhD thesis, University of Sussex, May 1994.

Aristotle. *The Rhetoric of Aristotle*. Appleton-Century-Crofts, New York, NY, 1960. An expanded translation with supplementary examples for students of composition and public speaking, by L. Cooper.

J. L. Armony, D. Servan-Schreiber, J. D. Cohen, and J. E. LeDoux. Computational modeling of emotion: Explorations through the anatomy and physiology of fear conditioning. *Trends in Cognitive Sciences*, 1(1):28–34, April 1997.

M. Arnold. *Emotion and personality: Vol. 1. Psychological aspects*. Columbia University Press, New York, 1960.

I. Asimov. *The Bicentennial Man and Other Stories*. Doubleday Science Fiction, Garden City, NY, 1976.

J. R. Averill. Inner feelings, works of the flesh, the beast within, diseases of the mind, driving force, and putting on a show: Six metaphors of emotion and their theoretical extensions. In D. E. Leary, editor, *Metaphors in the History of Psychology*, pages 104–132. Cambridge University Press, New York, 1990.

D. M. Badzinski. Children's cognitive representations of discourse: Effects of vocal cues on text comprehension. *Communication Research*, 18(6):715–736, 1991.

F. H. Baker. Assistive technology for the visually impaired, 1994. http://www.wilmer.jhu.edu/low_vis/lves.htm.

J. Bates. The role of emotion in believable agents. *Communications of the ACM*, 37(7):122–125, July 1994.

J. Bates, A. B. Loyall, and W. S. Reilly. An architecture for action, emotion, and social behavior. School of Computer Science CMU-CS-92-144, Carnegie Mellon University, Pittsburgh, PA, May 1992.

A. Bechara, H. Damasio, D. Tranel, and A. R. Damasio. Deciding advantageously before knowing the advantageous strategy. *Science*, 275:1293–1295, February 1997.

D. A. Becker and A. Pentland. Staying alive: A virtual reality visualization tool for cancer patients. In *Proceedings of the AAAI'96 Workshop on Entertainment and Alife/AI*, Portland, OR, August 1996. M.I.T. Media Laboratory TR 380.

C. H. Bennett. Quantum information and computation. *Physics Today*, 1995.

C. M. Bishop. *Neural Networks for Pattern Recognition*. Clarendon Press, Oxford, 1995.

M. J. Black and Y. Yacoob. Tracking and recognizing rigid and non-rigid facial motions using local parametric model of image motion. In *IEEE Int. Conf. on Comp. Vis.*, pages 374–381. IEEE Computer Society, Cambridge, MA, 1995.

P. H. Blaney. Affect and memory: A review. *Psychological Bulletin*, 99(2):229–246, 1986.

A. Bouhuys, G. M. Bloem, and T. G. Groothuis. Induction of depressed and elated mood by music influences the perception of facial emotional expression in healthy subjects. *Journal of Affective Disorders*, 33:215–226, 1995.

G. H. Bower and P. R. Cohen. Emotional influences in memory and thinking: Data and theory. In *Affect and Cognition: The Seventh Annual Carnegie Symposium on Cognition*, pages 291–233. Lawrence Erlbaum Associates, N.J., 1982.

M. M. Bradley, B. N. Cuthbert, and P. J. Lang. Picture media and emotion: Effects of a sustained affective context. *Psychophysiology*, 33:662–670, 1996.

V. Braitenberg. *Vehicles: Experiments in Synthetic Psychology*. The MIT Press, Cambridge, Massachusetts, 1984.

R. A. Brooks and L. A. Stein. Building brains for bodies. Technical Report 1439, MIT AI Lab, August 1993.

R. Brown and J. Kulik. Flashbulb memories. *Cognition*, 5:73–99, 1977.

V. Bruce and M. Burton. The human face—the organ of communication. In V. Bruce and M. Burton, editors, *Processing Images of Faces*. Ablex Publishing Corporation, 1992.

V. Bruce, M. Burton, and T. Doyle. Faces as surfaces. In V. Bruce and M. Burton, editors, *Processing Images of Faces*, chapter 10. Ablex Publishing Corporation, 1992.

R. Buck. *The Communication of Emotion*. Guilford Press, 1984.

S. Bury. *Interface*. Bantam Books, New York Toronto London, 1994.

J. T. Cacioppo and L. G. Tassinary. Inferring psychological significance from physiological signals. *American Psychologist*, 45(1):16–28, Jan. 1990.

J. E. Cahn. The generation of affect in synthesized speech. *Journal of the American Voice I/O Society*, 8:1–19, July 1990.

L. A. Camras. Expressive development and basic emotions. *Cognition and Emotion*, 6(3/4), 1992.

D. Canamero. Modeling motivations and emotions as a basis for intelligent behavior. In W. L. Johnson, editor, *Proceedings of the First International Conference on Autonomous Agents*, pages 148–155, New York, Feb. 1997. ACM Press.

W. B. Cannon. The James-Lange theory of emotions: A critical examination and an alternative theory. *American Journal of Psychology*, 39:106–124, 1927.

O. S. Card. *Speaker for the Dead*. Tom Doherty Associates, Inc., New York, NY, 1986.

M. Chekhov. *On the Technique of Acting*. HarperCollins Pub., New York, 1991. Chekhov, (1891–1955), Preface and Afterword by M. Powers.

S.-J. Chung. An acoustic and perceptual study on the emotive speech in Korean and French. In *ICPhS*, pages 266–269, Stockholm, 1995. Vol. 1, Session 11.7.

A. C. Clarke. *2001 A Space Odyssey*. New American Library, Inc., New York, NY, 1968. Based on the 1965 screenplay by S. Kubrick and A. C. Clarke.

G. L. Clore. Cognitive phenomenology: Feelings and the construction of judgment. In L. Martin and A. Tesser, editors, *The Construction of Social Judgments*. Lawrence Erlbaum Associates, 1992.

D. M. Clynes. *Sentics: The Touch of the Emotions*. Anchor Press/Doubleday, 1977.

M. Clynes, S. Jurisevic, and M. Rynn. Inherent cognitive substrates of specific emotions: Love is blocked by lying but not anger. *Perceptual and Motor Skills*, 70:195–206, 1990.

M. Clynes and N. S. Kline. Cyborgs and space. *Astronautics*, 14(9):26–27 and 74–76, Sept. 1960.

K. M. Colby. Computer simulation of a neurotic process. In S. S. Tomkins and S. Messick, editors, *Computer Simulation of Personality: Frontier of Psychological Theory*, pages 165–179. John Wiley and Sons, New York, London, 1963.

G. Collier. *Emotional Expression*. Lawrence Erlbaum Associates, Hillsdale, N.J., 1985.

G. W. Cottrell and J. Metcalfe. EMPATH: Face, emotion, and gender recognition using holons. In R. P. Lippmann, J. E. Moody, D. S. Touretzky, and B. M. Spatz, editors, *Neural Information Processing Systems*, volume 3, pages 564–571, San Mateo, CA, 1991. Morgan Kaufmann Publishers, Inc.

S. R. Covey. *The Seven Habits of Highly Effective People*. Fireside, Simon and Schuster, New York, 1989.

M. Csikszentmihalyi. *Flow: The Psychology of Optimal Experience*. Harper and Row, New York, 1990.

J. G. Cunningham and R. S. Sterling. Developmental change in the understanding of affective meaning in music. *Motivation and Emotion*, 12(4):399–413, 1988.

R. E. Cytowic. *Synesthesia: A union of the senses*. Springer-Verlag, New York, 1989.

R. E. Cytowic. *The Man Who Tasted Shapes*. G. P. Putnam's Sons, New York, NY, 1993.

R. E. Cytowic. *The Neurological Side of Neuropsychology*. MIT Press, Cambridge, MA, 1996.

A. R. Damasio. *Descartes' Error: Emotion, Reason, and the Human Brain*. Gosset/Putnam Press, New York, NY, 1994.

J. K. Darby. *Speech Evaluation in Psychiatry*. Grune and Stratton, Inc., 1981.

C. Darwin. *The Expression of the Emotions in Man and Animals*. The University of Chicago Press, Chicago, IL, 1965. Originally published in 1872.

R. J. Davidson. Temperament, affective style, and frontal lobe asymmetry. In G. Dawson and K. W. Fischer, editors, *Human Behavior and the Developing Brain*, pages 518–536. Guilford Press, New York, 1994.

J. R. Davitz. *The Communication of Emotional Meaning*. McGraw-Hill Book Company, New York, 1964.

D. Dennett. Where am I? In *Brainstorms: Philosophic Essays on Mind and Psychology*, Montgomery, VT, 1978. Bradford Books.

D. C. Dennett. Did Hal commit murder? In D. G. Stork, editor, *Hal's Legacy: 2001's Computer as Dream and Reality*, Cambridge, MA, 1997. MIT Press.

G. B. Duchenne. *The Mechanism of Human Facial Expression*. Cambridge University Press, New York, NY, 1990. Reprinting of original 1862 dissertation.

R. O. Duda and P. E. Hart. *Pattern Classification and Scene Analysis*. Wiley-Interscience, 1973.

M. G. Dyer. The role of affect in narratives. *Cognitive Science*, 7:211–242, 1983.

M. G. Dyer. Emotions and their computations: Three computer models. *Cognition and Emotion*, 1(3):323–347, 1987.

P. Ekman. Commentaries: Duchenne and facial expression of emotion. In R. A. Cuthbertson, editor, *The Mechanism of Human Facial Expression*, pages 270–284. Cambridge University Press, 1990.

P. Ekman. Are there basic emotions? *Psychological Review*, 99(3):550–553, 1992.

P. Ekman. An argument for basic emotions. *Cognition and Emotion*, 6(3/4):169–200, 1992.

P. Ekman. Facial expression and emotion. *American Psychologist*, 48(4):384–392, April 1993.

P. Ekman and W. Friesen. *Facial Action Coding System*. Consulting Psychologists Press, 1977.

P. Ekman, R. W. Levenson, and W. V. Friesen. Autonomic nervous system activity distinguishes among emotions. *Science*, 221:1208–1210, Sep. 1983.

P. Ekman and M. O'Sullivan. Who can catch a liar? *American Psychologist*, 46(9):913–920, Sep. 1991.

C. Elliott. Components of two-way emotion communication between humans and computers using a broad, rudimentary model of affect and personality. *Cognitive Studies: Bulletin of the Japanese Cognitive Science Society*, 1(2):16–30, 1994.

C. Elliott. I picked up catapia and other stories: A multimodal approach to expressivity for 'emotionally intelligent' agents. In *Proceedings of the First International Conference on Autonomous Agents*, pages 451–457, Marina del Rey, CA, February 1997.

I. A. Essa. *Analysis, Interpretation and Synthesis of Facial Expressions*. PhD thesis, MIT Media Lab, Cambridge, MA, Feb. 1995.

I. A. Essa and A. Pentland. Facial expression recognition using a dynamic model and motion energy. In *IEEE Int. Conf. on Comp. Vis.*, pages 360–367, Cambridge, MA, 1995. IEEE Computer Society.

I. Essa and A. Pentland. Coding, analysis, interpretation and recognition of facial expressions. *IEEE Transactions on Pattern Analysis and Machine Intelligence*, 19(7):757–763, July 1997.

I. Flatow. *They all laughed– : from light bulbs to lasers, the fascinating stories behind the great inventions that have changed our lives.* HarperCollins, New York, c1992.

L. N. Foner. A security architecture for multi-agent matchmaking. In *The Second International Conference on Multi-Agent Systems*, pages 80–86, Kyoto, Japan, Dec. 1996. AAAI Press.

J. P. Forgas and G. H. Bower. Mood effects on person-perception judgments. *Journal of Personality and Social Psychology*, 53(1):53–60, 1987.

J. P. Forgas and S. Moylan. After the movies: Transient mood and social judgments. *Personality and Social Psychology Bulletin*, 13(4):467–477, 1987.

W. J. Freeman. *Societies of Brains. A Study in the Neuroscience of Love and Hate.* Lawrence Erlbaum Associates, Publishers, Hillsdale, NJ, 1995.

N. H. Frijda. *The Emotions.* Studies in Emotion and Social Interaction. Cambridge University Press, Cambridge, 1986.

N. H. Frijda and J. Swagerman. Can computers feel? Theory and design of an emotional system. *Cognition and Emotion*, 1(3):235–257, 1987.

K. Fukunaga. *Introduction to Statistical Pattern Recognition.* Academic Press, Inc., New York, 1972.

H. Gardner. *Frames of Mind.* BasicBooks, New York, 1983.

H. Gardner. *Multiple Intelligences: The Theory in Practice.* Basic Books, New York, 1993.

D. Gelernter. *The Muse in the Machine.* The Free Press, Macmillan, Inc., Ontario, 1994.

D. Goleman. *Emotional Intelligence.* Bantam Books, New York, 1995.

J. Gray. *Men are from Mars, Women are from Venus.* Harper Collins, New York, 1992.

S. Grossberg and W. E. Gutowski. Neural dynamics of decision making under risk: Affective balance and cognitive-emotional interactions. *Psychological Review*, 94(3):300–318, 1987.

U. Hagen with H. Frankel. *Respect for Acting*, chapter on Emotional Memory and Sense Memory. MacMillan, New York, 1983.

J. B. Halberstadt, P. M. Niedenthal, and J. Kushner. Resolution of lexical ambiguity by emotional state. *Psychological Science*, 6(5):278–282, September 1995.

S. Hassan. *Combatting Cult Mind Control*, chapter Four: Understanding Mind Control, pages 53–75. Park St. Press, 1988.

B. Hayes-Roth, L. Brownston, and E. Sincoff. Directed improvisation by computer characters. Technical Report KSL-95-04, Stanford University Knowledge Systems Laboratory, Palo Alto, California, 1995.

D. O. Hebb. *A Textbook of Psychology.* W. B. Saunders Co., Philadelphia, 1966.

W. R. Hess. *The functional organization of the diencephalon.* Grune & Stratton, New York, 1957.

S. G. Hofmann and D. H. Barlow. Ambulatory psychophysiological monitoring: A potentially useful tool when treating panic relapse. *Cognitive and Behavioral Practice*, 3:53–61, 1996.

D. Hofstadter and the Fluid Analogies Research Group. *Fluid Concepts and Creative Analogies: Computer Models of the Fundamental Mechanisms of Thought*. Basic Books, New York, 1995.

D. R. Hofstadter. *Godel, Escher, Bach: an Eternal Golden Braid*. Basic Books, New York, 1979.

D. R. Hofstadter and D. C. Dennett. *The Mind's I*. Bantam Books, New York, 1981.

E. H. Hovy. Putting affect into text. In *Proceedings of the Eighth Annual Conference of the Cognitive Science Society*, pages 669–775, Englewood Cliffs, NJ, 1986. Erlbaum.

E. Hudlicka and J.-M. Fellous. Review of computational models of emotion. Technical Report 9612, Psychometrix, Arlington, MA, April 1996.

A. Huxley (1894–1963). *Brave new world & Brave new world revisited*. Harper & Row, New York, NY, 1965.

A. M. Isen, K. A. Daubman, and G. P. Nowicki. Positive affect facilitates creative problem solving. *Journal of Personality and Social Psychology*, 52(6):1122–1131, 1987.

A. M. Isen, M. M. Johnson, E. Mertz, and G. F. Robinson. The influence of positive affect on the unusualness of word associations. *Journal of Personality and Social Psychology*, 48(6):1413–1426, 1985.

A. M. Isen, T. E. Shalker, M. Clark, and L. Karp. Affect, accessibility of material in memory, and behavior: A cognitive loop? *Journal of Personality and Social Psychology*, 36(1):1–12, Jan. 1978.

C. E. Izard. Facial expressions and the regulation of emotions. *Journal of Personality and Social Psychology*, 58(3):487–498, 1990.

C. E. Izard. Four systems for emotion activation: Cognitive and noncognitive processes. *Psychological Review*, 100(1):68–90, 1993.

W. James. *William James: Writings 1878–1899*, chapter on Emotion, pages 350–365. The Library of America, 1992. Originally published in 1890.

K. R. Jamison. *Touched with Fire: Manic-Depressive Illness and the Artistic Temperament*. The Free Press, 1993.

K. R. Jamison. Manic-depressive illness and creativity. *Scientific American*, 272(2):62–67, Feb. 1995.

R. V. Jensen. Classical chaos. *American Scientist*, 75:168–181, March-April 1987.

P. N. Johnson-Laird and K. Oatley. The language of emotions: An analysis of a semantic field. *Cognition and Emotion*, 3(2):81–123, 1989.

P. N. Johnson-Laird and E. Shafir. The interaction between reasoning and decision making: an introduction. *Cognition*, 49:1–9, 1993.

J. Kagan, N. Snidman, D. Arcus, and J. S. Reznick. *Galen's Prophecy: Temperament in Human Nature*. Basic Books, Division of HarperCollins, New York, 1994.

D. Kahneman. Arousal and attention. In *Attention and Effort*, pages 28–49. Prentice-Hall, Englewood Cliffs, N.J., 1973.

M. Kamppinen. *Consciousness, Cognitive Schemata, and Relativism*. Kluwer Academic Pub., Norwell, MA, 1993.

P. R. Kleinginna, Jr. and A. M. Kleinginna. A categorized list of emotion definitions, with suggestions for a consensual definition. *Motivation and Emotion*, 5(4):345–379, 1981.

T. Koda. Agents with faces: A study on the effects of personification of software agents. Master's thesis, MIT Media Lab, Cambridge, MA, Sept. 1996.

O. Kroeger and J. M. Thuesen. *Type Talk at Work*. Delacorte Press, Bantam Doubleday Dell Publishing Group, Inc., New York, 1992.

J. D. Laird, J. J. Wagener, M. Halal, and M. Szegda. Remembering what you feel: Effects of emotion on memory. *Journal of Personality and Social Psychology*, 42(4):646–657, 1982.

P. J. Lang. Cognition in emotion: Concept and action. In C. E. Izard, J. Kagan, and R. B. Zajonc, editors, *Emotions, Cognition, and Behavior*, pages 192–226, Cambridge, 1984. Cambridge University Press.

P. J. Lang. The emotion probe: Studies of motivation and attention. *American Psychologist*, 50(5):372–385, 1995.

E. J. Langer. *Mindfulness*. Addison-Wesley, 1989.

A. Lanitis, C. Taylor, and T. Cootes. A unified approach to coding and interpreting face images. In *Fifth International Conference on Computer Vision*, pages 368–373, Cambridge, MA, June 1995. IEEE Computer Society Press.

Y. Z. Lashkari. Feature guided automated collaborative filtering. Master's thesis, MIT Media Lab, Cambridge, MA, September 1995.

B. Laurel. Interface agents: Metaphors with character. In B. Laurel, editor, *The Art of Human-computer Interface Design*, pages 355–365, Reading, MA, 1990. Addison-Wesley.

R. S. Lazarus. *Emotion & Adaptation*. Oxford University Press, New York, NY, 1991.

J. LeDoux. *The Emotional Brain*. Simon & Schuster, New York, 1996.

J. E. LeDoux. Information flow from sensation to emotion: Plasticity in the neural computation of stimulus value. In M. Gabriel and J. Moore, editors, *Learning and Computational Neuroscience: Foundations of Adaptive Networks*, pages 3–51. MIT Press, 1990.

J. E. LeDoux. Emotion, memory and the brain. *Scientific American*, pages 50–57, June 1994.

G. W. V. Leibniz. *Monadology and Other Philosophical Essays*. The Bobbs-Merrill Company, Inc., Indianapolis, 1965. Essay: Critical Remarks Concerning the General Part of Descartes' Principles (1692), Translated by: P. Schrecker and A. M. Schrecker.

D. B. Lenat. Artificial intelligence. *Scientific American*, pages 80–82, Sept. 1995.

D. B. Lenat and R. V. Guha. *Building Large Knowledge-Based Systems: Representation and Inference in the CYC Project*. Addison-Wesley, Reading, MA, 1989.

R. W. Levenson. Autonomic nervous system differences among emotions. *American Psychological Society*, 3(1):23–27, Jan. 1992.

M. Lewis. Ch 16: The emergence of human emotions. In M. Lewis and J. Haviland, editors, *Handbook of Emotions*, pages 223–235, New York, NY, 1993. Guilford Press.

M. Lewis. Self-conscious emotions. *American Scientist*, 83:68–78, Jan.–Feb. 1995.

V. E. Lewis and R. N. Williams. Mood-congruent vs. mood-state-dependent learning: Implications for a view of emotion. In D. Kuiken, editor, *Mood and Memory: Theory, Research, and Applications*, volume 4 of *Special Issue of the Journal of Social Behavior and Personality*, pages 157–171. Journal of Social Behavior and Personality, 1989. No. 2.

A. M. Ludwig. Creative achievement and psychopathology: Comparison among professions. *American Journal of Psychotherapy*, XLVI(3):330–356, July 1992.

D. G. Luenberger. *Introduction to Dynamic Systems*. John Wiley & Sons, New York, 1979.

T. Machover. Hyperinstruments: A composer's approach to the evolution of intelligent musical instruments. *CyberArts*, pages 67–76, Jan. 1992.

P. D. MacLean. The triune brain, emotion, and scientific bias. In F. Schmitt, editor, *The Neurosciences: Second Study Program*, pages 336–349. Rockefeller University Press, New York, 1970.

P. Maes. Agents that reduce work and information overload. *Communications of the ACM*, 37(7):31–40, July 1994.

P. Maes, T. Darrell, B. Blumberg, and A. Pentland. The ALIVE system: Full-body interaction with autonomous agents. *Proceedings of Computer Animation*, Apr. 1995.

G. Mandler. *Mind and Body: Psychology of Emotion and Stress*. W. W. Norton & Company, New York, NY, 1984.

S. Mann. Wearable computing: A first step toward personal imaging. *Computer*, pages 25–31, February 1997.

S. Marquis and C. Elliott. Emotionally responsive poker playing agents. In *Notes for the Twelfth National Conference on Artificial Intelligence AAAI-94 Workshop on Artificial Intelligence, Artificial Life, and Entertainment*. AAAI, 1994.

K. Mase. Recognition of facial expression from optical flow. *IEICE Transactions, Special Issue on Computer Vision and its Applications*, E74(10):3474–3483, October 1991.

K. Matsuno, C.-W. Lee, S. Kimura, and S. Tsuji. Automatic recognition of human facial expressions. In *IEEE Int. Conf. on Comp. Vis.*, pages 352–359, Cambridge, MA, June 1995. IEEE Computer Society Press.

J. D. Mayer and P. Salovey. The intelligence of emotional intelligence. *Intelligence*, 17:433–442, 1993.

D. J. Mayhew. *Principles and Guidelines in Software User Interface Design*. Prentice Hall, Englewood Cliffs, New Jersey, 1992.

J. McCarthy. Ascribing mental qualities to machines. In V. Lifschitz, editor, *Formalization of common sense*. Ablex, 1990. Originally published in 1979.

J. McCarthy. Making robots conscious of their metal state. In *Proceedings of Machine Intelligence Workshop*, Oxford, Aug. 1995.

H. McGurk and J. MacDonald. Hearing lips and seeing voices. *Nature*, 23(30):746–748, December 1976.

M. E. Metral. Motormouth: A generic engine for largescale, real-time automated collaborative filtering. Master's thesis, MIT Media Lab, Cambridge, MA, June 1995.

T. P. Minka and R. W. Picard. Interactive learning with a society of models. *Pattern Recognition*, 30(4):565–581, 1997.

M. Minsky. *The Society of Mind*. Simon & Schuster, New York, NY, 1985.

O. H. Mowrer. *Learning Theory and Behavior*. John Wiley & Sons, Inc., New York, 1960.

E. T. Mueller. *Daydreaming in Humans and Machines: A Computer Model of the Stream of Thought*. Ablex Publishing Corporation, Norwood, NJ, 1990.

I. R. Murray and J. L. Arnott. Toward the simulation of emotion in synthetic speech: A review of the literature on human vocal emotion. *Journal Acoustical Society of America*, 93(2):1097–1108, Feb. 1993.

C. Nass and S. S. Sundar. Is human-computer interaction social or parasocial?, 1994.

C. I. Nass, J. S. Steuer, and E. Tauber. Computers are social actors. In *Proceeding of the CHI '94 Proceedings*, pages 72–78, Boston, MA, Apr. 1994.

W. S. Neal Reilly. *Believable Social and Emotional Agents*. PhD thesis, School of Computer Science, Carnegie Mellon University, Pittsburgh, PA, May 1996.

N. Negroponte. *Being Digital*. Alfred A. Knopf, New York, 1995.

P. M. Niedenthal and S. Kitayama, editors. *Heart's Eye: Emotional Influences in Perception and Attention*. Academic Press, San Diego, 1994.

D. A. Norman. Twelve issues for cognitive science. In D. A. Norman, editor, *Perspectives on Cognitive Science*, pages 265–295, Hillsdale, NJ, 1981. Erlbaum.

A. V. Oppenheim and R. W. Schafer. *Discrete-Time Signal Processing*. Prentice-Hall, Inc., Englewood Cliffs, New Jersey, 1989.

A. Ortony, G. L. Clore, and A. Collins. *The Cognitive Structure of Emotions*. Cambridge University Press, Cambridge, MA, 1988.

A. Ortony and T. J. Turner. What's basic about basic emotions? *Psychological Review*, 97(3):315–331, 1990.

J. Panksepp. A critical role for 'affective neuroscience' in resolving what is basic about emotions. *Psychological Review*, 1992.

A. Pentland. Smart rooms. *Scientific American*, 274(4):68–76, Apr. 1996.

R. Pfeifer. Artificial intelligence models of emotion. In V. Hamilton, G. H. Bower, and N. H. Frijda, editors, *Cognitive Perspectives on Emotion and Motivation*, volume 44 of *Series D: Behavioural and Social Sciences*, pages 287–320, Netherlands, 1988. Kluwer Academic Publishers.

R. Pfeifer. The 'fungus eater approach' to emotion: A view from artificial intelligence. *Cognitive Studies, The Japanese Society for Cognitive Science*, 1(2):42–57, 1994.

R. Pfeifer and D. W. Nicholas. Toward computational models of emotion. In L. Steels and J. A. Cambell, editors, *Progress in Artificial Intelligence*, pages 184–192. Chichester: Ellis Horwood, 1985.

R. W. Picard. A society of models for video and image libraries. *IBM Systems Journal*, 35(3/4):292–312, 1996.

R. W. Picard. Does HAL cry digital tears?: Emotion and computers. In D. G. Stork, editor, *HAL's Legacy: 2001's Computer as Dream and Reality*, Cambridge, MA, 1997. MIT Press.

R. W. Picard and J. Healey. Affective wearables. In *Proceedings of the First International Symposium on Wearable Computers*, Cambridge, MA, Oct. 1997. To appear.

R. W. Picard and T. P. Minka. Vision texture for annotation. *Journal of Multimedia Systems*, 3:3–14, 1995.

R. W. Picard, T. P. Minka, and M. Szummer. Modeling user subjectivity in image libraries. In *Proceedings International Conference on Image Processing*, volume 2, pages 777–780, Lausanne, Switzerland, Sept. 1996. IEEE.

J. Pittam, C. Gallois, and V. Callan. The long-term spectrum and perceived emotion. *Speech Communication*, 9:177–187, 1990.

R. Plutchik. A general psychoevolutionary theory of emotion. In R. Plutchik and H. Kellerman, editors, *Emotion Theory, Research, and Experience*, volume 1, Theories of Emotion. Academic Press, 1980.

R. Plutchik and H. Kellerman, editors. *Emotion Theory, Research, and Experience*, volume 1–5. Academic Press, 1980–1990. Series of selected papers.

K. Popat and R. W. Picard. Novel cluster-based probability models for texture synthesis, classification, and compression. In *Proceedings SPIE Visual Communication and Image Processing*, volume 2094, pages 756–768, Boston, Nov. 1993.

K. H. Pribram. The biology of emotions and other feelings. In R. Plutchik and H. Kellerman, editors, *Emotion Theory, Research, and Experience*, volume 1, Theories of Emotion. Academic Press, 1980.

L. R. Rabiner. A tutorial on hidden Markov models and selected applications in speech recognition. *Proceedings IEEE*, 77(2):257–286, Feb. 1989.

L. R. Rabiner and B. H. Juang. An introduction to hidden Markov models. *IEEE ASSP Magazine*, pages 4–16, Jan. 1986.

E. Raymond, editor. *The New Hacker's Dictionary, third edition*. MIT Press, Cambridge, MA, 1996.

B. Reeves and C. Nass. *The Media Equation*. Center for the Study of Language and Information, 1996.

B. J. Rhodes and T. Starner. Remembrance agent: A continuously running automated information retrieval system. In *Proceedings of the First International Conference on the Practical Application of Intelligent Agents and Multi Agent Technology*, pages 487–495, 1996.

E. T. Rolls. A theory of emotion, and its application to understanding the neural basis of emotion. *Cognition and Emotion*, 4(3):161–190, 1990.

D. Romer. The Kodak picture exchange, Apr. 1995. Seminar at MIT Media Lab.

I. J. Roseman. Appraisal determinants of discrete emotions. *Cognition and Emotion*, 5(3):161–200, 1991.

I. J. Roseman, A. A. Antoniou, and P. E. Jose. Appraisal determinants of emotions: Constructing a more accurate and comprehensive theory. *Cognition and Emotion*, 10(3):241–277, 1996.

I. J. Roseman, M. S. Spindel, and P. E. Jose. Appraisals of emotion-eliciting events: Testing a theory of discrete emotions. *Journal of Personality and Social Psychology*, 59(5):899–915, 1990.

D. Roy and A. Pentland. Automatic spoken affect analysis and classification. In *Proceedings of the Second International Conference on Automatic Face and Gesture Recognition*, pages 363–367, Killington, VT, Oct. 1996.

T. Sakaguchi and S. Morishima. Face feature extraction from spatial frequency for dynamic expression recognition. In *Proceedings of ICPR'96*, pages 451–455, 1996.

P. Salovey and J. D. Mayer. Emotional intelligence. *Imagination, Cognition and Personality*, 9(3):185–211, 1990.

S. Schachter. The interaction of cognitive and physiological determinants of emotional state. In L. Berkowitz, editor, *Advances in Experimental Psychology*, volume 1, pages 49–80. Academic Press, New York, 1964.

L. F. Schaffer, B. Gilmer, and M. Schoen. *Psychology*. Haper and Brothers, New York, 1940.

R. J. Schalkoff. *Pattern Recognition: Statistical, Structural and Neural Approaches*. John Wiley & Sons, New York, 1992.

K. R. Scherer. Ch. 10: Speech and emotional states. In J. K. Darby, editor, *Speech Evaluation in Psychiatry*, pages 189–220. Grune and Stratton, Inc., 1981.

K. R. Scherer. Criteria for emotion-antecedent appraisal: A review. In V. Hamilton, G. H. Bower, and N. H. Frijda, editors, *Cognitive perspectives on emotion and motivation*, pages 89–126, Norwell, MA, 1988. Kluwer Academic.

K. R. Scherer. Neuroscience projections to current debates in emotion psychology. *Cognition and Emotion*, 7(1):1–41, 1993.

K. R. Scherer, D. R. Ladd, and K. E. A. Silverman. Vocal cues to speaker affect: Testing two models. *Journal Acoustical Society of America*, 76(5):1346–1355, Nov. 1984.

H. Schlosberg. Three dimensions of emotion. *Psychological Review*, 61(2):81–88, Mar. 1954.

T. Selker. Coach: A teaching agent that learns. *Communications of the ACM*, 37(7):92–99, July 1994.

C. E. Shannon and W. Weaver. *The Mathematical Theory of Communication*. University of Illinois Press, Urbana and Chicago, 1963.

M. W. Shelley. *Frankenstein*. University of California Press, Berkeley, 1984. Originally published in 1816.

A. Sherstinsky and R. W. Picard. Orientation-sensitive image processing with M-Lattice: A novel non-linear dynamical system. In *Proceedings IEEE First International Conference on Image Processing*, volume III, pages 152–156, Nov. 1994.

T. Shibata and R. Irie. Artificial emotional creature for human-robot interaction: A new direction for intelligent systems. In *Proceedings of the IEEE/ASME International Conference on Advanced Intelligent Mechatronics*, Tokyo, June 1997.

H. A. Simon. Motivational and emotional controls of cognition (1967). In *Models of Thought*, pages 29–38. Yale University Press, New Haven, 1979.

A. Sloman and M. Croucher. Why robots will have emotions. In *Proceedings Seventh International Conference on AI*, pages 197–202, Aug. 1981.

C. A. Smith and P. C. Ellsworth. Patterns of cognitive appraisal in emotion. *Journal of Personality and Social Psychology*, 48(4):813–838, 1985.

C. A. Smith and P. C. Ellsworth. Patterns of appraisal and emotion related to taking an exam. *Journal of Personality and Social Psychology*, 52(3):475–488, 1987.

J. T. Spence and K. W. Spence. The motivational components of manifest anxiety: Drive and drive stimuli. In C. Spielberger, editor, *Anxiety and Behavior*, pages 291–326. Academic Press, London, 1966.

K. Stanislavsky. *An Actor Prepares*. Theatre Arts Books, New York, 1936.

T. Starner, S. Mann, B. Rhodes, J. Levine, J. Healey, D. Kirsch, R. W. Picard, and A. Pentland. Augmented reality through wearable computing. *Presence*, 1997. To appear. Also appears as MIT Media Lab Perceptual Computing TR 397.

T. Starner, J. Weaver, and A. Pentland. A wearable computer based American sign language recognizer. In *Proceedings of the First International Symposium on Wearable Computers*, Cambridge, MA, Oct. 1997. To appear.

T. E. Starner. Human powered wearable computing. *IBM Systems Journal*, 35(3/4):618–629, 1996.

N. L. Stein and K. Oatley, editors. *Basic Emotions*. Lawrence Erlbaum Associates, Hove, UK, 1992. Book is a special double issue of the journal *Cognition and Emotion*, Vol. 6, No. 3 & 4, 1992.

D. Tannen. *You Just Don't Understand: Women and Men in Conversation*. Ballantine Books, New York, 1990.

C. W. Therrien. *Decision Estimation and Classification*. John Wiley and Sons, Inc., New York, 1989.

F. Thomas and O. Johnson. *Disney Animation: The Illusion of Life*. Walt Disney Productions, 1981.

M. Toda. Design of a fungus-eater. *Behavioral Science*, 7:164–183, 1962. Reprinted also in Toda, 1982, Man, Robot, and Society, The Hague: Nijhoff.

M. Toda. The urge theory of emotion and cognition (English version). Technical Report 93-1-01, School of Computer and Cognitive Sciences, Institute for Advanced Studies in Artificial Ingelligence, Chukyo University, 101 Tokodate, Kaizu-cho, Toyota, 470-03, Japan, Dec. 1993.

M. Toda. The urge theory of emotion and cognition, chapter 2: Basic structure of the urge operations. Technical Report 94-1-01, School of Computer and Cognitive Sciences, Institute for Advanced Studies in Artifical Intelligence, Chukyo University, 101 Tokodate, Kaizu-cho, Toyota, 470-03, Japan, Aug. 1994.

M. Toda. The urge theory of emotion and cognition, chapter 3: A decision theoretical model of urge operations. Technical Report 95-1-01, School of Computer and Cognitive Sciences, Institute for Advanced Studies in Artifical Intelligence, Chukyo University, 101 Tokodate, Kaizu-cho, Toyota, 470-03, Japan, Apr. 1995.

M. Toda. The urge theory of emotion and cognition, chapter 4: The problems of altruism and evolution of systems. Technical Report 95-1-04, School of Computer and Cognitive Sciences, Institute for Advanced Studies in Artifical Intelligence, Chukyo University, 101 Tokodate, Kaizu-cho, Toyota, 470-03, Japan, Mar. 1995.

S. S. Tomkins. *Affect, Imagery, Consciousness*, volume 1: The Positive Affects. Springer, New York, 1962.

S. S. Tomkins. *Affect, Imagery, Consciousness*, volume 2: The Negative Affects. Springer, New York, 1962.

N. Tosa and R. Nakatsu. Life-like communication agent—emotion sensing character 'MIC' and feeling session character 'MUSE'. In *Proceedings of the International Conference on Multimedia Computing and Systems*, pages 12–19. IEEE, 1996.

J. T. Tou. *Pattern Recognition Principles*. Addison-Wesley, Reading, MA, 1974.

A. M. Turing. Computing machinery and intelligence. *Mind*, LIX(236):433–460, Oct. 1950.

S. Turkle. *The second self: Computers and the human spirit*. Simon and Schuster, New York, 1984.

R. van Bezooyen. *Characteristics and Recognizability of Vocal Expressions of Emotion*. Foris Publications, Dordrecht, Holland; Cinnaminson, N.J., 1984.

J. D. Velasquez. Cathexis: A computational model for the generation of emotions and their influence in the behavior of autonomous agents. Master's thesis, MIT Media Lab, Sep. 1996.

J. D. Velasquez. Modeling emotions and other motivations in synthetic agents. In *AAAI 97*, pages 10–15. ACM, 1997.

S. R. Vrana. The psychophysiology of disgust: Differentiating negative emotional contexts with facial EMG. *Psychophysiology*, 1993.

J. S. Wachman. A video browser that learns by example. Master's thesis, MIT Media Lab, Cambridge, MA, May 1996.

H. G. Wallbott and K. R. Scherer. Assessing emotion by questionnaire. In R. Plutchik and H. Kellerman, editors, *Emotion Theory, Research, and Experience*, volume 4, The Measurement of Emotions. Academic Press, 1989.

J. Weizenbaum. Eliza - a computer program for the study of natural language communication between man and machine. *Communications of the ACM*, 9(1):36–45, Jan. 1966.

P. Werbos. The brain as a neurocontroller: New hypotheses and new experimental possibilities. In K. H. Pribram, editor, *Origins: Brain and Self-Organization*. Erlbaum, 1994.

S. Wewerka, K. Miller, and J. M. R. Doman. Together forever. *Life Magazine*, pages 46–56, Apr. 1996.

C. E. Williams and K. N. Stevens. On determining the emotional state of pilots during flight: An exploratory study. *Aerospace Medicine*, 40(12):1369–1372, Dec. 1969.

C. E. Williams and K. N. Stevens. Emotions and speech: Some acoustical correlates. *Journal Acoustical Society of America*, 52(4):1238–1250, 1972. part 2.

W. M. Winton, L. Putnam, and R. Krauss. Facial and autonomic manifestations of the dimensional structure of emotion. *Journal of Experimental Social Psychology*, 20:195–216, 1984.

I. Wright, A. Sloman, and L. Beaudoin. Towards a design-based analysis of emotional episodes. *Philosophy, Psychiatry and Psychology*, 3(2):101–126, 1996.

J. J. Wurtman. *Managing your mind and mood through food*. Rawson Associates, New York, 1986.

Y. Yacoob and L. S. Davis. Recognizing human facial expressions from log image sequences using optical flow. *IEEE Transactions on Pattern Analysis and Machine Intelligence*, 18(6):636–642, June 1996.

R. M. Yerkes and J. D. Dodson. The relation of strength of stimulus to rapidity of habit formation. *Journal of Comparative and Neurology and Psychology*, 18:459–482, 1908.

R. B. Zajonc. On the primacy of affect. *American Psychologist*, 39(2):117–123, Feb. 1984.

T. Zimmerman. Personal area networks (PAN): Near-field intra-body communication. *IBM Systems Journal*, 35:609–618, 1996.

Index

Digital disk jockey, 234–235
Digitally altered views, 232–233
Digital music libraries, 98
Digital video libraries, 99–100
Dimensions in emotion
  recognition, 168–170
Discrete states in emotion
  recognition, 169
Disgust
  as basic emotion, 167–168
  computer recognition rates for,
    176–177
  vocal intonation in, 179, 181
Dislike, EEG signals for, 188
Disney Animation (Thomas and
  Johnson), 200
Distress, piano tutor recognition
  of, 82
Dogs, emotion recognized by,
  26–27
Doing, learning by, 135–136
Doman, J. M. R., 147
"Don't worry; be happy", 35
Doom game, feedback for, 91,
  163–164
Dragging the tail phenomenon,
  121
Drives
  in Cathexis model, 211
  vs. emotions, 24
  influence on emotion, 67
Duchenne, G. B., 26, 41–42
Duncker's candle task, 40
Duplicating emotions, 82–83
Duration of emotions and
  moods, 145
Dyer, M. G., 222
Dynamical systems theory, 191

Eastman, George, 230
EEG (electroencephalogram)
  signals, 188
Ekman, Paul, 23
  on anger expression, 171
  on basic emotions, 168
  emotional plots by, 169
  on facial expression, 25–26,
    178
  facial expression recognition
    system by, 175–176
  on lie detection, 120
  on pan-cultural signals, 32
  on posing faces, 43
  on smiles, 42

Elan vital, 136
Electrodermal response. *See*
  Galvanic skin response
  (GSR)
Electroencephalogram (EEG)
  signals, 188
Electromyogram (EMG),
  185–188
  for emotion recognition, 53
  signals from, 161–162
  in wearables, 236
Elicitors for emotion, 209–211
Eliza program, 116
Elliot (Damasio patient), 11,
  35–37, 64
Elliott, Clarke
  affective reasoner system by,
    116
  on emotion expression, 58
  and OCC model, 204–206
Email
  affective channel capacity in,
    57–58
  tone in, 87
Embodied computers, 71–73,
  224
Emergent emotions, 61–62
EMG (electromyogram),
  185–188
  for emotion recognition, 53
  signals from, 161–162
  in wearables, 236
Em generation system, 200,
  202–203
Emoticons, 87–88
Emotion
  in Affective Reasoner system,
    204–205
  in animated characters, 200,
    202–204
  basic, 167–168
  and behavior, 61–62, 203
  body-mind interaction in,
    66–69
  categories of, 167–168
  cognitive appraisal model for,
    206–209
  cognitive aspects of, 35–42,
    63–64
  computers with, 60–71
  and consciousness, 73–75
  for creativity, 1, 39–40
  in decision making, 1, 9–12,
    37, 133

definitions of, 21
developing and learning,
  36–37, 48–50
duration of, 145
and effective computing, 3
elicitors for, 209–211
emergent, 61–62
in Em system, 202–203
evaluation of, 69–70
experience of, 24, 64–66, 70
expression of. *See* Emotion
  expression; Facial
  expressions
fast primary, 62–63, 70
as feminine, 10
in film, 108–109
gratuitous, 117–118
in health, 29–30
imitating vs. duplicating,
  82–83
in inanimate objects, 15
inducement of, 30, 42–44, 58
inhibiting and hiding,
  172–173
in learning, 1, 93–96, 216–218
memory affected by, 40–41,
  222–224
in motivation, 1, 76–77
necessity of, 249–252
in perception, 5–7
physical aspects of. *See* Physical
  component of emotions
primary vs. secondary, 35–36,
  62–63
as rational, 126
in reasoning, 1–2, 135
reasoning about, 195
recognition of. *See* Emotion
  recognition
relevant, 81
representations for, 141–144
in robots, 61
sentographs for, 28–29
signals for. *See* Signals for
  emotion
sincerity of, 54
from situations, 198
in social relationships, 2,
  204–206
synthesis of. *See* Synthesis
system modeling of, 142–144
system properties of, 145–160
temperament in, 147–148
terminology for, 24–25

Printed in the United States
By Bookmasters